IMAGES
of America

ALAMANCE COUNTY

IMAGES
of America

ALAMANCE COUNTY

William Kerr Lasley Jr.

ARCADIA
PUBLISHING

ISBN 978-0-7385-0036-2

Published by Arcadia Publishing
Charleston, South Carolina

Printed in the United States of America

Library of Congress Catalog Card Number: 99-61284

For all general information contact Arcadia Publishing at:
Telephone 843-853-2070
Fax 843-853-0044
E-mail sales@arcadiapublishing.com
For customer service and orders:
Toll-Free 1-888-313-2556

Visit us on the Internet at www.arcadiapublishing.com

Contents

Acknowledgments

In my quest to compile images for this publication, I was constantly stunned by an immediate and unhesitating eagerness to be helpful from almost all of those of whom I made a request. A major source of photographs and postcards came in the form of Dr. William Murray Vincent, curator of the Alamance County Historical Museum, Inc. After making available much material from the museum archives, Bill directed me to Gail Knauff of the Haw River Historical Association Museum. Gail enthusiastically offered for use a vast amount of images and then opened her mental storehouse of knowledge, providing information about each and every picture that I borrowed.

When informed of my efforts, representatives of several local governments jumped at the chance to be generous. Alamance County Planner Steve M. Hundley loaned photographs and gave me copies of history columns written by my grandfather. Graham City Planner Russell M. Smith, Mebane Recreation and Parks Director D. Dean Ray Jr., and Howard Henry of Gibsonville's governmental office each presented visual material and, in some cases, included additional information that was vital in creating the scope and variety that I had envisioned for this book.

Other institutions in Graham joined the city government in lending support. Amy E. Jordan of the Graham Public Library helped out by showing me old images from around the county seat. Amy then personally escorted me to the Graham Fire Department where she introduced me to John Andrews and Chief Kenneth Evans. The firemen did not allow me to leave without at least one great 8-by-10 black-and-white glossy under my arm.

I wish to thank several more individuals for their contributions to this project. Austin Holt McCormick, who conducts interesting tours through the Alamance County Historical Museum, allowed the use of photographs of some of his ancestors who were pioneer industrialists and businessmen in the county. He also bestowed upon me an original receipt from my great-great-grandfather's store, a treasure that I never imagined existed.

When my grandmother, Nell Holt Lasley, got wind of this endeavor, she exposed me to visual and written material in her possession of which I was previously unaware. I direct my deepest appreciation to her and my late grandfather, W.T. Lasley, who I hope enjoyed the time he spent instilling in me an appreciation for history at an early age. Finally, special gratitude is extended to my mother, Carrie Trollinger Lasley, who spent great portions of time typing what I had written out in longhand.

The overwhelming interest and outpouring of selflessness and willingness to lend a helping hand that I have experienced from my fellow citizens indicates that the American ideal of living in a community of friendly neighbors is not a fantasy but an existing situation destined to continue far into the future of Alamance County.

Introduction

In the late 1600s, the first traders and explorers from the Old World made their way from Virginia into what was known as Haws Old Fields. About 1720, after the Royal Proprietors began offering cheap land, settlers headed south to the country around the Haw River. From Pennsylvania came Quakers, Scotch-Irish Presbyterians, and Lutherans as well as a large number of Reformed families. For the next few decades, the organization of churches was among the most important activities in what would become Alamance County. Businesses such as saloons, taverns, and gristmills sprang up.

Being part of a British colony meant that the people were ruled by the provincial government headquartered in New Bern, far to the east. The fact that living conditions were better toward the coast was just one reason for growing tension between the wealthier royals and the colonists in the wilder Piedmont area. As a result of this tension, pioneers near Alamance Creek shed the first blood in defiance of an oppressive empire.

After the Revolution, the rebels-turned-Americans continued to work. The gristmills flourished, and farmlands bore harvest. The crop of cotton was plentiful, and eventually, cotton mills were established in this land that was still part of the large Orange County. Alamance County was created in 1849 by dividing it from Orange. Soon textile production dominated the new county, and the railroad made its inevitable way through the area, becoming a major player in the creation and growth of new communities.

Various towns waxed and waned as the new industry of rail transport underwent growing pains. Hotels that were built either did not pan out or were resounding successes. Locomotive repair shops were established, begetting a village, but the shops would not stay put. Some passenger and freight depots had a heyday and then became obsolete. By the turn of the century, after a civil war of which Alamance County saw little, textile mills re-emerged as the life-blood of the county's economy and would remain so for a long time to come.

This book is a collection of images, both famous and obscure, from a community's past. It is not intended to be a definitive photographic history of Alamance County. A great deal of good work has been done on the subject, and the reader is encouraged to seek out the volumes listed in the bibliography. This publication is a compilation of visual material from the area including photographs, postcards, bank notes, business receipts, and covers to programs and bulletins. Never before has such a great quantity of images from Alamance County's past been reproduced with this level of clarity and compiled into such a high-quality publication. An attempt has been made to present these illustrations in an interesting way that will serve as both entertainment and education for future generations who possess an interest in history.

One

Events Big and Small

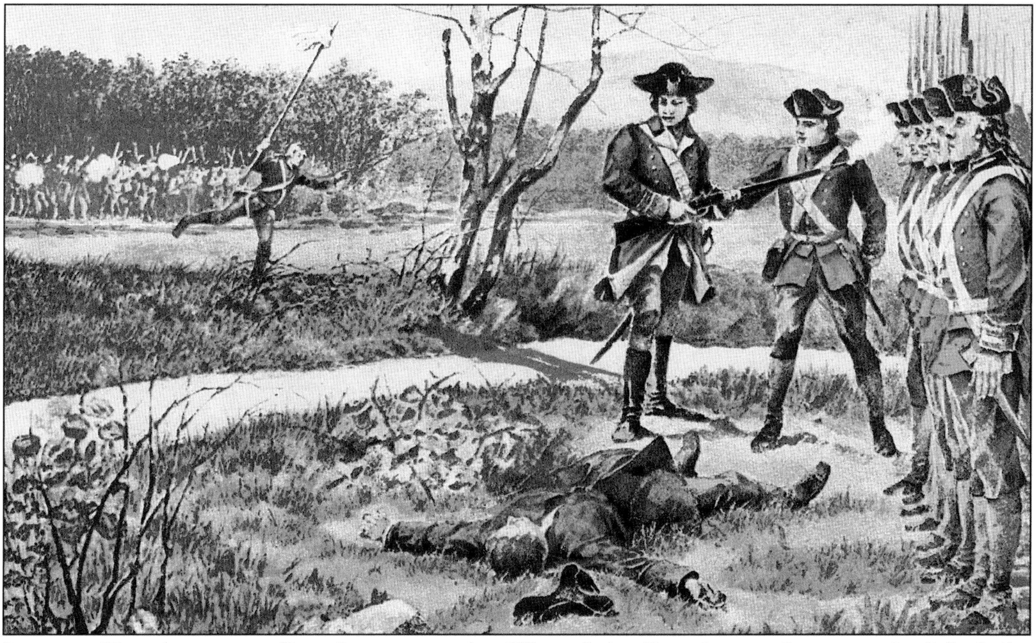

In a pre-Revolution conflict, known as the War of the Regulation, brave souls defied the royal militia near Alamance Creek. This postcard image features artwork by J. Steeple Davis and depicts an incident that immediately preceded the Battle of Alamance. A colonist, sent to negotiate, is shot by Governor Tryon himself, triggering the bloody fight that would be remembered more than two centuries later. Although they were defeated, this early act of bold resistance by North Carolinians foreshadowed the coming upheaval that would give birth to our country. (Courtesy Alamance County Historical Museum, Inc.)

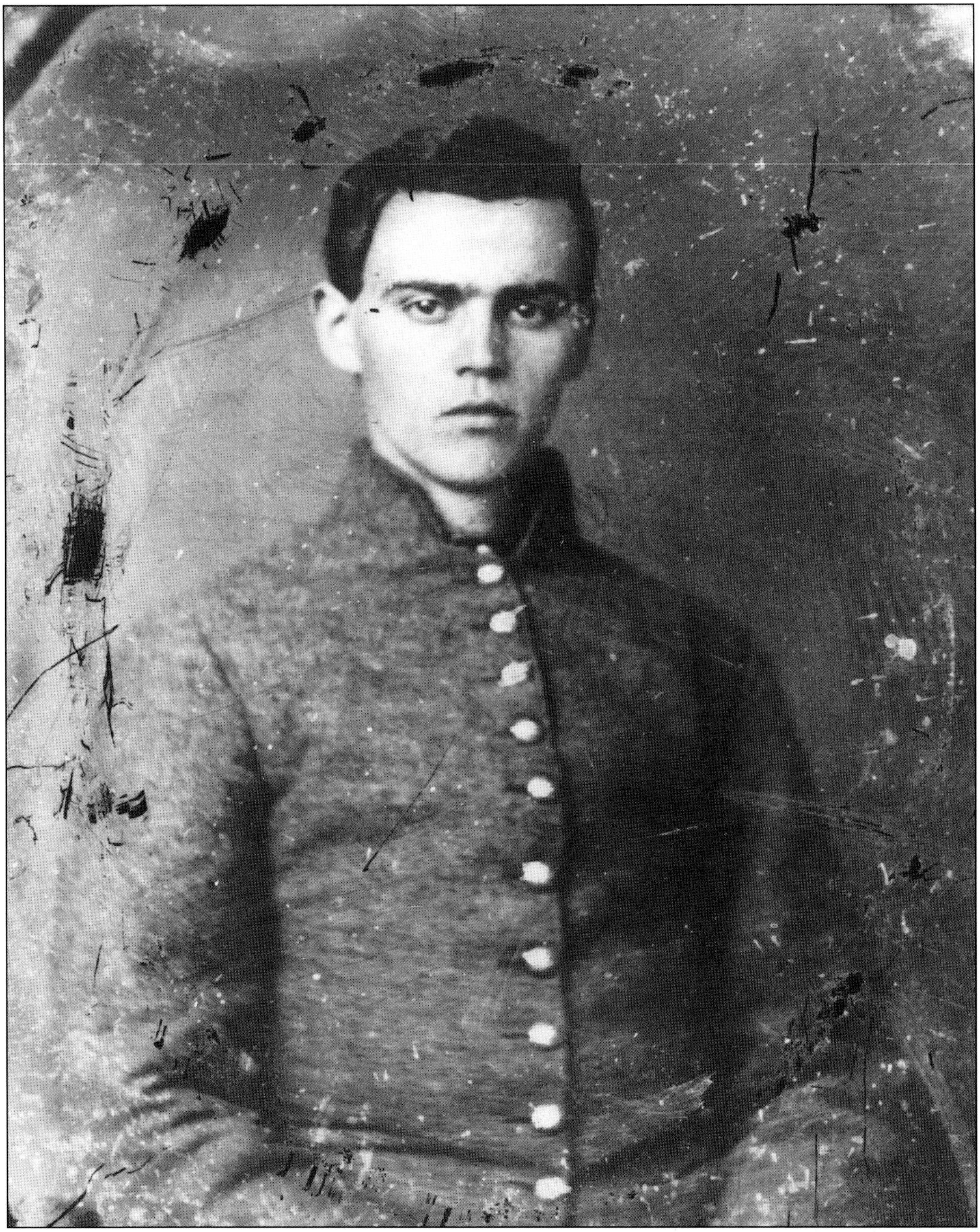

On May 20, 1861, North Carolina became the final state to secede from the Union. Alamance County native Daniel Foust Morrow was 19 years old and a student at the University of North Carolina. This photograph was taken upon his leaving to join Company G of the 28th North Carolina Infantry, Branch's Brigade. (Courtesy Alamance County Historical Museum, Inc.)

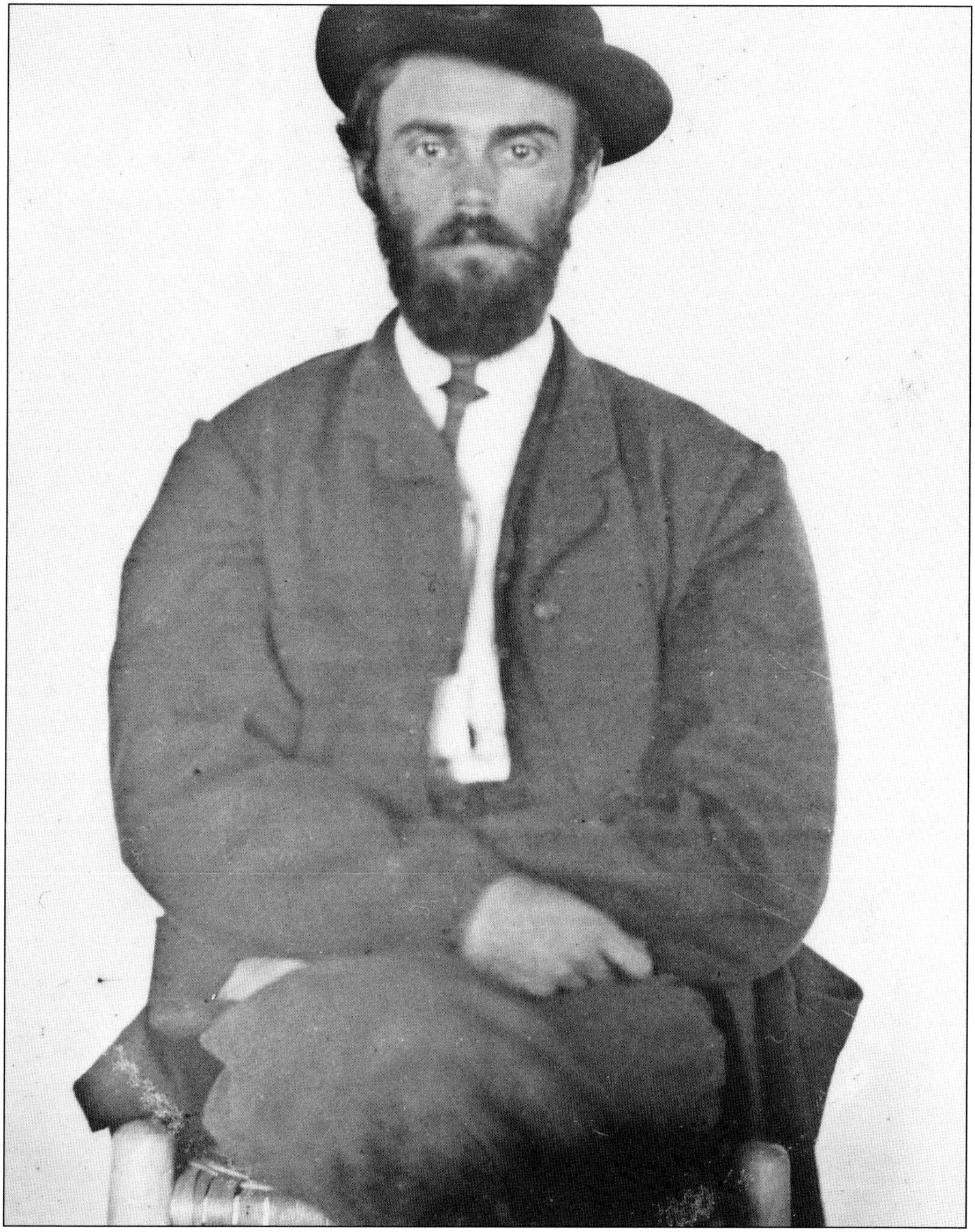

Daniel Foust Morrow survived the War Between the States, which ended on April 9, 1865. Any doubt about that fact was erased after he posed for this photograph in 1868, displaying the clothing of a more peaceful time. (Courtesy Alamance County Historical Museum, Inc.)

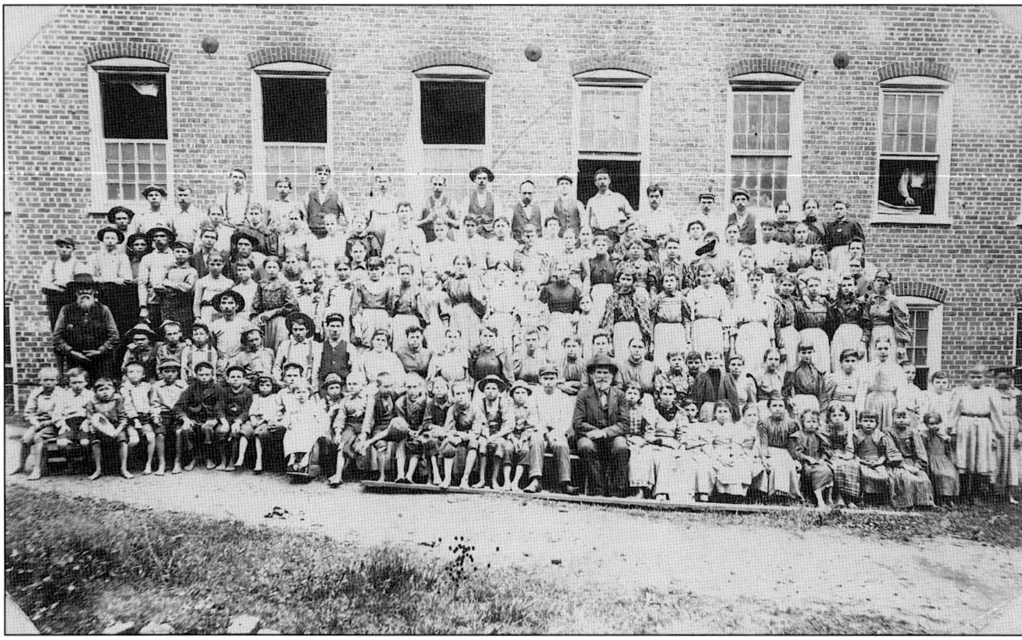

By the late nineteenth century, Independence Day had been celebrated in the United States of America for as long as any living person could remember. On July 4, 1899, this group of Alamance County citizens, probably from Haw River, gathered to remember the anniversary of the adoption of the Declaration of Independence.

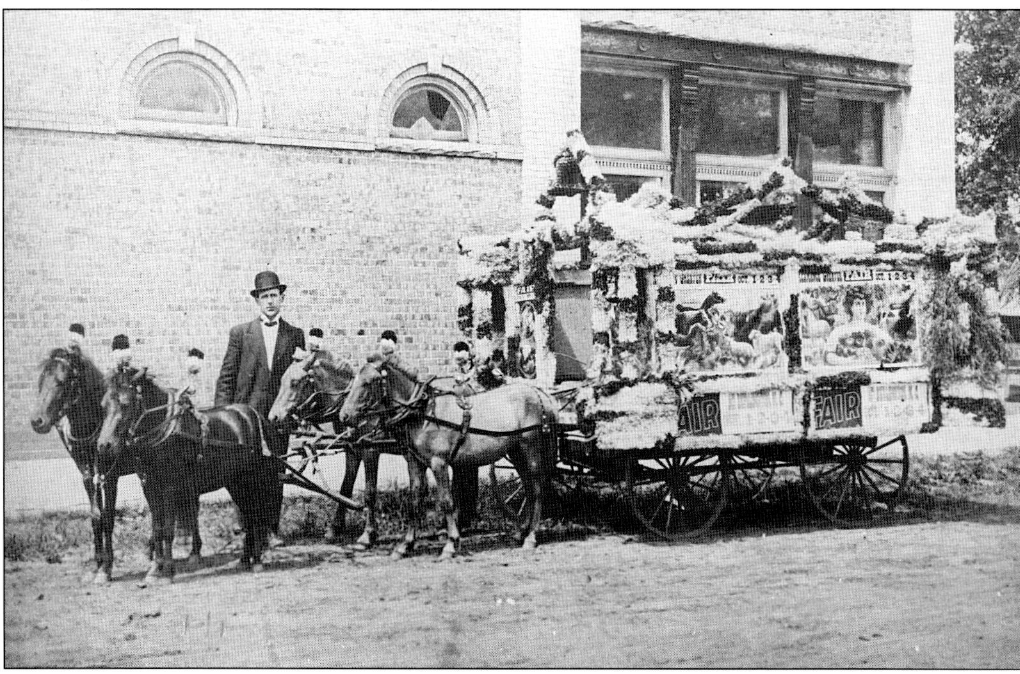

This pony-driven wagon is a good example of a method of old-time advertising. Both ears and eyes were alerted when this garish display came near with ringing bell and colorful signs. The mobile announcement hailed the coming of the Alamance County Fair to take place in Burlington on October 1, 2, 3, and 4.

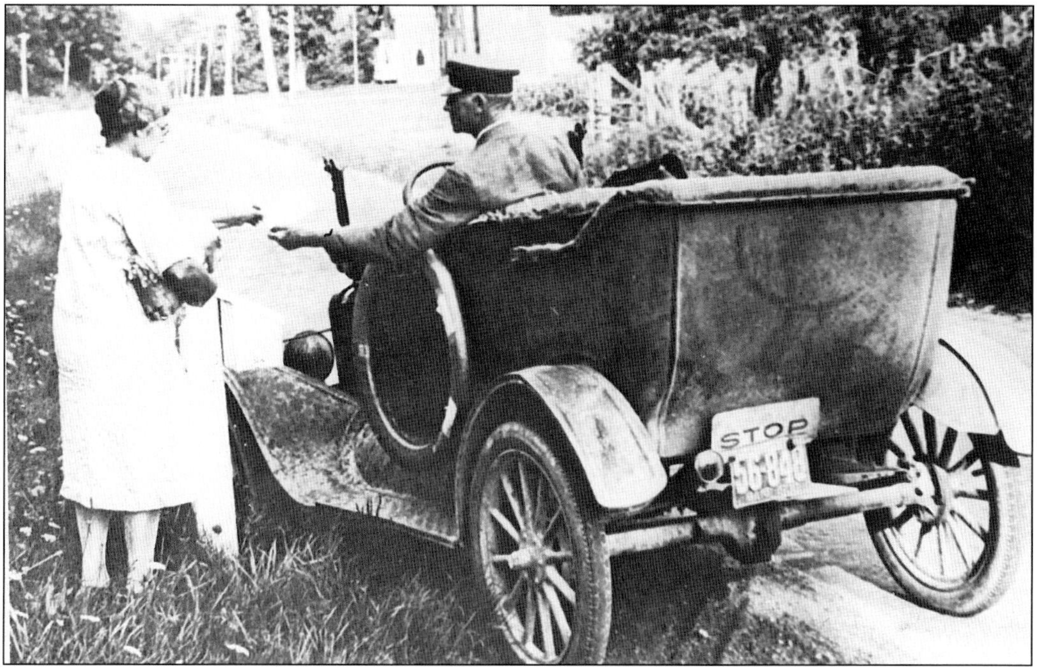

In 1863 the United States Post Office Department introduced free city mail service. By 1896, at the request of farmers, rural-free delivery had been established. Here we see an early twentieth-century Burlington woman receiving mail from her friendly neighborhood postman.

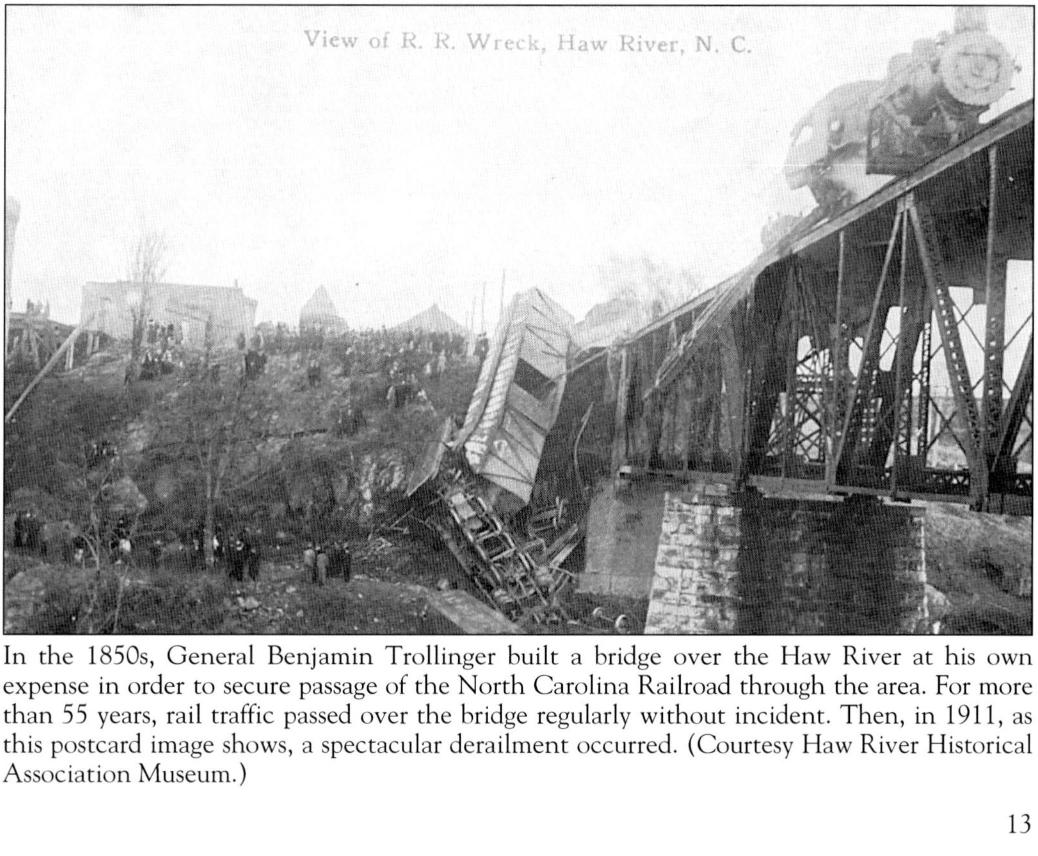

In the 1850s, General Benjamin Trollinger built a bridge over the Haw River at his own expense in order to secure passage of the North Carolina Railroad through the area. For more than 55 years, rail traffic passed over the bridge regularly without incident. Then, in 1911, as this postcard image shows, a spectacular derailment occurred. (Courtesy Haw River Historical Association Museum.)

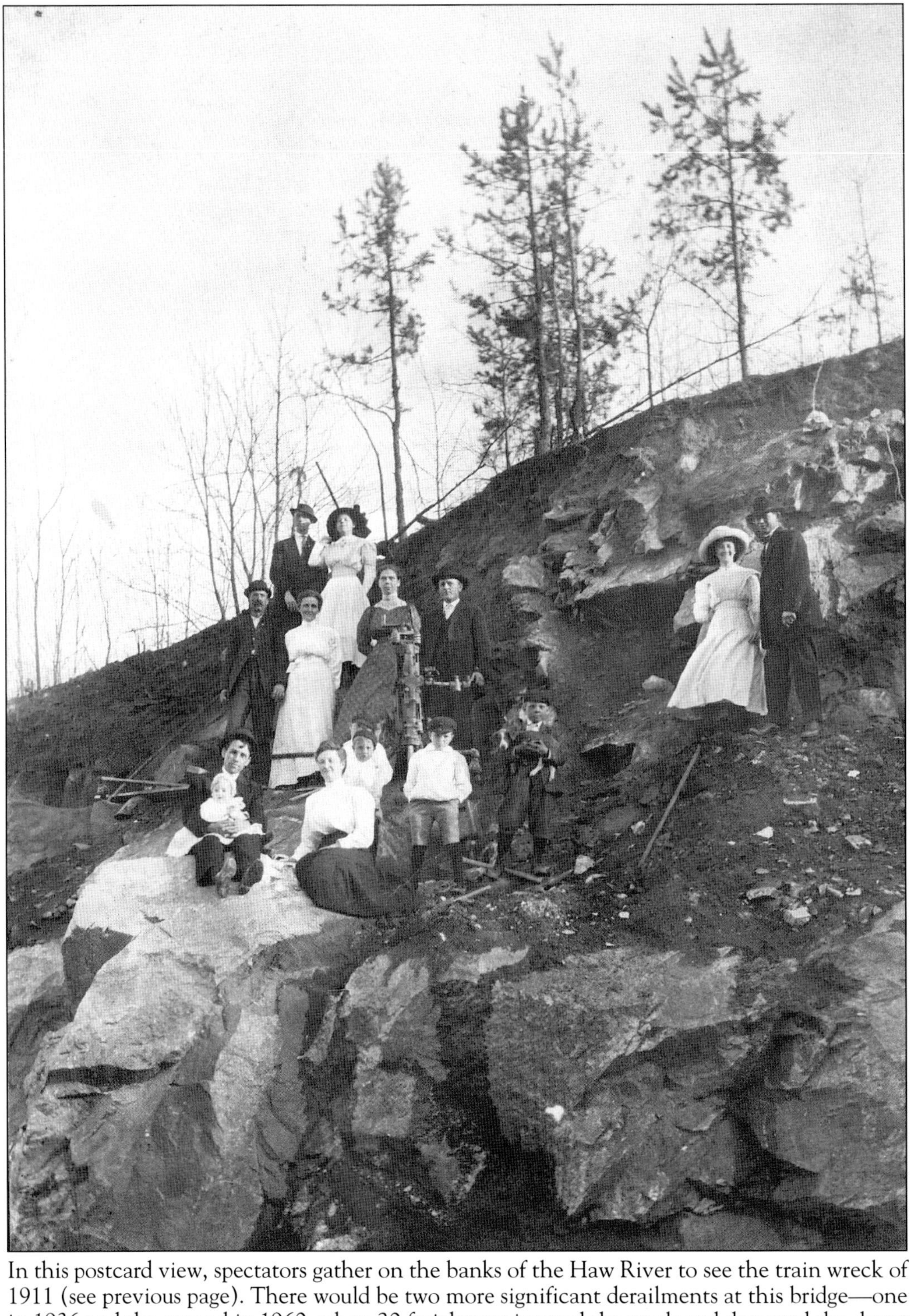

In this postcard view, spectators gather on the banks of the Haw River to see the train wreck of 1911 (see previous page). There would be two more significant derailments at this bridge—one in 1936 and the second in 1960, when 20 freightcars jumped the track and damaged the depot beyond repair. (Courtesy Haw River Historical Association Museum.)

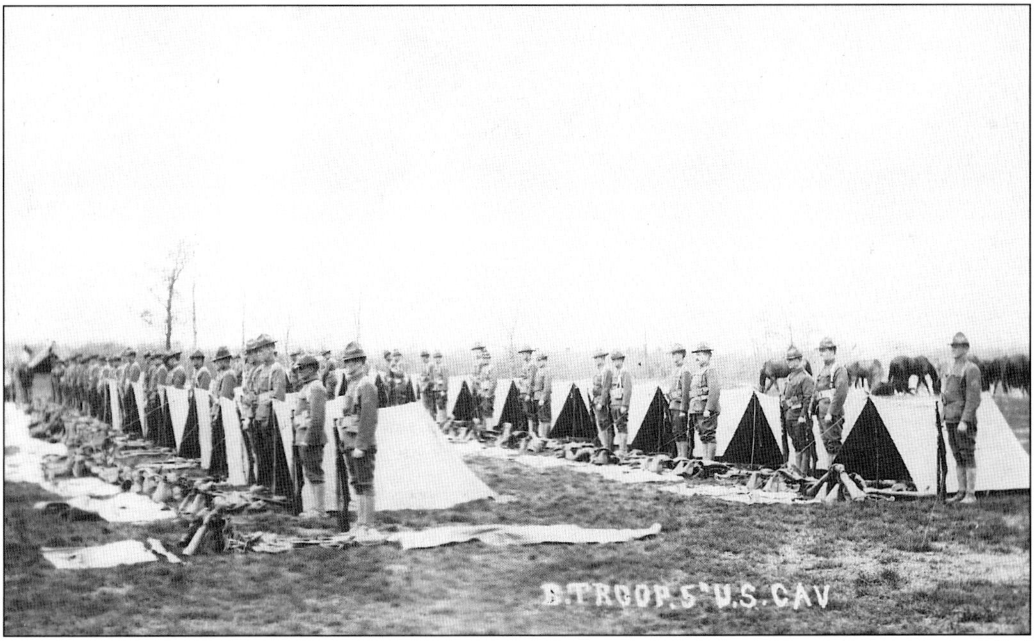

Between April 1917 and April 1919, more than 1,000 Alamance County citizens were called to serve their country in World War I. Ben Hugh was one such native son from Haw River. He wound up in this cavalry unit. (Courtesy Haw River Historical Association Museum.)

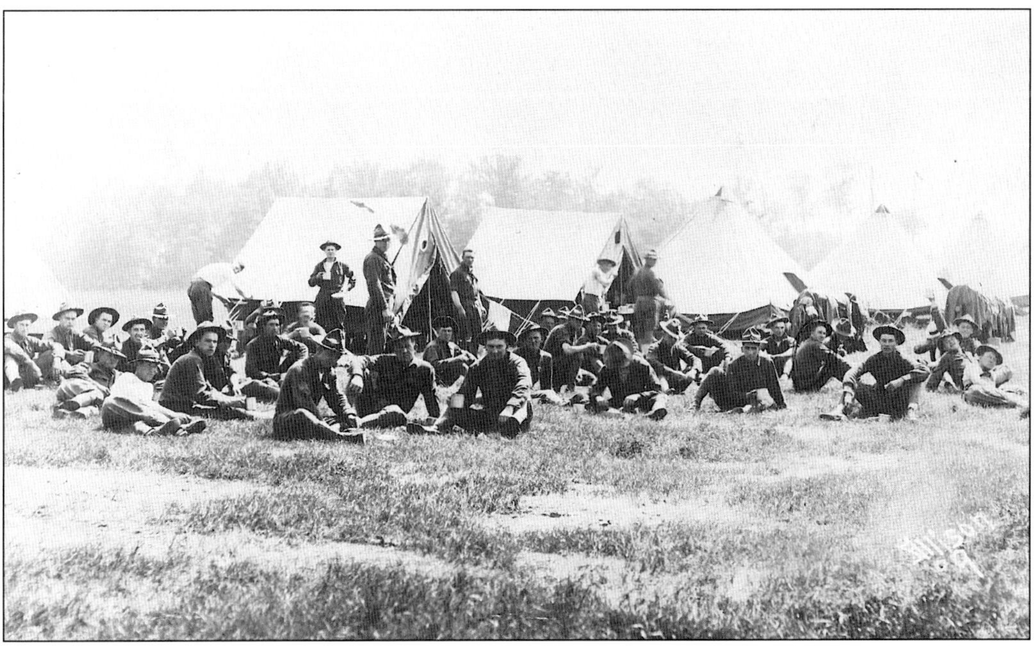

This is another view of Ben Hugh's cavalry unit, now bivouacked and at ease. Hugh is the soldier standing farthest to the right. We know too well the loss suffered in war. More than 100 of the county's servicemen did not come home. (Courtesy Haw River Historical Association Museum.)

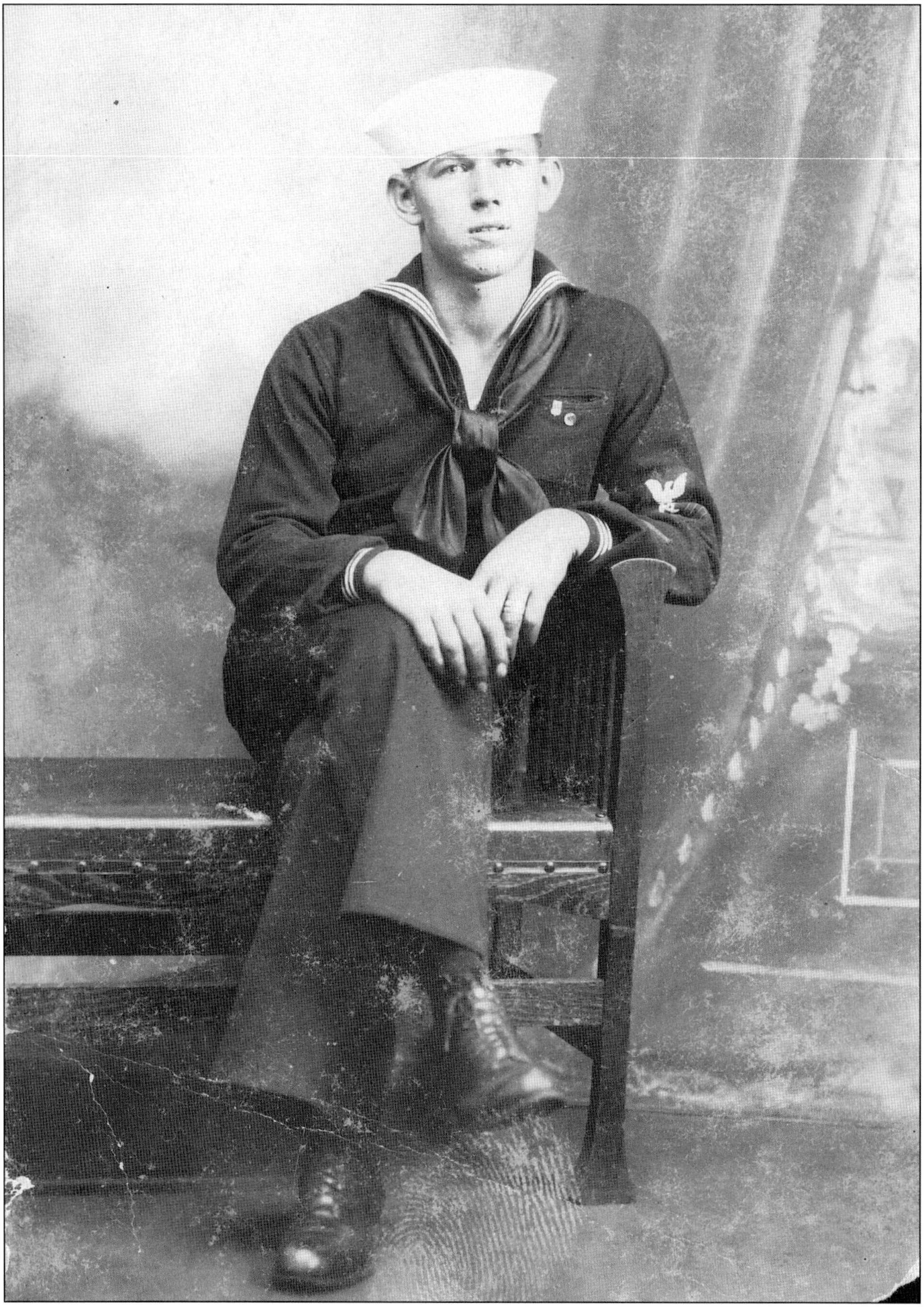

Records reveal that 85 people from the county served in the Navy during the great conflict. A young sailor from Haw River named Sammie posed for this photograph and had it made into a postcard. (Courtesy Haw River Historical Association Museum.)

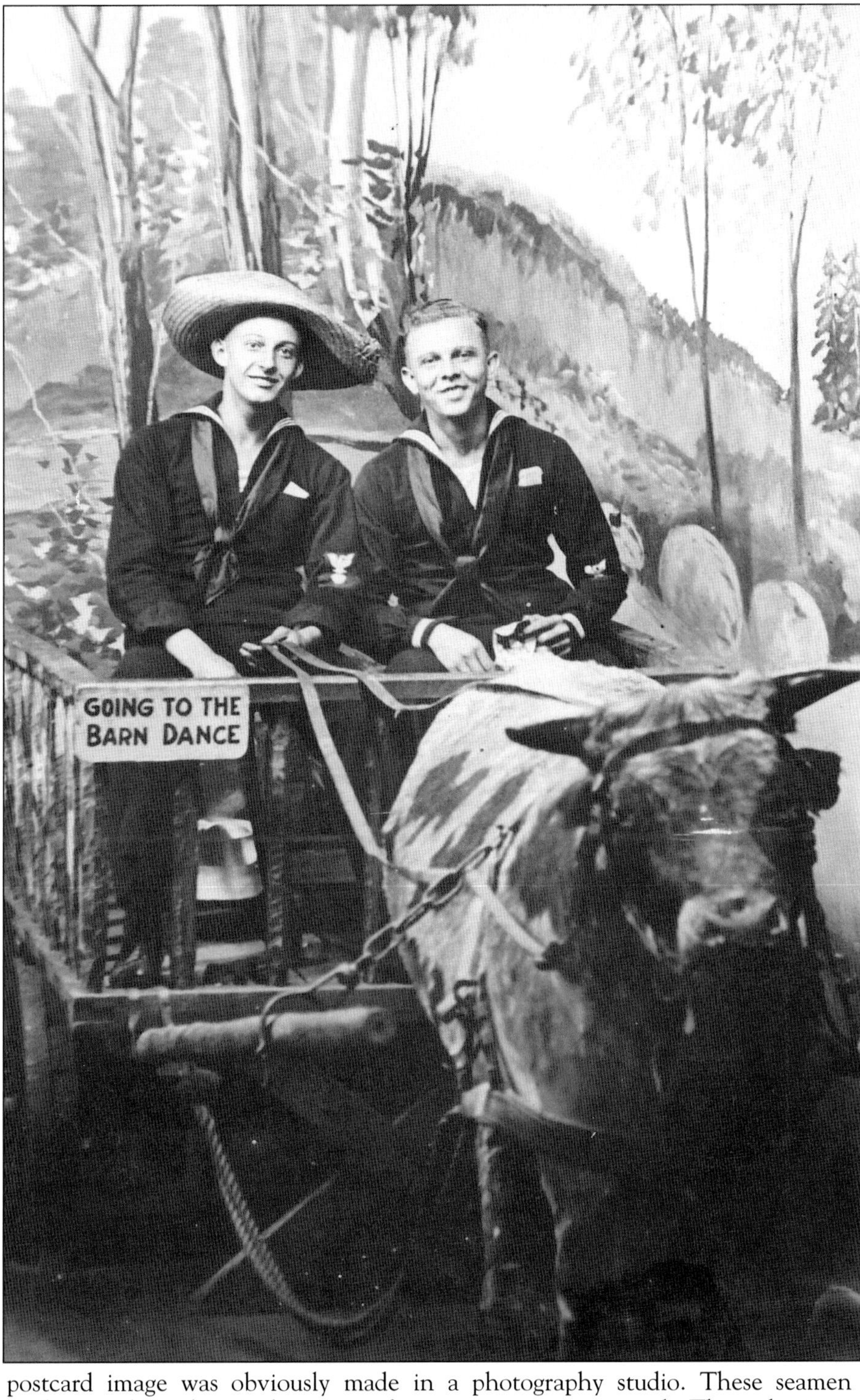

This postcard image was obviously made in a photography studio. These seamen would soon exchange this whimsical ox cart for an ocean-going vessel. Their destination was probably France, where most of the fighting took place. (Courtesy Haw River Historical Association Museum.)

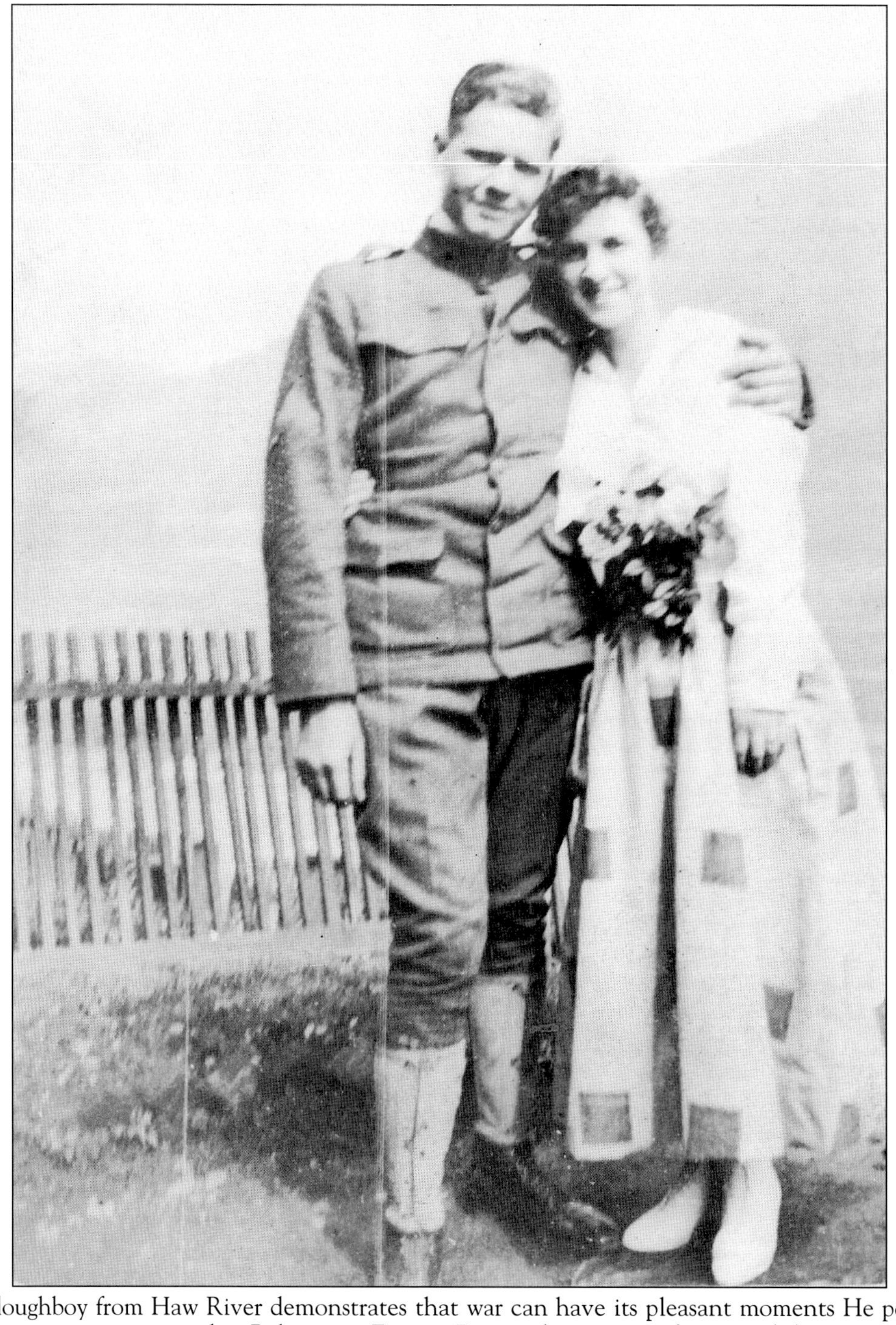

A doughboy from Haw River demonstrates that war can have its pleasant moments He poses with a companion in either Belgium or France. Due to the passage of time and the mysterious origin of this photograph, it is probably safe to reveal what was scribbled on the back: "This is Hubert, but not his wife . . . a girl he went with a little during the war." (Courtesy Haw River Historical Association Museum.)

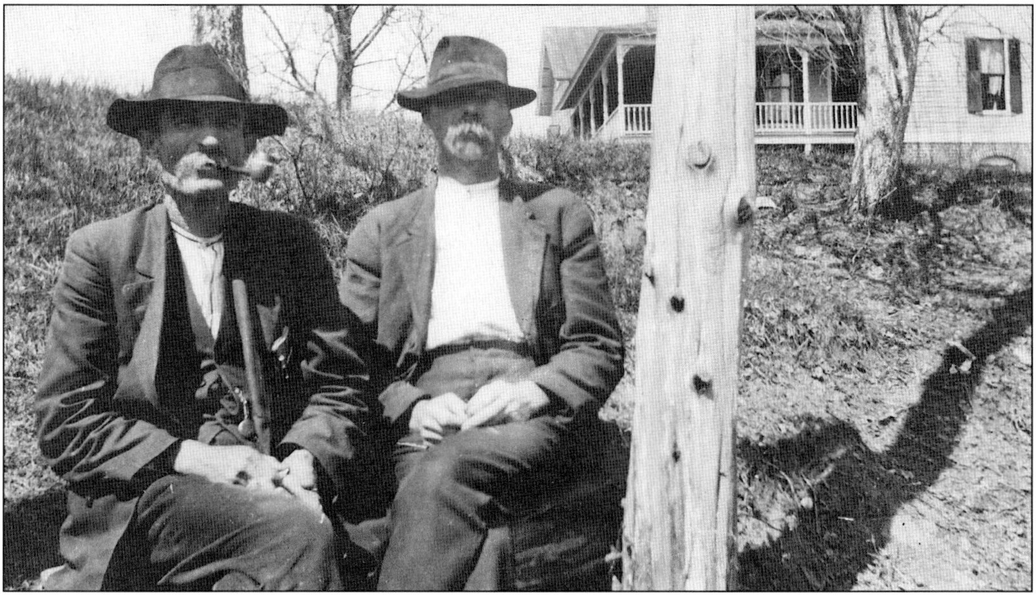

In 1923 Route 10 was laid across the expanse of Alamance County. Two men, one named David Jarrett, watch the construction crews do their work. Running east to west, the road was later deemed U.S. Highway 70 and became the main transportation link between Durham and Greensboro. (Courtesy Haw River Historical Association Museum.)

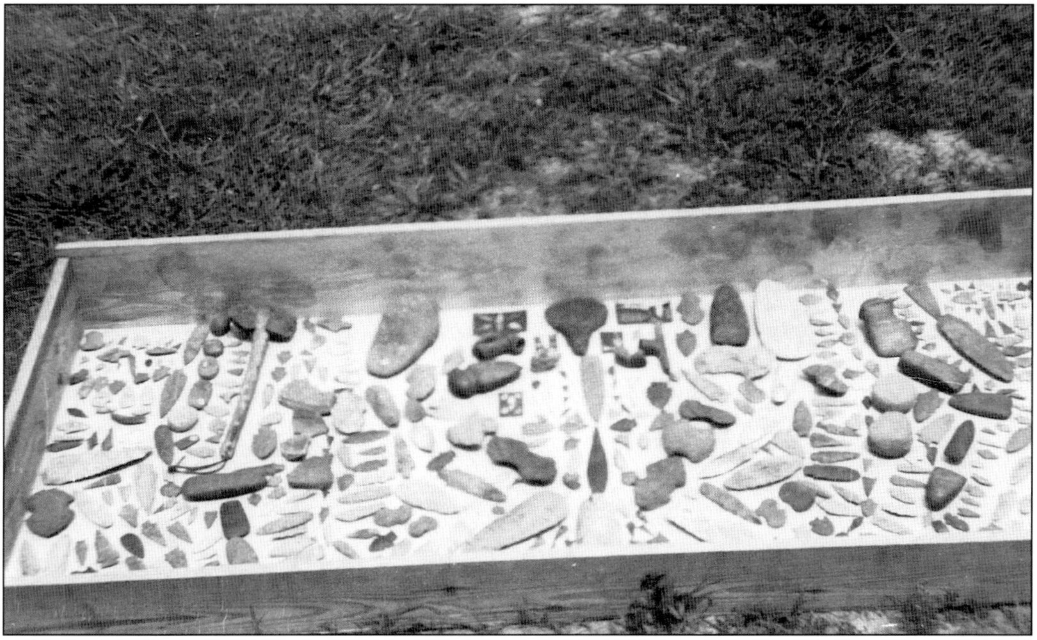

By the 1930s, a wealth of Native American artifacts had been discovered in the area. The Sissipahaw or Saxapahaw Indians made arrowheads from white quartz, multicolored flints, and a rare transparent crystal quartz. Soapstone or clay pipes have also been found. The "tomahawk" at left has a bone handle.

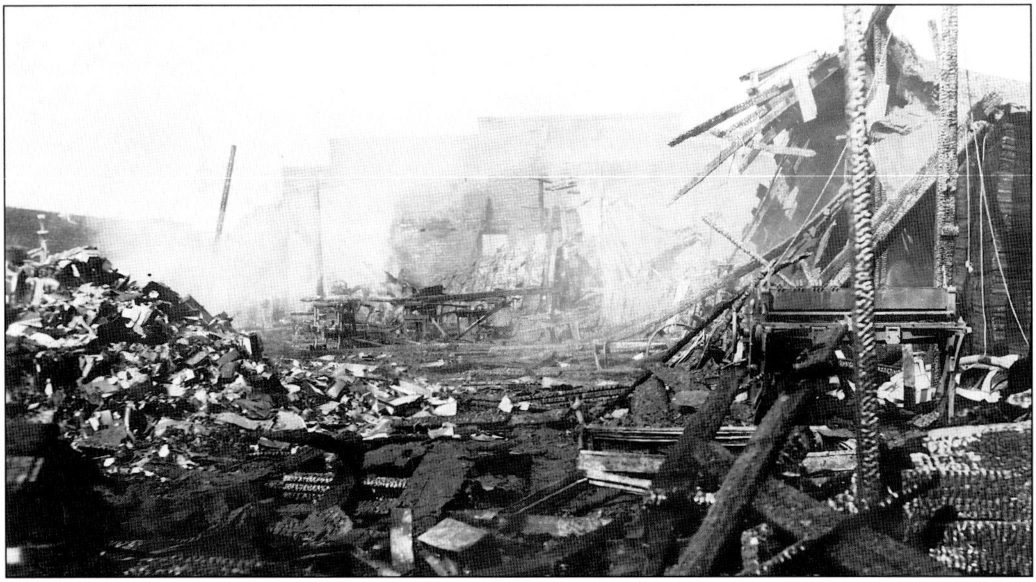

Most areas have at least one disastrous fire somewhere in their history, and Alamance County is no stranger to catastrophe. The Farmer's Warehouse burned on Sunday, October 29, 1933.

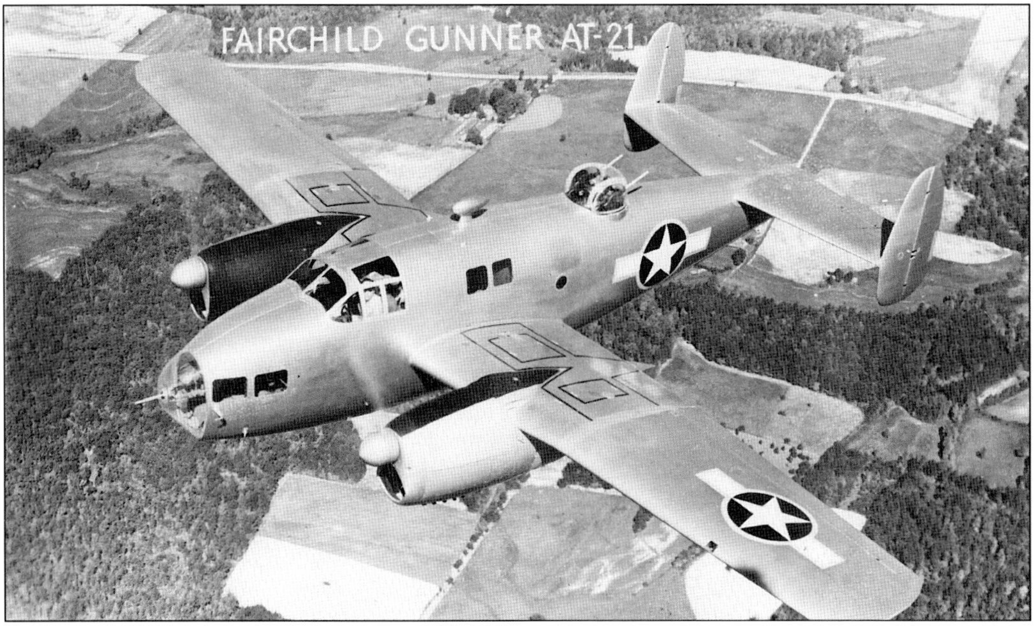

During World War II, training planes for the Army Air Force were produced at a plant in Burlington that had been established by Fairchild Aircraft Corporation. Many people from all over the United States came to work there. This Fairchild Gunner AT-21 makes a successful test flight.

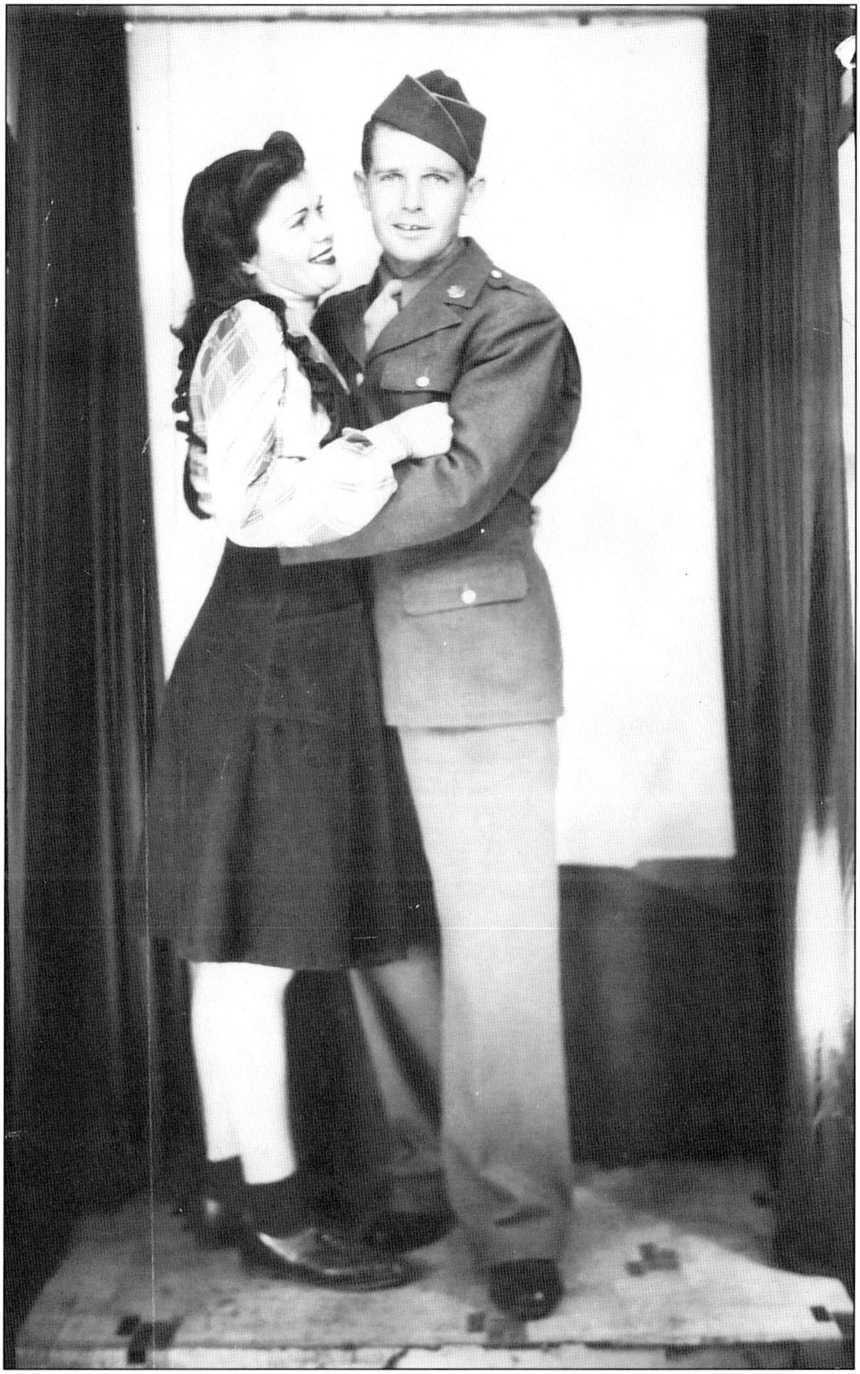

As in previous times of military action, the Second World War saw many brave Americans in Europe and away from home for long periods of time. This young man from Haw River embraces a friend while overseas. In many ways, America's military presence represented some of our highest ideals, but the writing on the back side of this photograph reveals the imperfections that some of us possess: "Russell the cook and his girl but his wife doesn't know it." (Courtesy Haw River Historical Association Museum.)

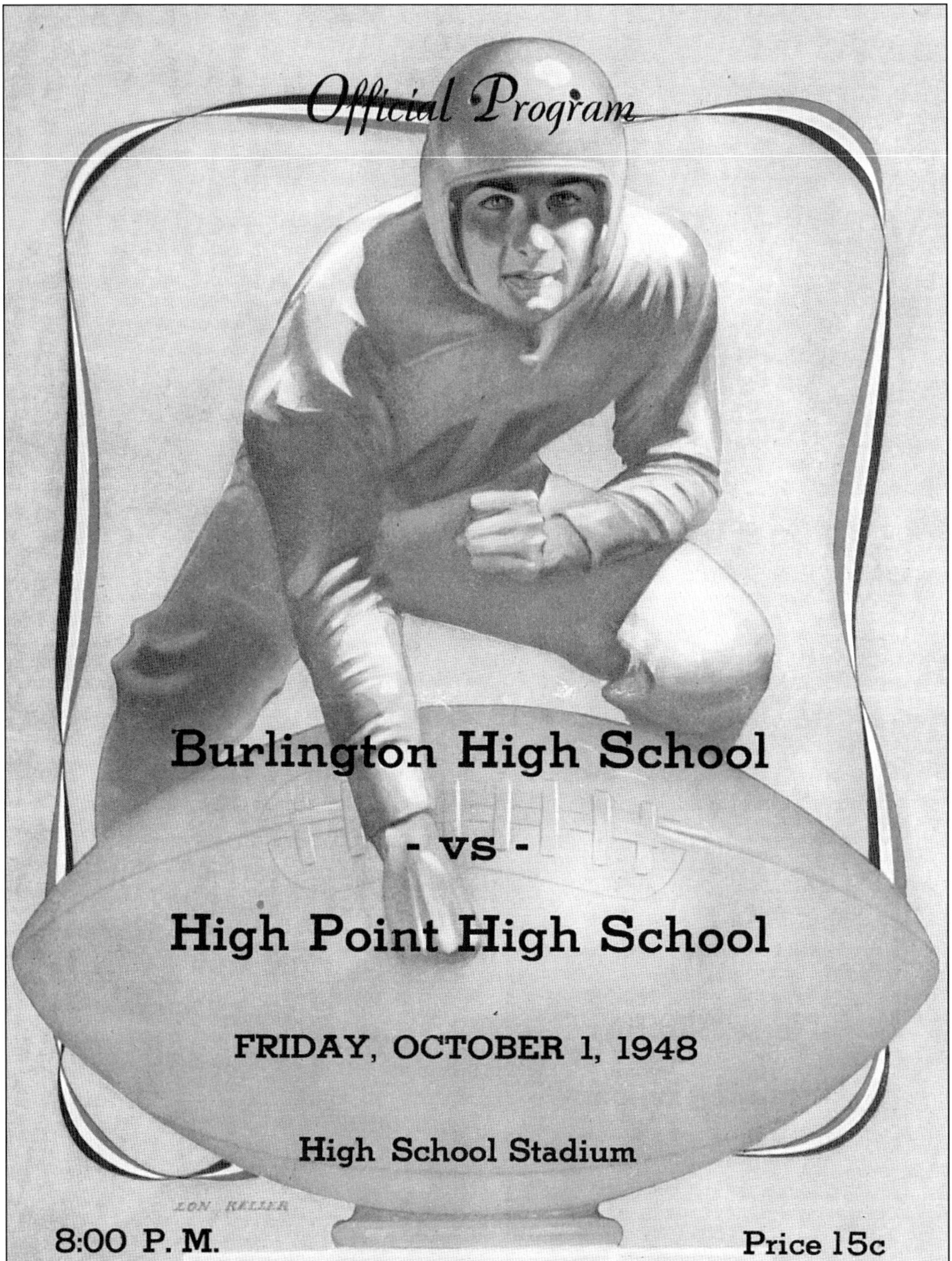

A Burlington High School football game was always a big event. Programs like this one were printed by Alamance Printing Company in Burlington. When the team played High Point High School (now Central High School) in 1948, Stanley Huffman was the head coach, and Lester Ridenhour was the director of athletics.

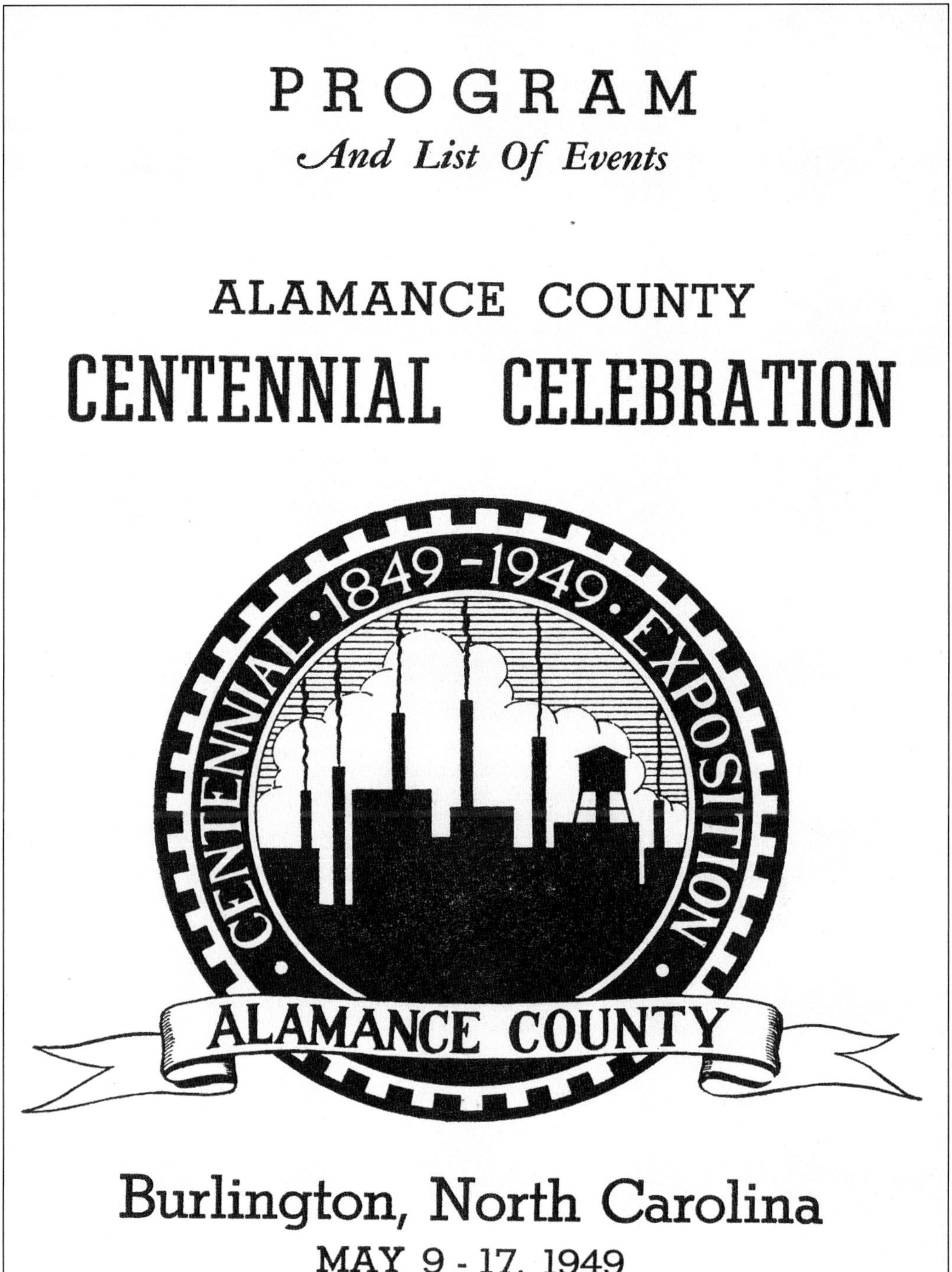

PROGRAM

And List Of Events

ALAMANCE COUNTY

CENTENNIAL CELEBRATION

Burlington, North Carolina

MAY 9 - 17, 1949

In 1949 Alamance County celebrated 100 years of existence. The centennial celebration was extremely popular with area residents, and events drew massive crowds. Goings on included a Miss Alamance Pageant, a visit by the governor, automobile giveaways, a folk music and dance festival, a ball, an outdoor historical drama, an antique show, and a combined service of all county churches in Burlington stadium.

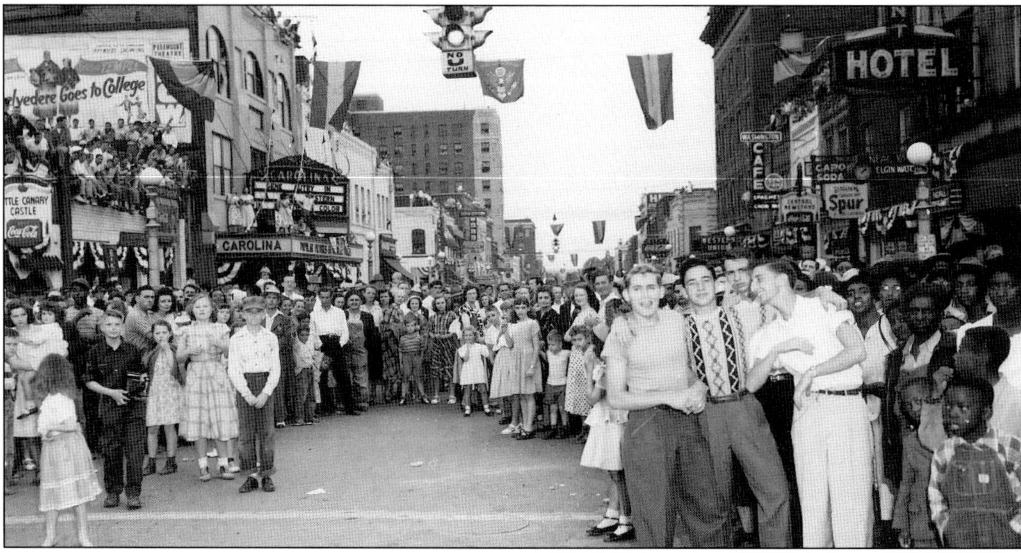

Spectators eagerly await the Centennial Parade at the intersection of Main Street and Andrews (now Webb Avenue) in Burlington. The procession started at the courthouse in Graham. One can see that the Paramount Theatre is advertising *Mr. Belvedere Goes to College*, while the Carolina plays a Gene Autry Western filmed in color. (Courtesy Nell Holt Lasley.)

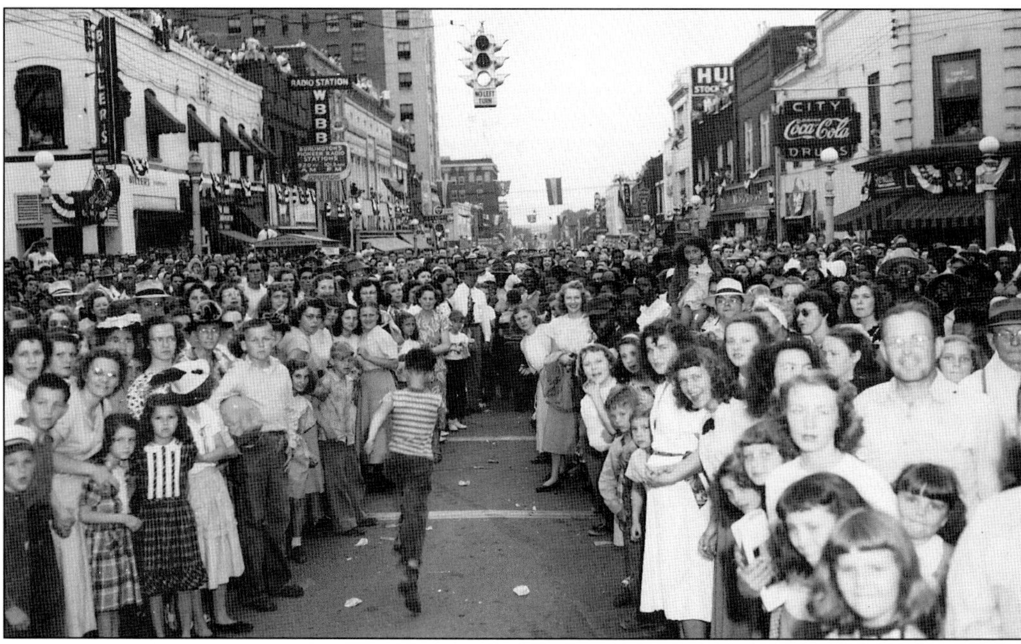

The photographer has proceeded to the next intersection to capture more parade watchers. Here, at the point where Main Street is crossed by Front Street, an even larger crowd anticipates the coming spectacle. We see that one could purchase Bulova watches at Biller's Jewelers and that radio station WBBB broadcast on both 920 AM and 101.3 FM. Many thirsty customers walked out of City Drugs with a glass bottle of Coca-cola and then gazed up at the nine-story Security Bank building. Originally the Atlantic Bank & Trust Company tower, and later the NCNB building, this building is the closest Alamance County has ever come to possessing a skyscraper. (Courtesy Nell Holt Lasley.)

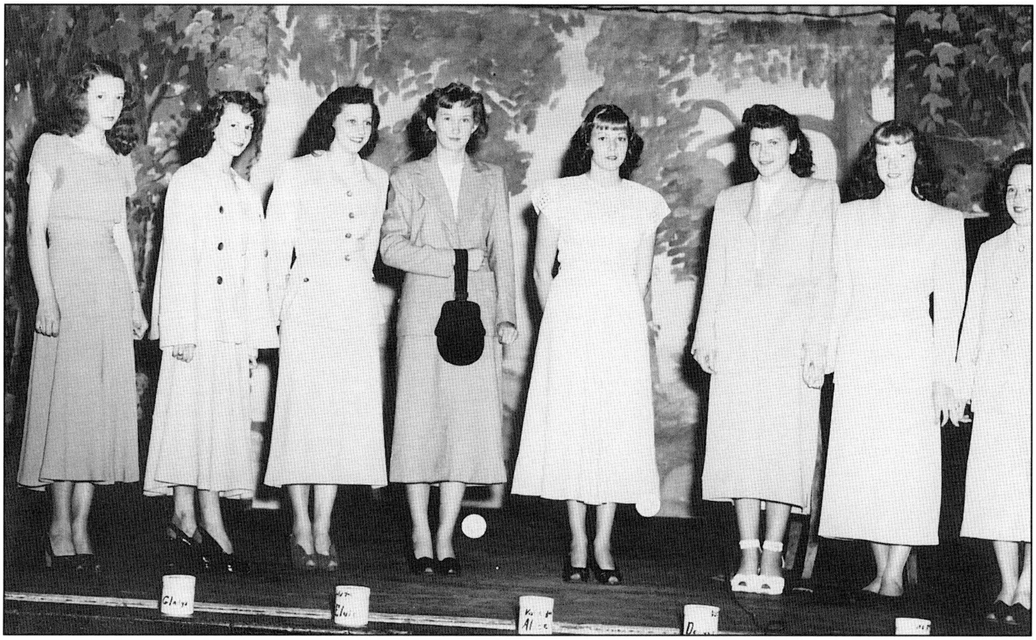

These beautiful young ladies are participants in a 1949 beauty and scholarship program sponsored by the Haw River Kiwanis Club. The contestants, from left to right, are as follows: Elaine Helms Martindale, Gladys Ray, Deanne Keck, Doris Buford, Alice Ray, Ruby Lamb, Betty Lou Byrd, and Doris Chatman Fogleman. Miss Ray was the winner of the pageant. (Courtesy Haw River Historical Association Museum.)

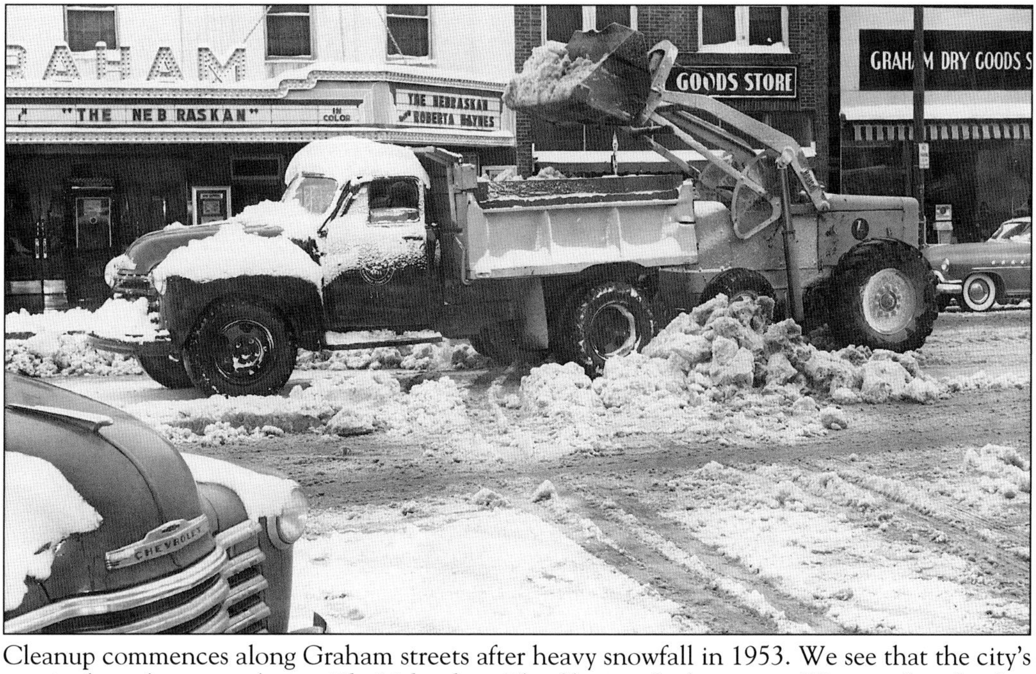

Cleanup commences along Graham streets after heavy snowfall in 1953. We see that the city's movie showplace was playing *The Nebraskan*. The film is a fairly routine Western, but the fact that it was filmed in color was enough of a selling point to get audiences out of their houses for a trek through the snow. (Courtesy City of Graham.)

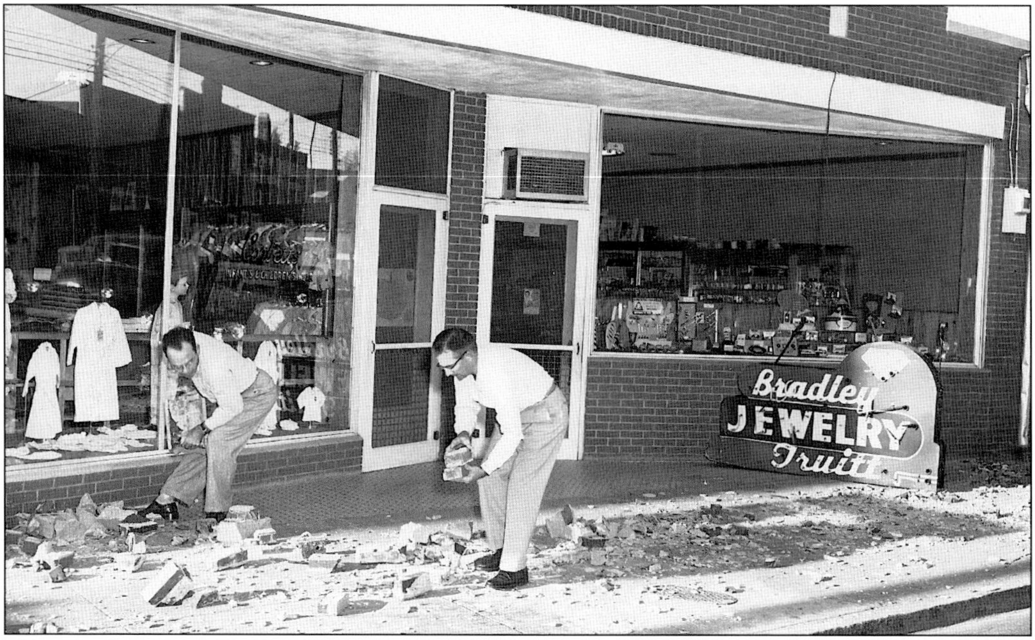

The windstorm caused by Hurricane Hazel reached far inland and is well remembered by longtime Alamance County residents. Pete Bradley and Keith Truitt clean up their storefront in Mebane on October 8, 1954. (Courtesy Town of Mebane.)

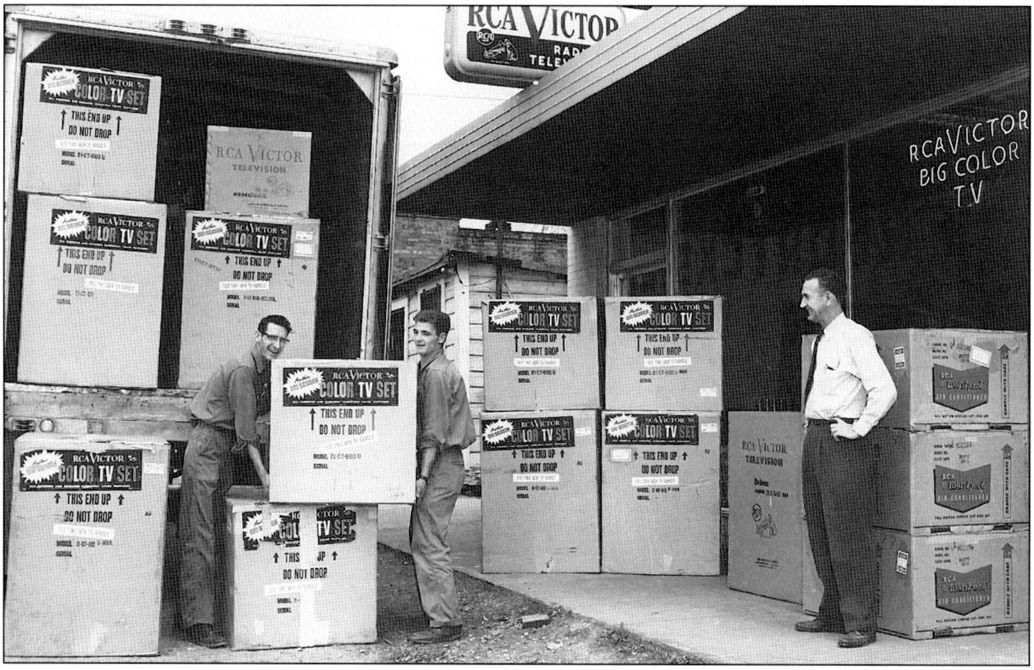

Much excitement was caused by a certain long-anticipated delivery to the Home and Farm Center in Haw River. Welcomed by a new neon sign, this was the first truckload of RCA color television sets shipped south of the Mason-Dixon line and east of the Mississippi River. From left to right are as follows: A. Reid Bayliff, Marco Mora, and Adrian L. Barger. (Courtesy Haw River Historical Association Museum.)

Two

Towns and Cities

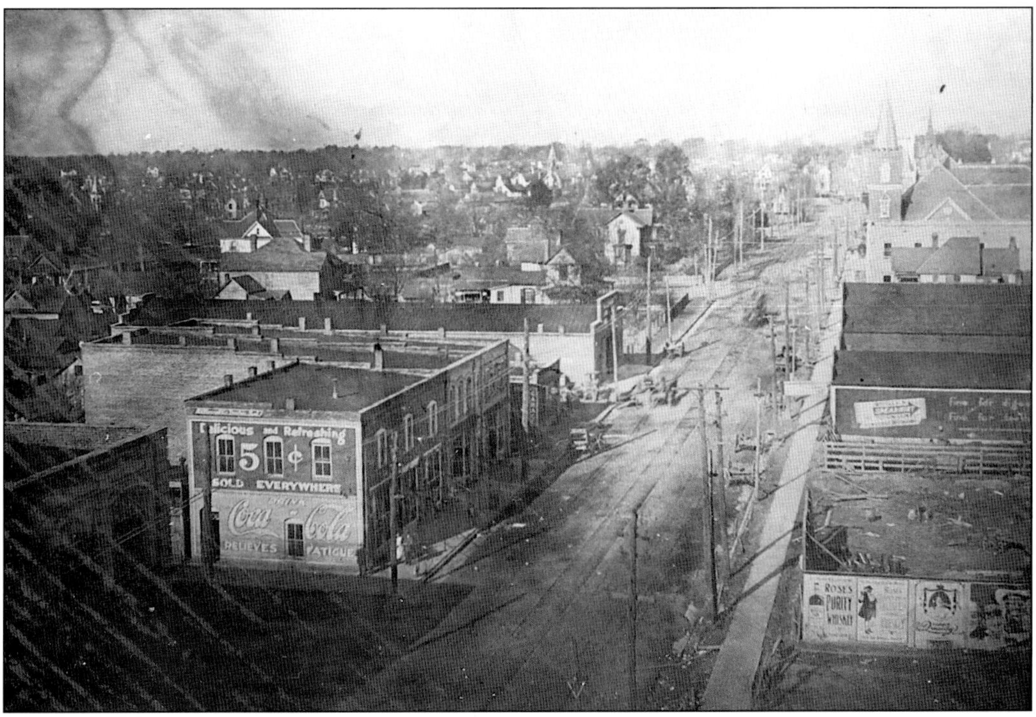

Around 1914 this photograph of Front Street in Burlington was taken from an upper story of the First National Bank building. Trolley tracks are clearly visible along the length of the unpaved street. One or more horse-drawn vehicles may be spotted, but no automobiles are in view. The building at left, with the advertisement for fatigue-relieving Coca-cola, housed the offices of the town government. On the right, Wrigley's Spearmint Gum is painted on the wall of a livery stable. Riding the streetcar toward the horizon, one would pass the Presbyterian and Methodist churches. (Courtesy Nell Holt Lasley.)

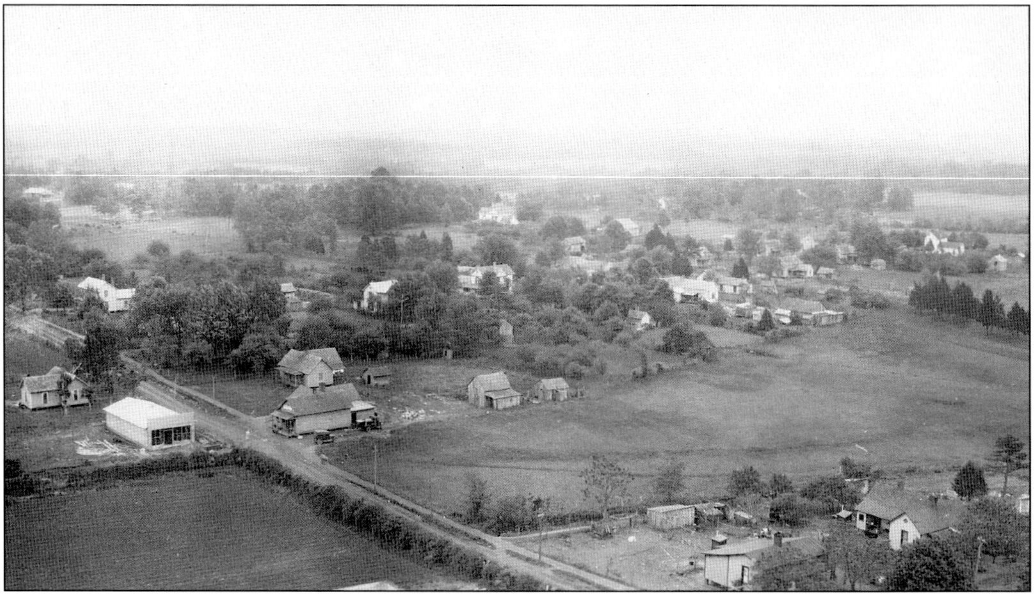

The person who took this photograph of 1920s Gibsonville stood with his/her back to Guilford County and looked across to the Alamance County portion of the town. The community was known as Gibsonville at least as far back as 1855, and the town was incorporated in 1871. (Courtesy Town of Gibsonville.)

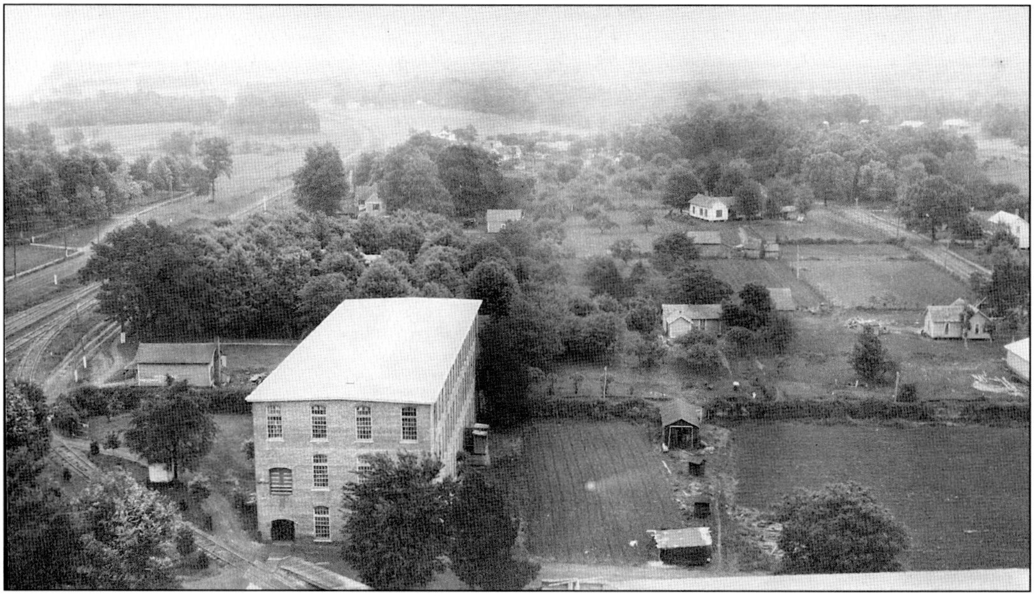

This is another view from Guilford County of the Alamance section of Gibsonville in the 1920s. Over the years, the town has faced many complex problems because of its division between two counties. (Courtesy Town of Gibsonville.)

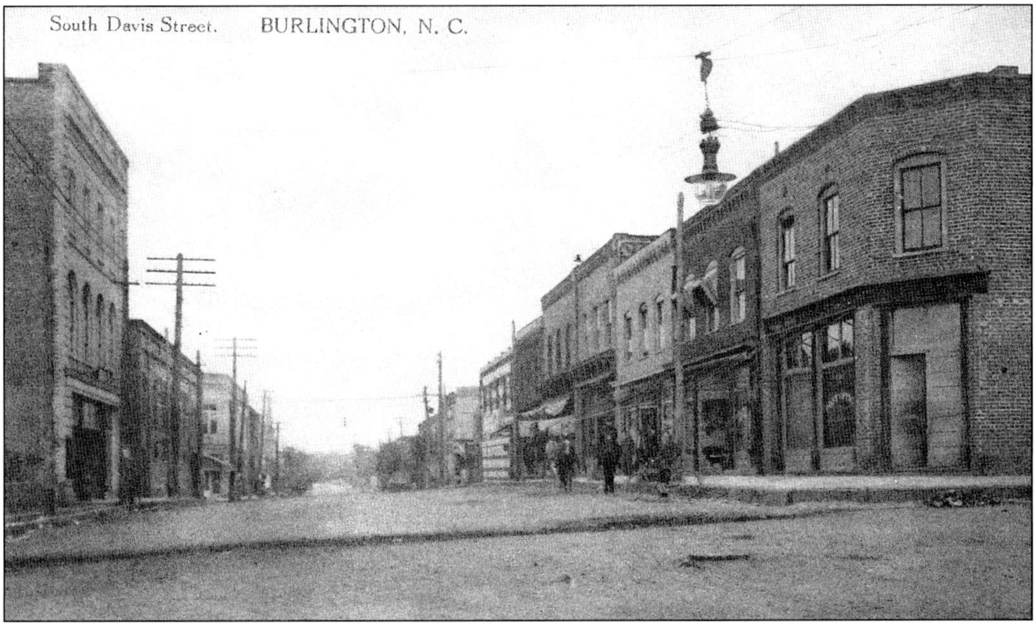

This postcard scene of Davis Street in Burlington is from around 1910 and was published by C.V. Sellers Art Store. (Courtesy Nell Holt Lasley.)

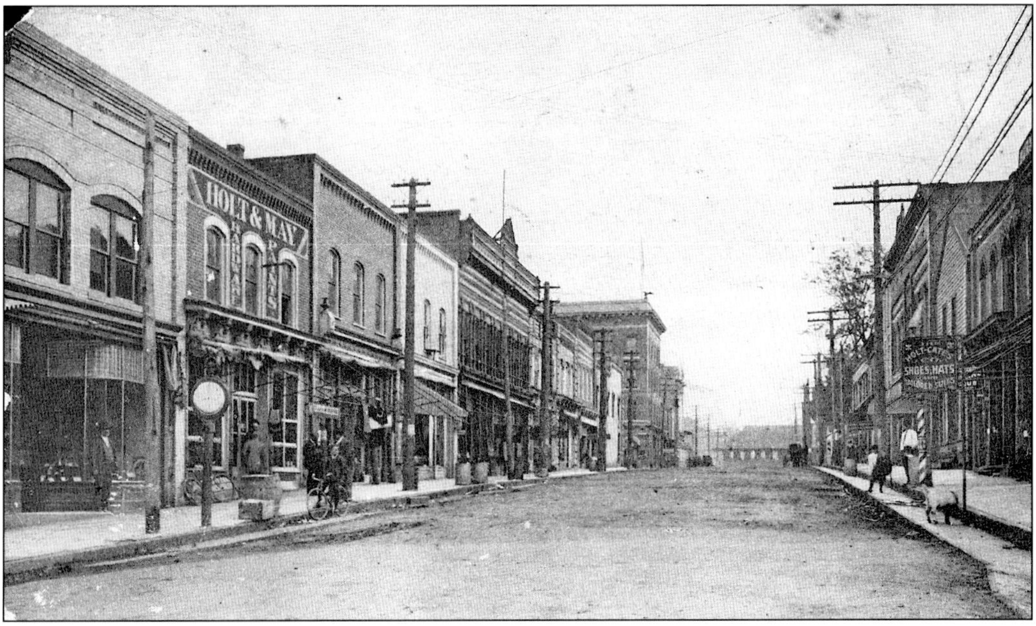

Another in the series of Burlington postcards from Sellers Art Store, this image reveals much about the community during the first 12 or so years of the twentieth century. As in other photographs from the time, no automobiles are in evidence, but two bicycles can be seen at left awaiting use as a mode of transportation. Also at left, behind a convenient street-side clock stands the store of Holt and May, offering a supply of hardware and a selection of paints. Following the utility poles across the scene to the right, we see the Holt Cates Co., dealer in shoes, hats, and tailored suits. A barber's pole stands out prominently as pedestrians and a dog seem to pose as permanent fixtures in this setting. (Courtesy Nell Holt Lasley.)

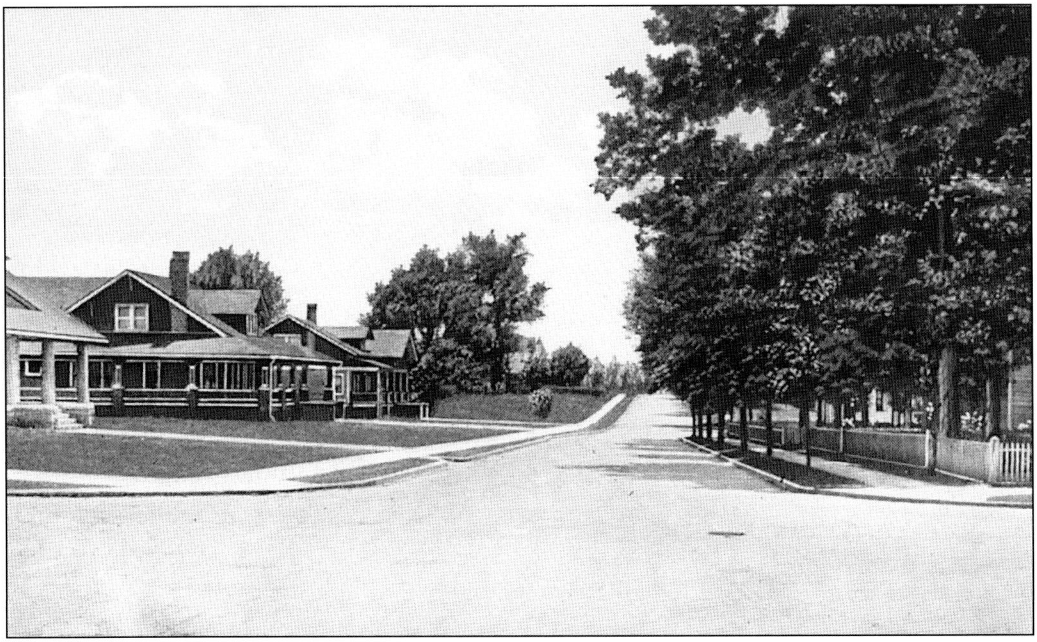

This postcard view of a Mebane residential area was taken in the 1920s. We are facing south down Fifth Street from the intersection of Jackson Street. (Courtesy Town of Mebane.)

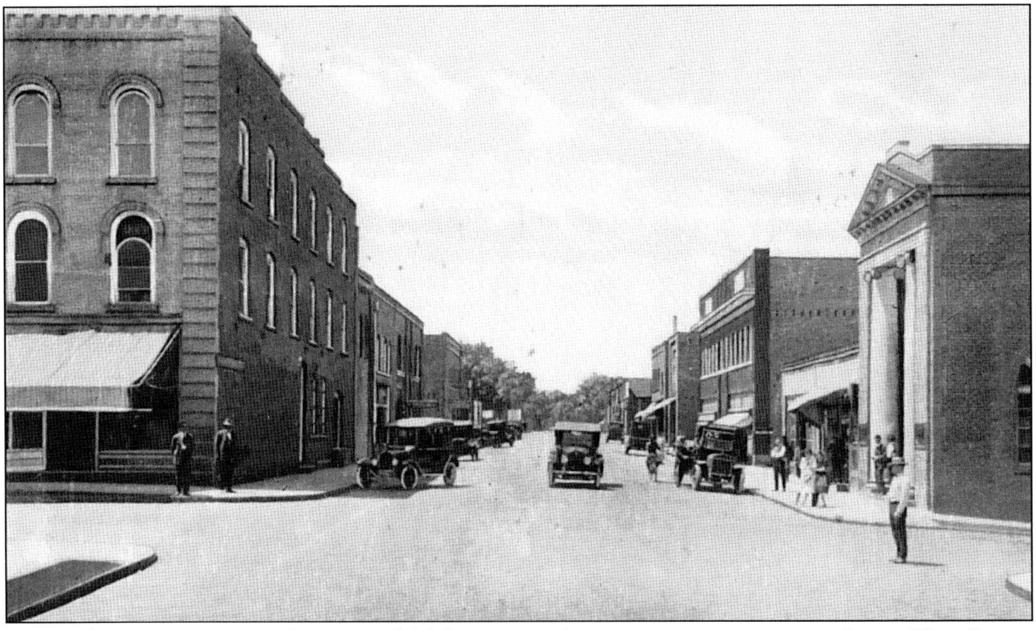

In another 1920s postcard image of Mebane, one has opportunity to gaze down Clay Street from the vantage point of the Fourth Street crossing. While in the teens, it would have been difficult to spot an automobile in or near Alamance County. A decade later, motorcars were commonplace. (Courtesy Town of Mebane.)

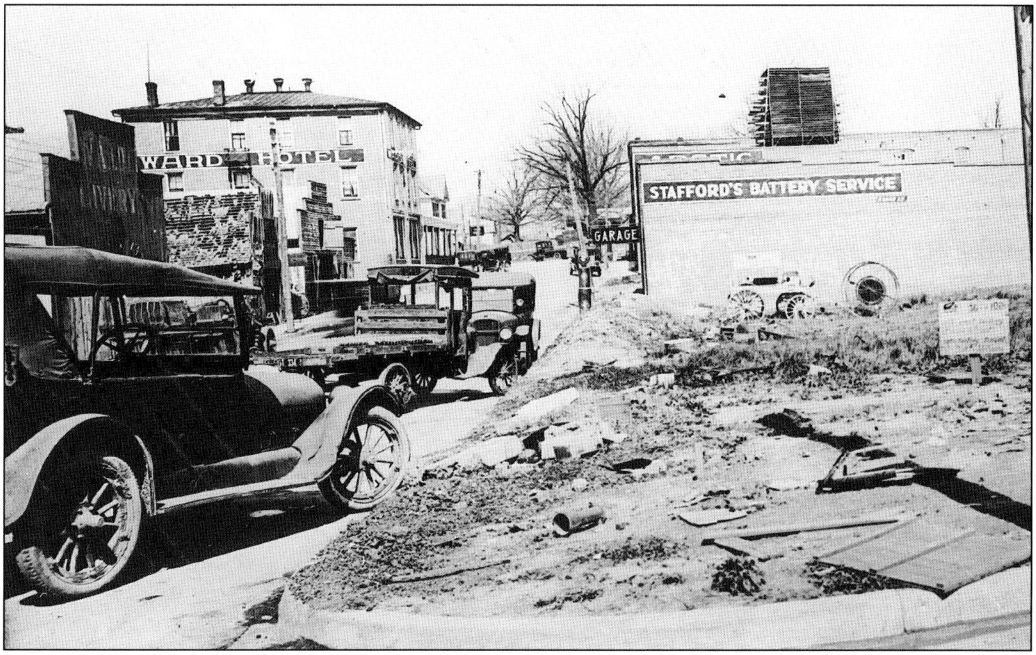

In the 1920s, Webb Avenue was still known as Andrews Street. On the left the Ward Hotel stands at the North Church Street intersection. Jane Elizabeth Cheatham Ward built the hotel in 1904, and it thrived as Burlington's main and, for a time, only inn.

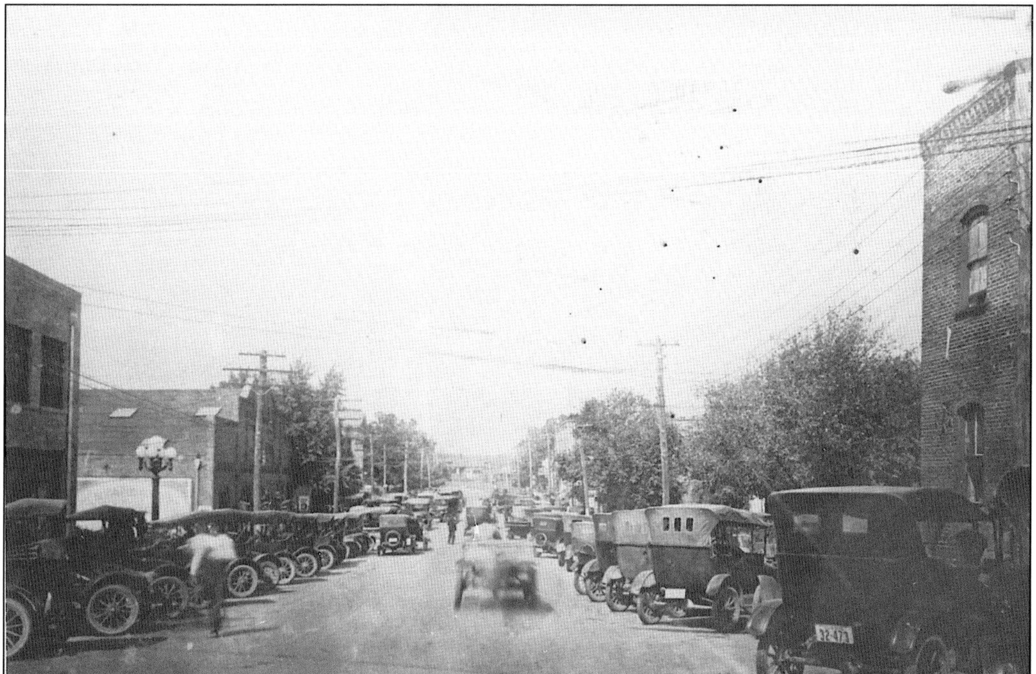

This photograph of a street in Mebane was made during a big event. A barely visible overhead banner advertises the four-county fair, which was first organized in 1919 and expanded to include six counties in 1926.

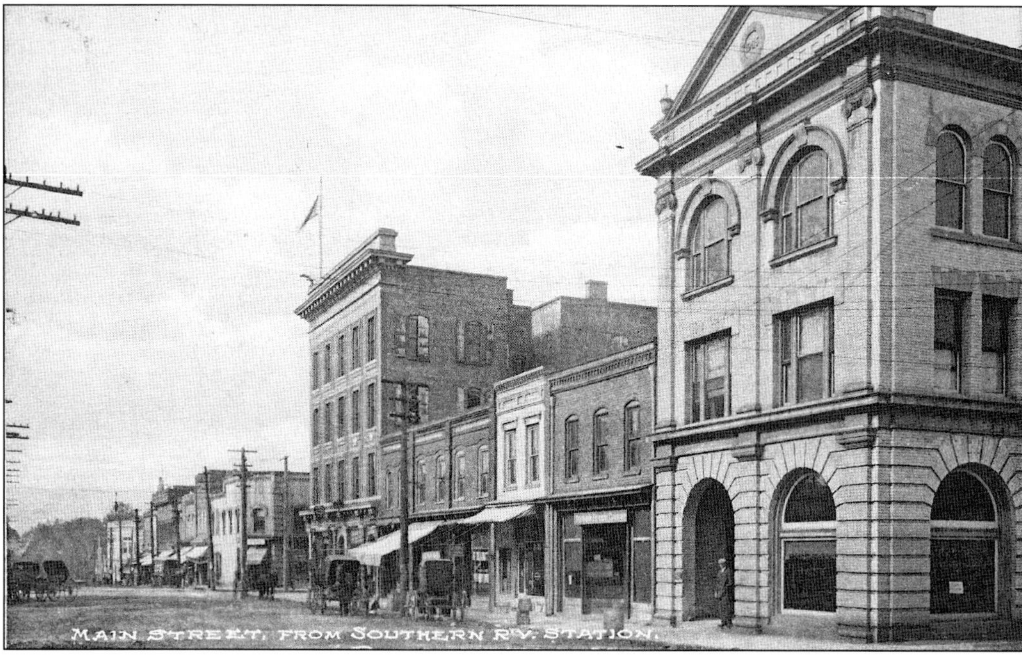

In this turn-of-the-century-era postcard of Burlington, we see Main Street from the Southern Railway station.

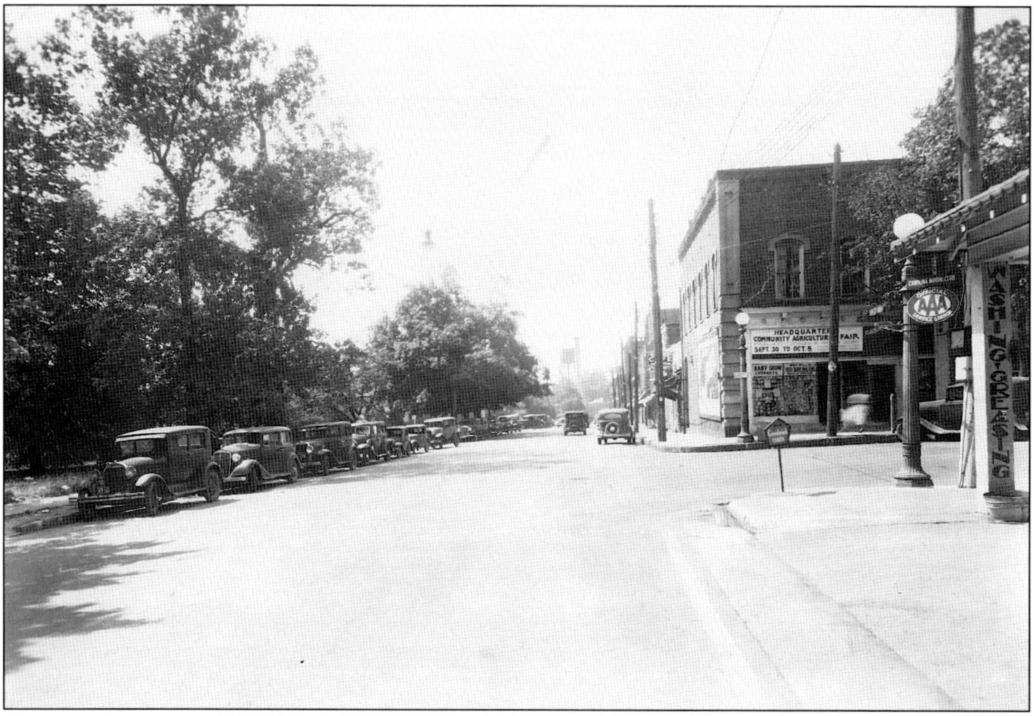

A view of downtown Burlington is represented in this photograph made in the 1930s. This is the corner of East Front Street and South Spring Street.

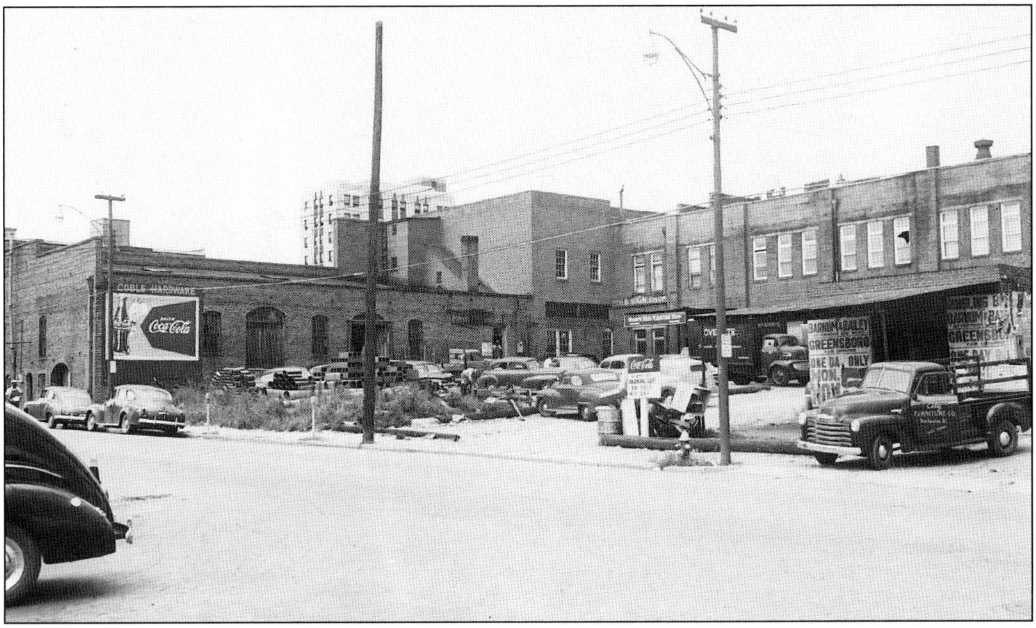

Security Bank Building rises in the background of this 1940s view of Worth Street in Burlington. Coble Hardware is at left, and at center is the location of Cobb Sign Shop. The truck on the right hauled merchandise for City Furniture Company. Behind it are advertisements for Ringling Brothers Barnum and Bailey Circus.

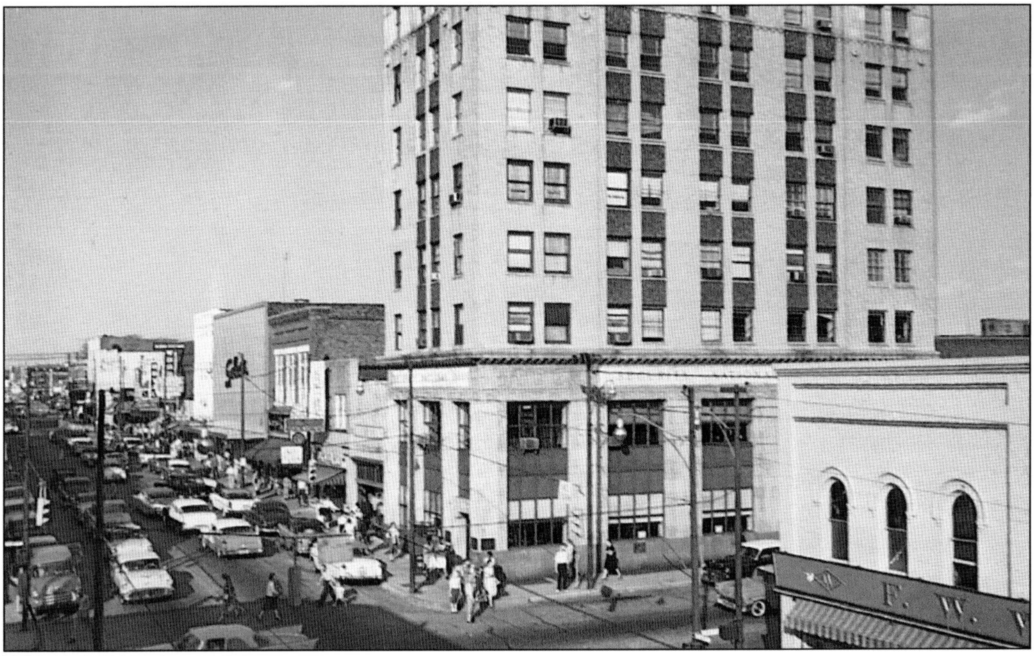

This late 1950s postcard image communicates the hustle and bustle of Burlington's downtown business district. The ever-visible Security Bank Building dominates this view of South Main Street. (Courtesy Alamance County Historical Museum, Inc.)

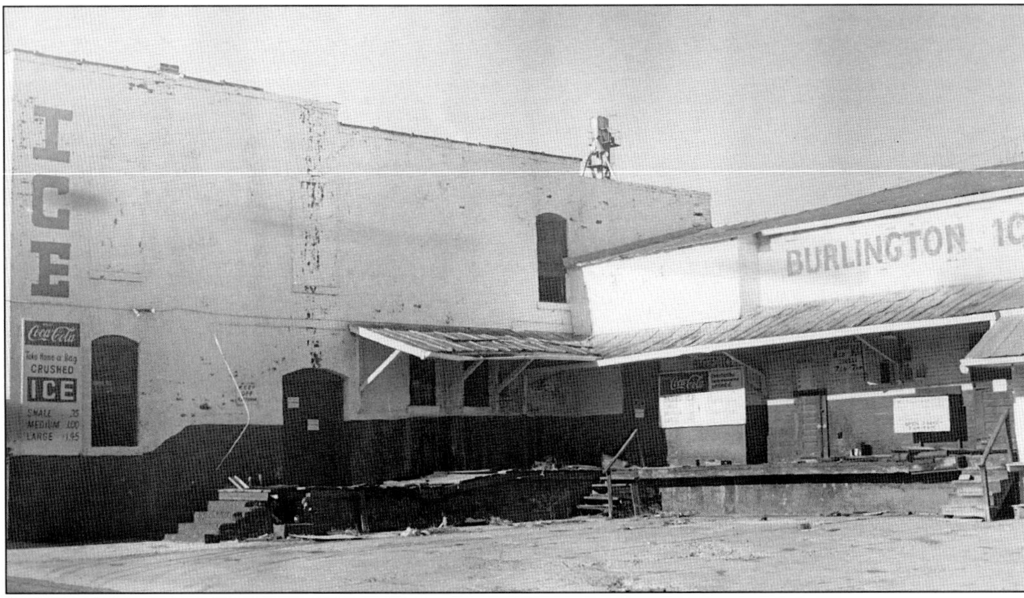

Burlington Ice Company was open seven days a week. (Courtesy Nell Holt Lasley.)

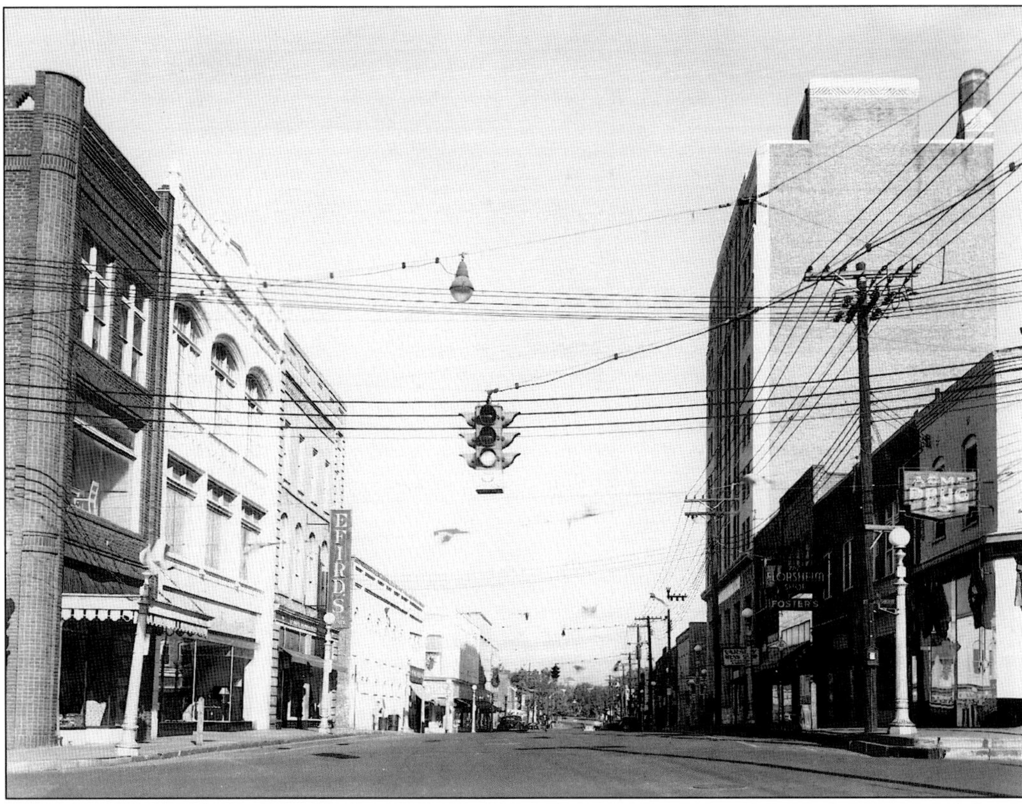

By the 1940s, Burlington's downtown area, near the intersection of Spring Street and Davis Street, was composed of such a great number of establishments offering so many services that almost any imaginable need could be satisfied.

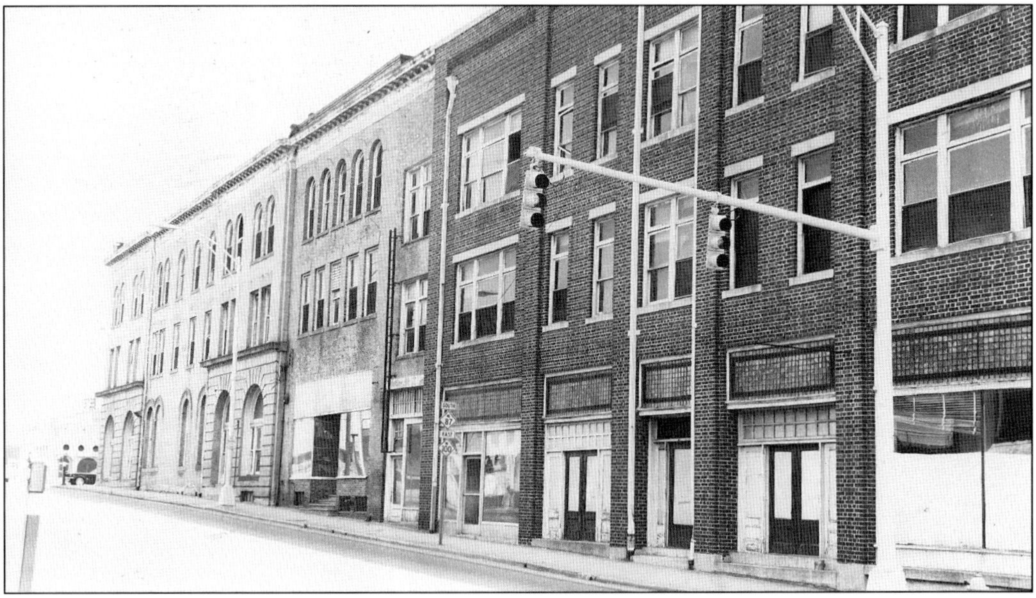

After the 1960s, this view of these buildings on Webb Avenue would never be seen again. The section was demolished.

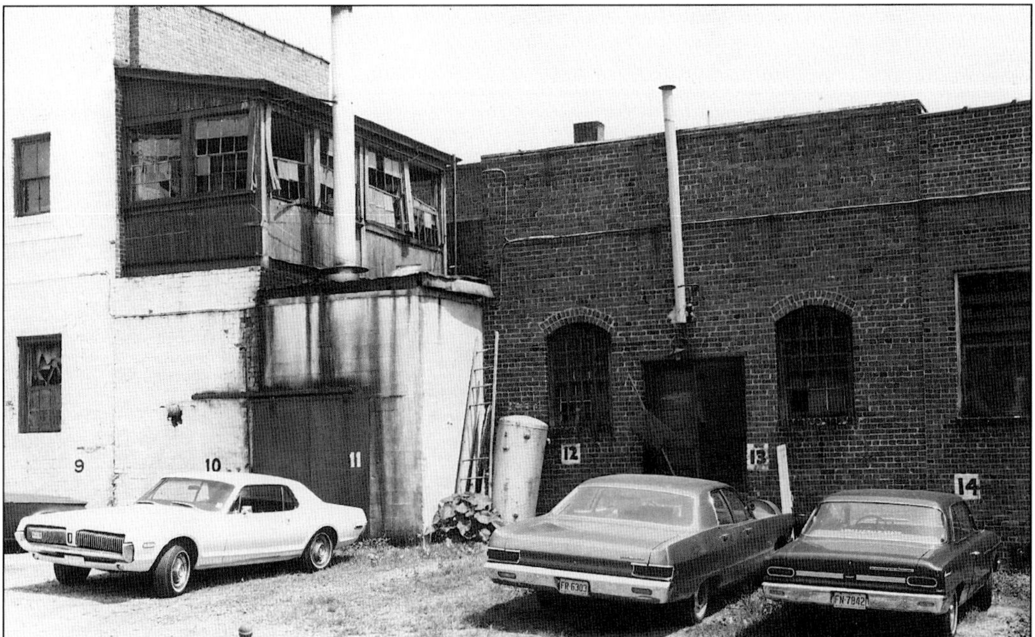

This photograph from the late 1960s has preserved a sign indicating reserved parking spaces for customers of Northwestern Bank. Many Alamance County citizens relied on Northwestern Bank year after year until it became First Union Bank in the 1980s.

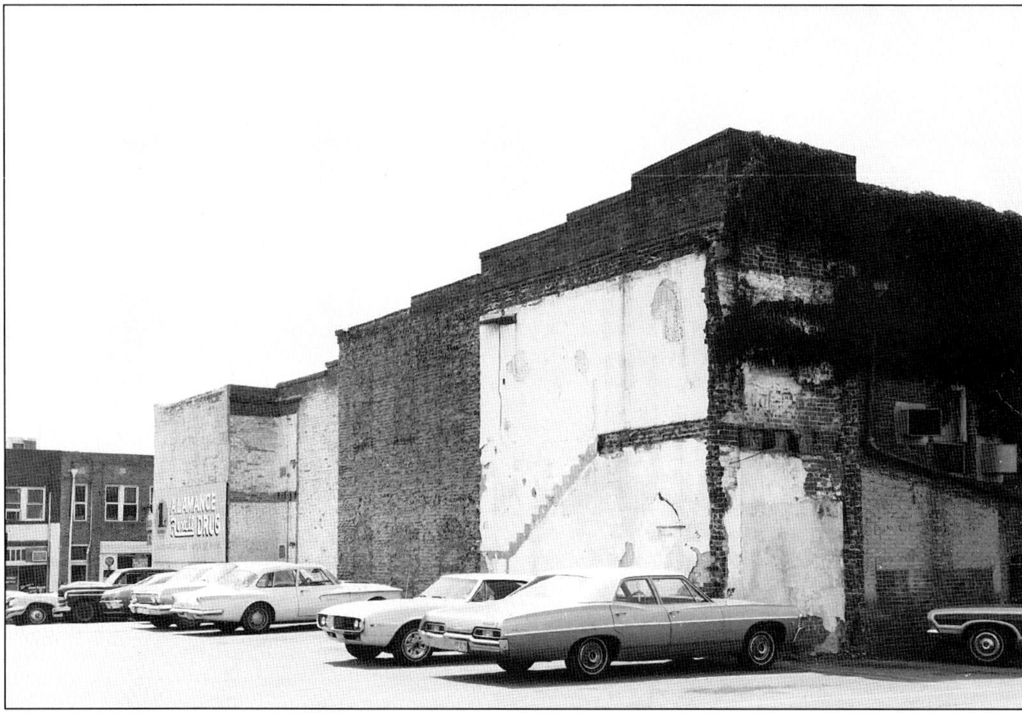

On the left of this picture, across the street from Herman's Shoe Shine, a sign boasts that Alamance Rexall Drug is "#1 in Service." By the late 1960s, when this photograph was taken, they were offering a 24-hour prescription service.

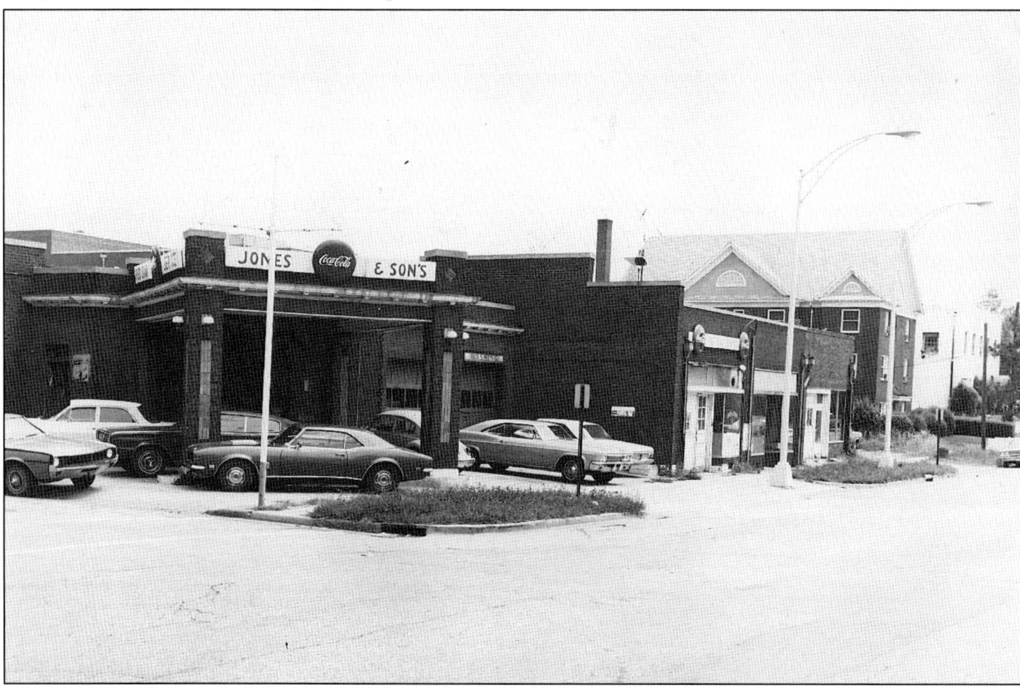

Jones and Son's Red Star Service Station was a busy place in the Burlington of the late 1960s. Car washing was only one of many services available.

Three

Public Places

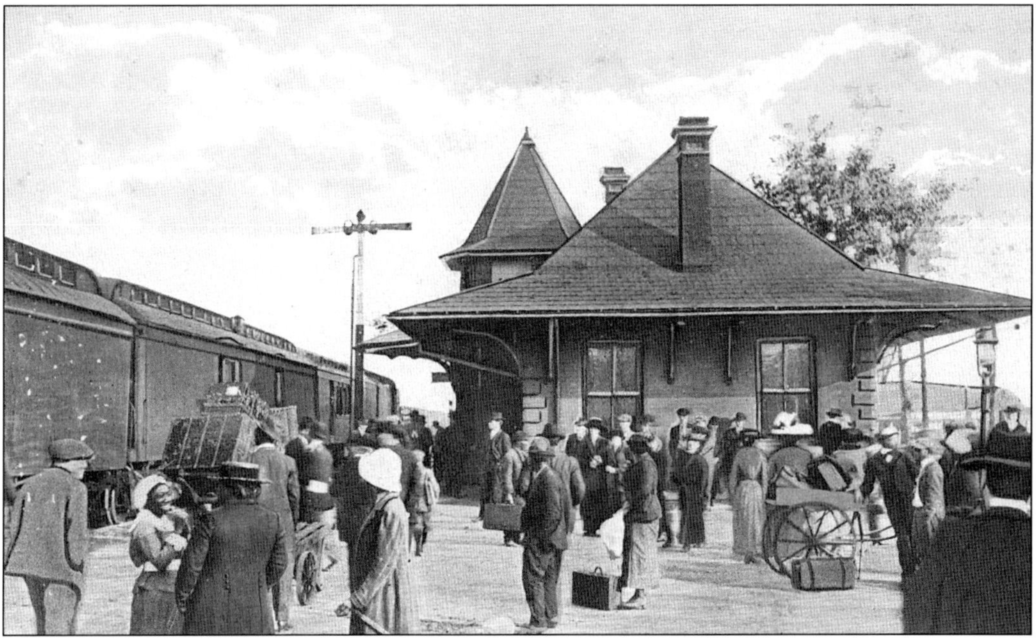

This postcard image is one of the most fascinating views of times past in Burlington. If one were to choose a frozen moment to use as a symbol of the city's history, this gem could very well be the winner. The Burlington Passenger Depot, also known as Southern Railway Station-Burlington, was built in late 1892 and/or early 1893. African-American ladies are part of the animated throng seen congregating around the depot awaiting either an arrival or a departure. Could the abundance of hats be evidence of cold weather or merely proof that the people of the county were always outfitted in proper attire?

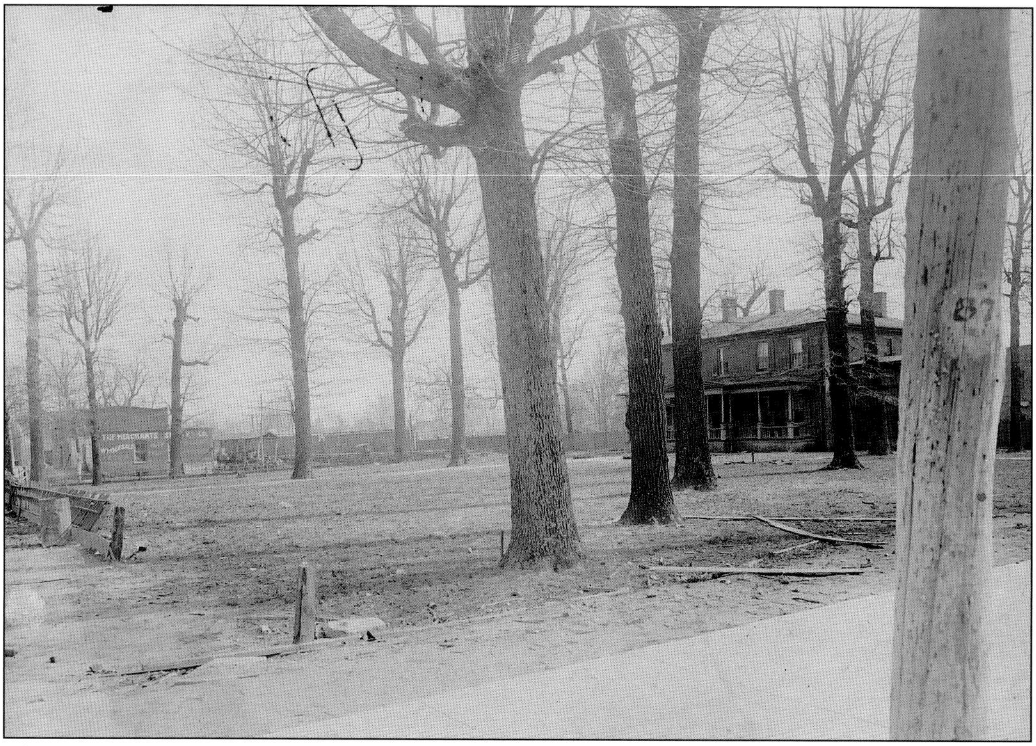

The house on the right served as the office of the North Carolina Railroad for many years and was located in Burlington. It was one of the original buildings constructed in the 1850s for the village then known as Company Shops. The structure was torn down in 1929.

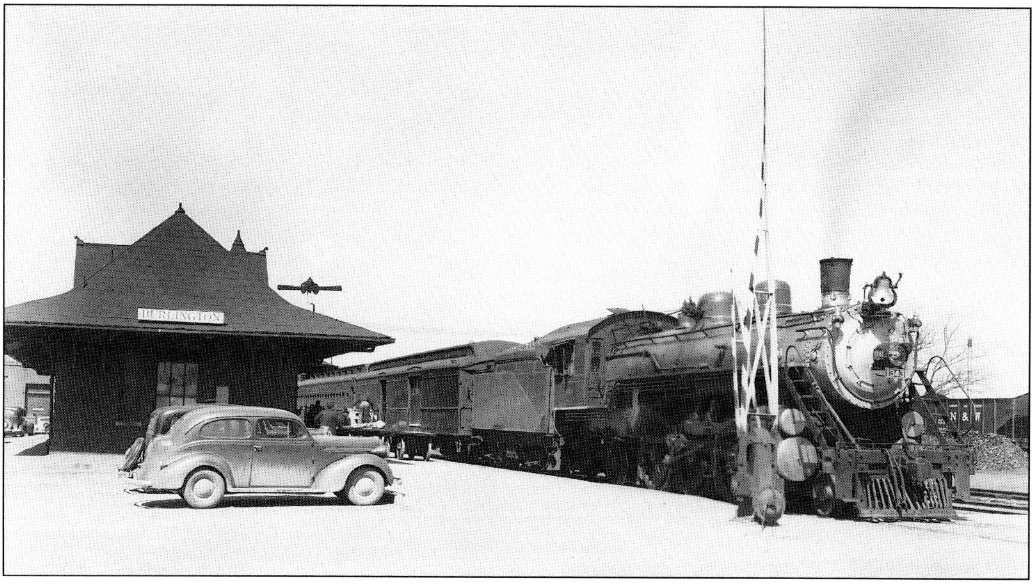

At first glance, one may get the impression that this locomotive is roaring down the track. Upon further study, it becomes quite evident that the train is at rest, awaiting the transfer of passengers at the still-charming Burlington Depot in the late 1930s or early 1940s. (Courtesy Alamance County Historical Museum, Inc.)

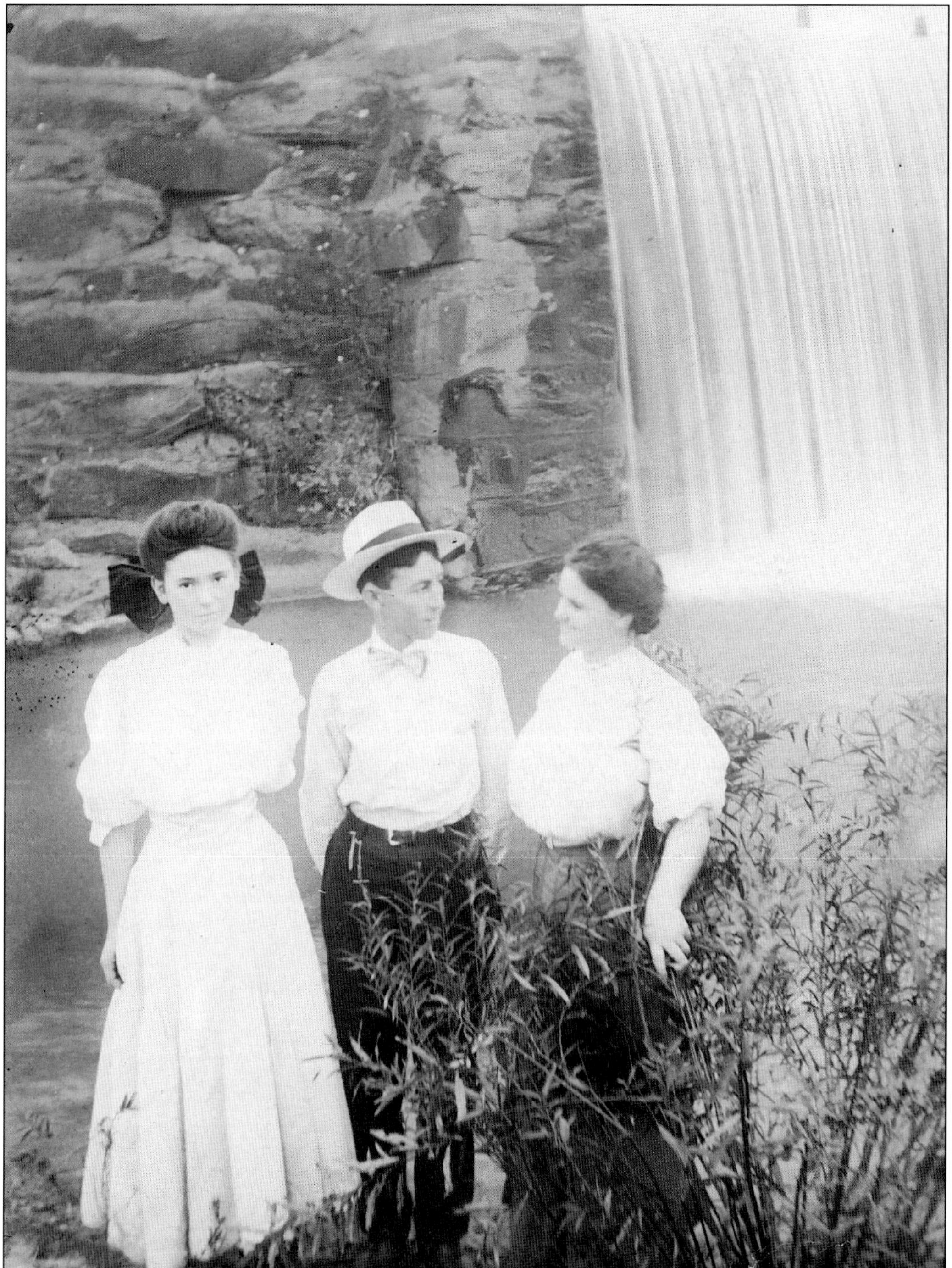

This interesting postcard image was made around 1915. The three people are standing on the banks of the Haw River and enjoying the soothing sound of the man-made waterfall. During this time period, it was a common practice to have a photograph of one's friends or family transformed into a postcard. (Courtesy Haw River Historical Association Museum.)

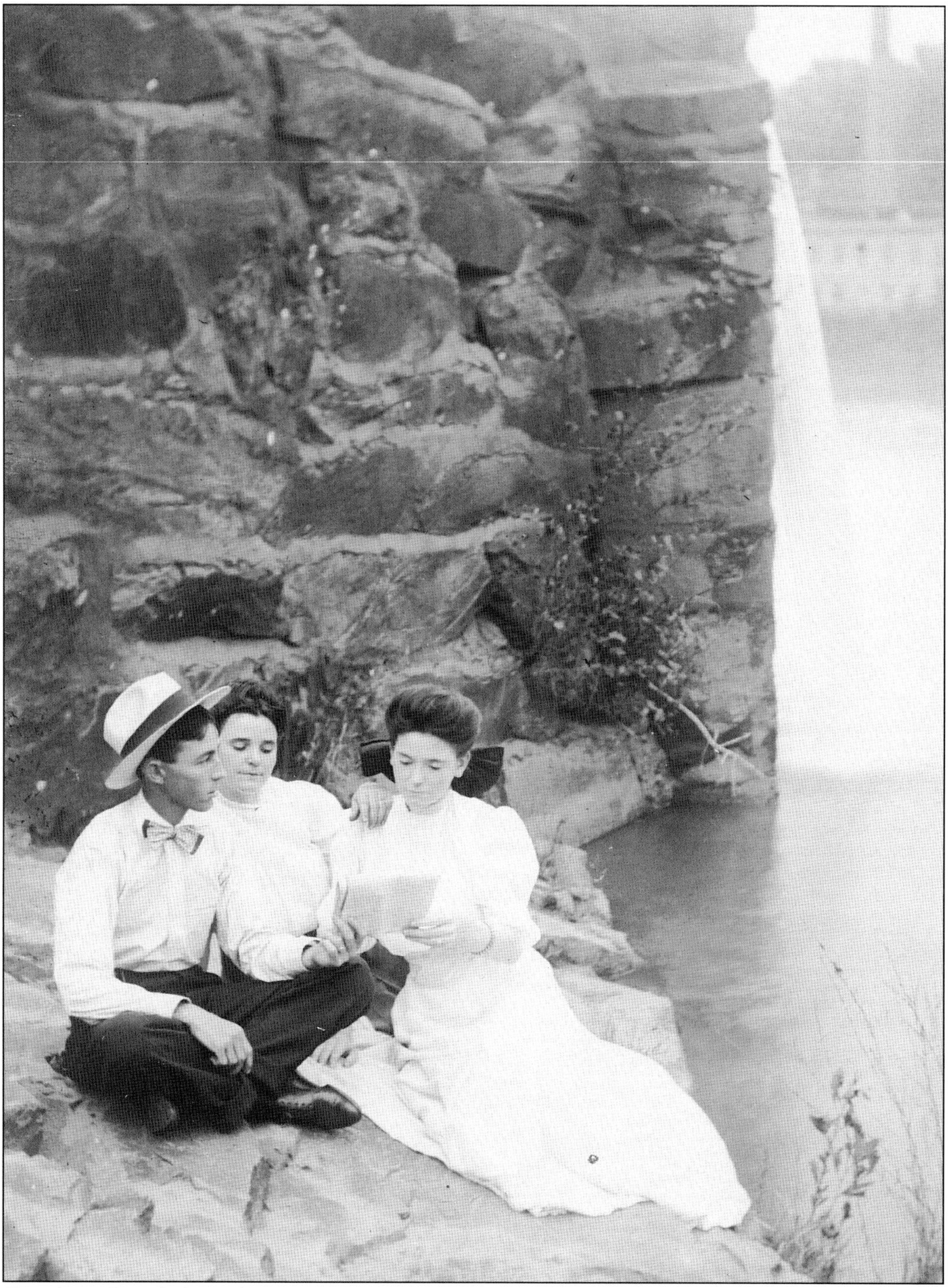

Our three friends from the previous page now strike a different pose in their efforts to provide postcards for distant mailboxes. They seem to have crossed to the other side of the river previous to reclining before a background view of the old Granite factory. One wonders what they could have chosen as riverside reading material. (Courtesy Haw River Historical Association Museum.)

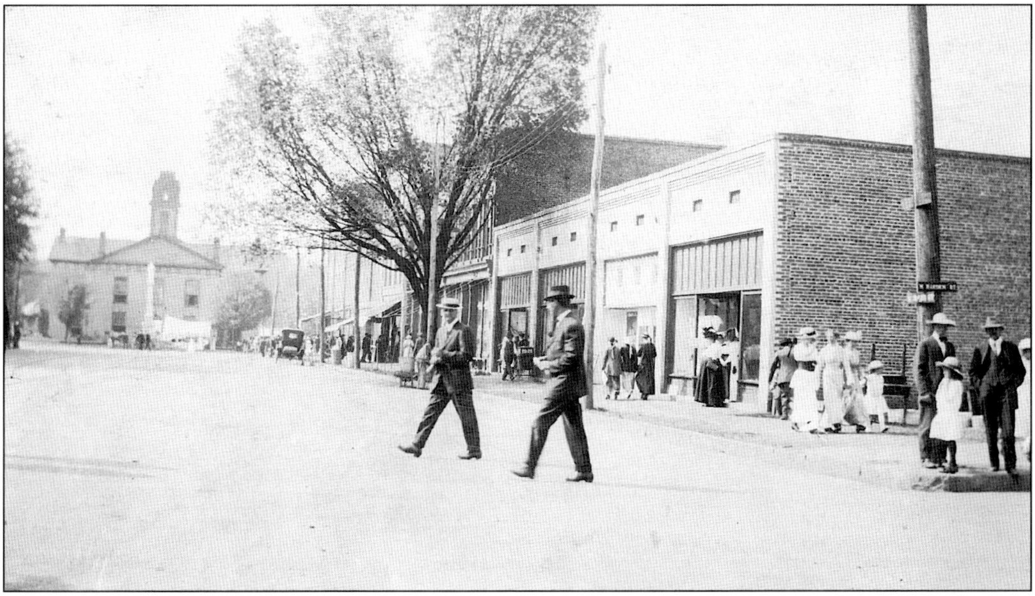

Sent to Miss Swanna Albright, Delgado Office, Wilmington, this postcard from Graham is postmarked May 13, 1915. Complete with bell tower, Alamance County's original courthouse stands down the street behind the Civil War monument. The structure was built a short time after the county came into existence in 1849. After serving the citizens for almost 74 years, it was torn down in 1923.

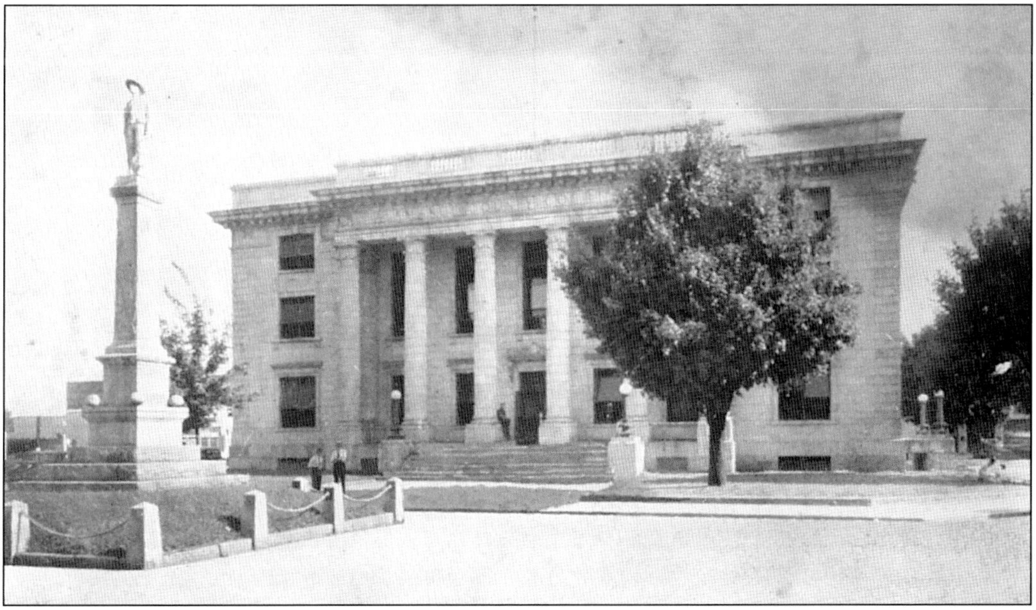

When the old courthouse was demolished, it was decided to keep the statue of the Confederate soldier. As seen in this postcard image from mid-century, the monument is still standing before the new courthouse, which opened in 1924. Now, near the turn of the millennium, little has changed in this scene of Graham. (Courtesy Amy E. Jordan of the Graham Public Library.)

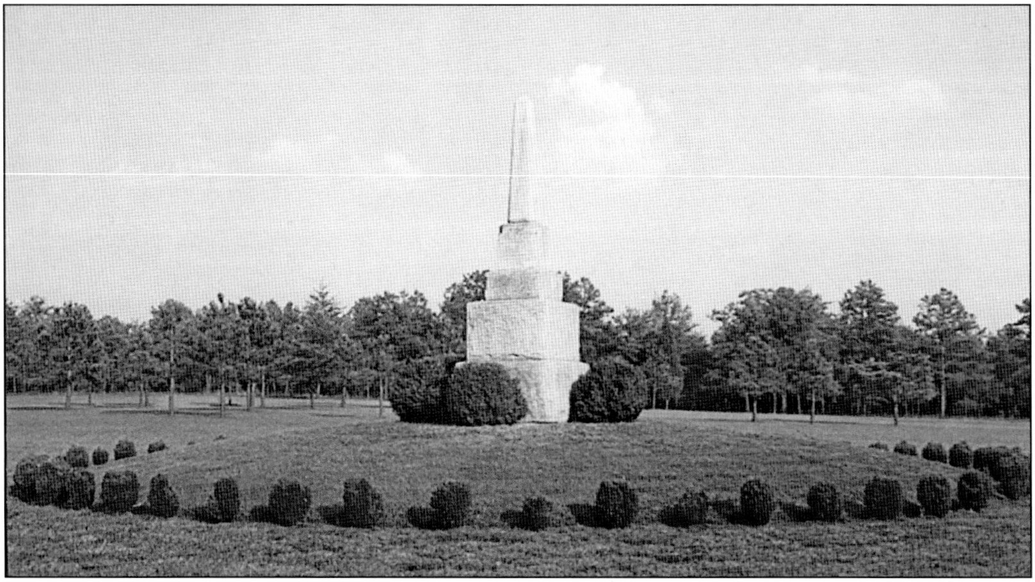

This photograph from 1960 shows a portion of Alamance Battleground on Highway 62 southwest of the town of Alamance. The monument was erected in 1880 to commemorate the battle in which colonists defied the royal militia in 1771.

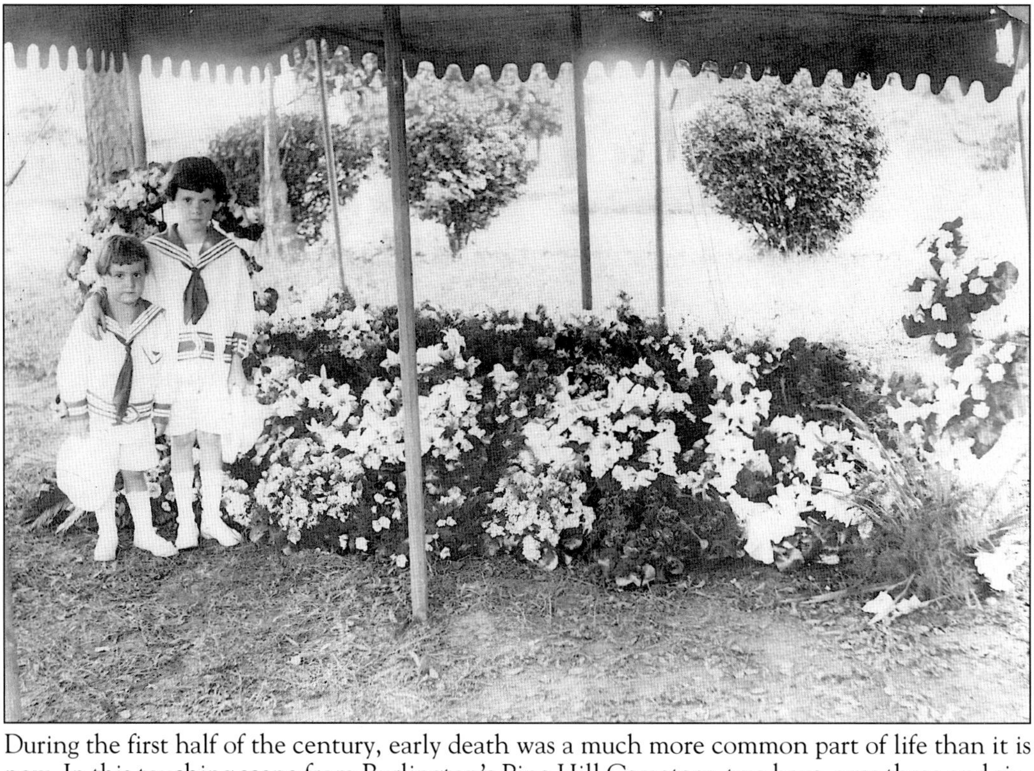

During the first half of the century, early death was a much more common part of life than it is now. In this touching scene from Burlington's Pine Hill Cemetery, two boys, ages three and six, mourn the passing of their 34-year-old father in July of 1917. (Courtesy Nell Holt Lasley.)

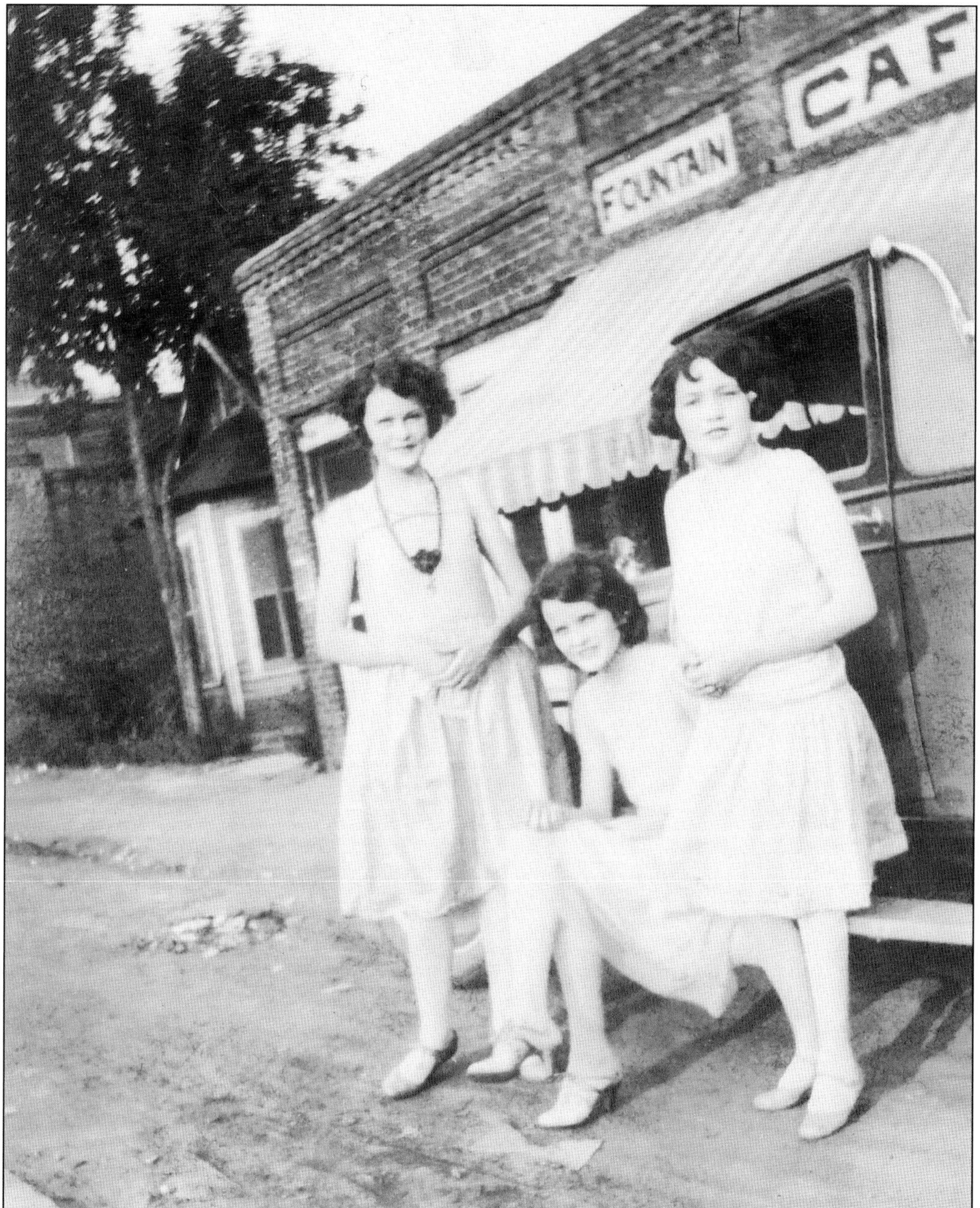

A 1959 edition of *Webster's* defined "flapper" this way: "In the 1920s, a young girl considered bold and unconventional in actions and dress." A more recent edition describes her as follows: "A young woman of the period of World War I and the following decade who showed freedom from conventions (as in conduct)." Whatever your definition, the '20s were certainly roaring in Haw River when these three young ladies were captured by a photographer. The one on the right is Bonnie Pearson. (Courtesy Town of Mebane.)

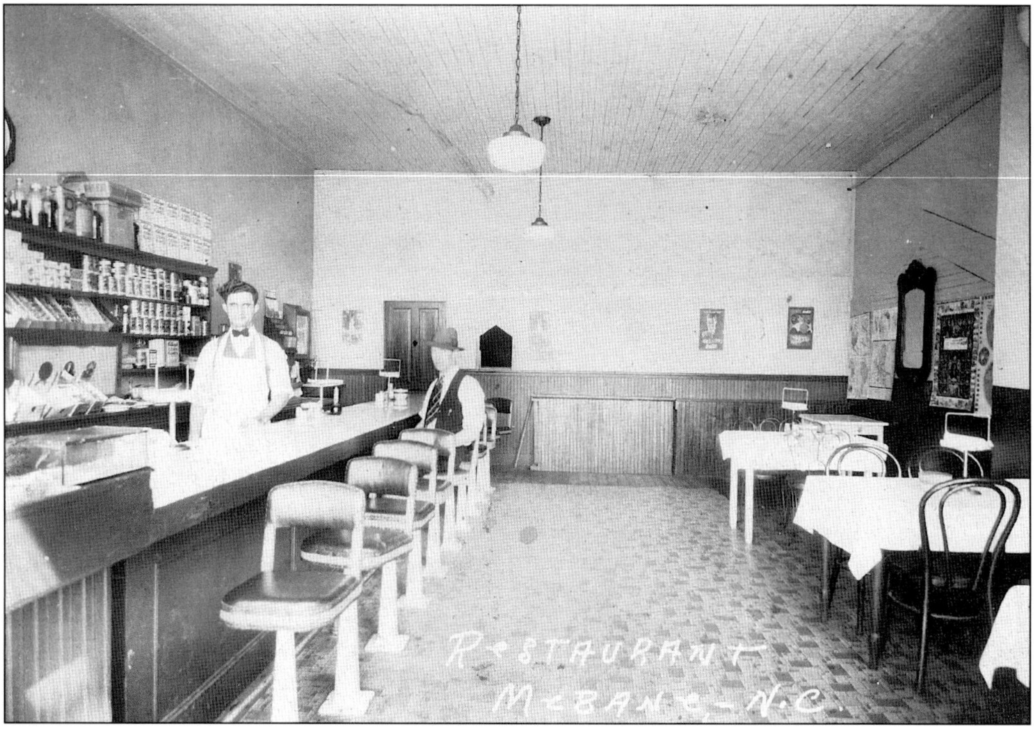

Two gentlemen pose in a Mebane dining establishment during the first half of the century. The bow-tied, apron-clad fellow behind the counter is Gus Bartis. (Courtesy Town of Mebane.)

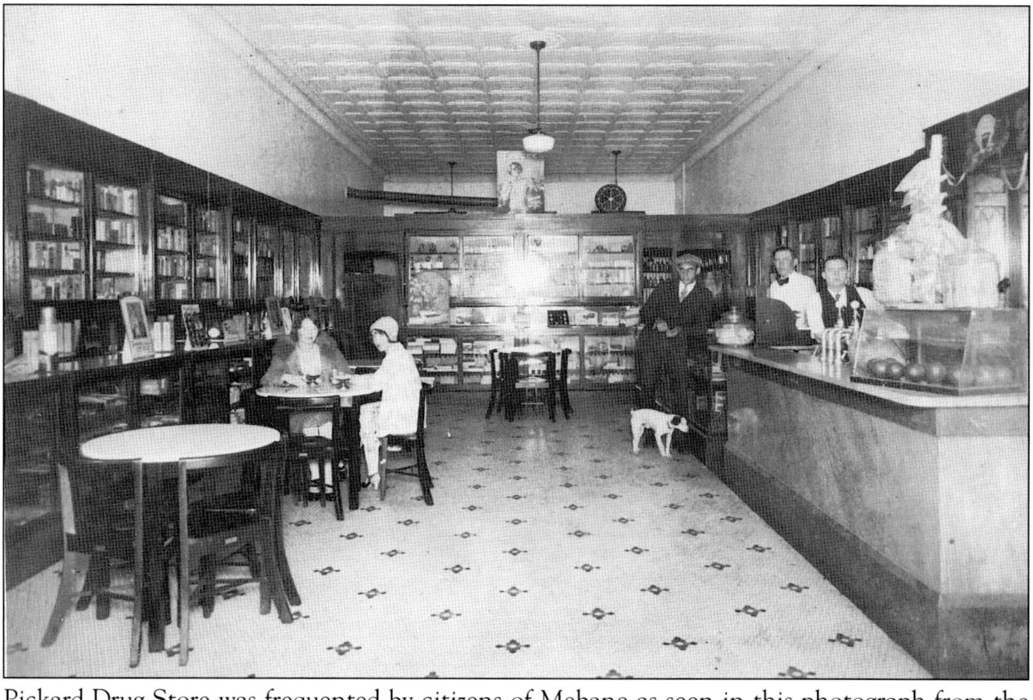

Pickard Drug Store was frequented by citizens of Mebane as seen in this photograph from the 1920s or 1930s. (Courtesy Town of Mebane.)

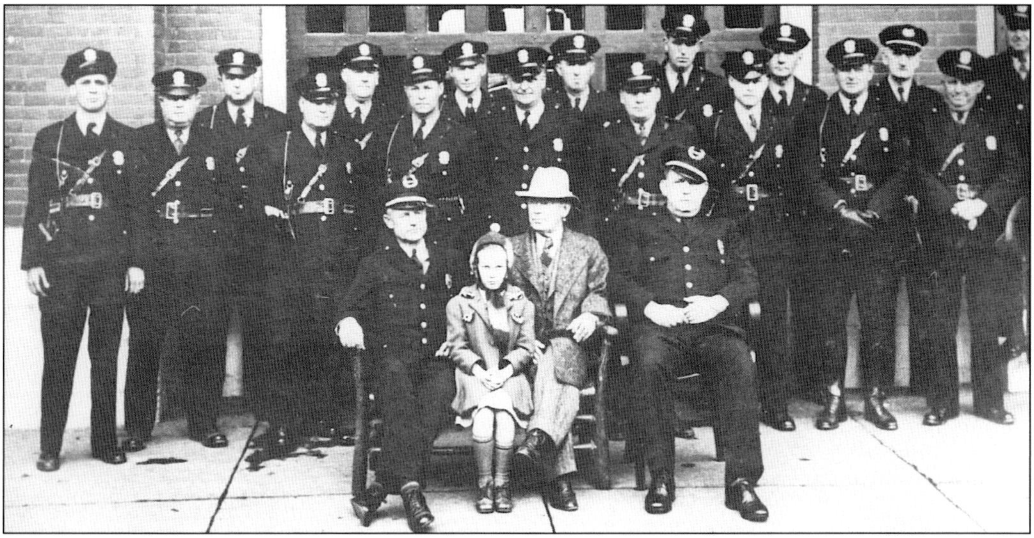

Early in the development of any community, the need arises for a governmental department charged with enforcing the law, insuring safety, keeping order, and preventing and detecting crimes. Members of the Burlington Police Department are pictured here with Mayor Earl Horner and his daughter, Ann, *c.* 1940.

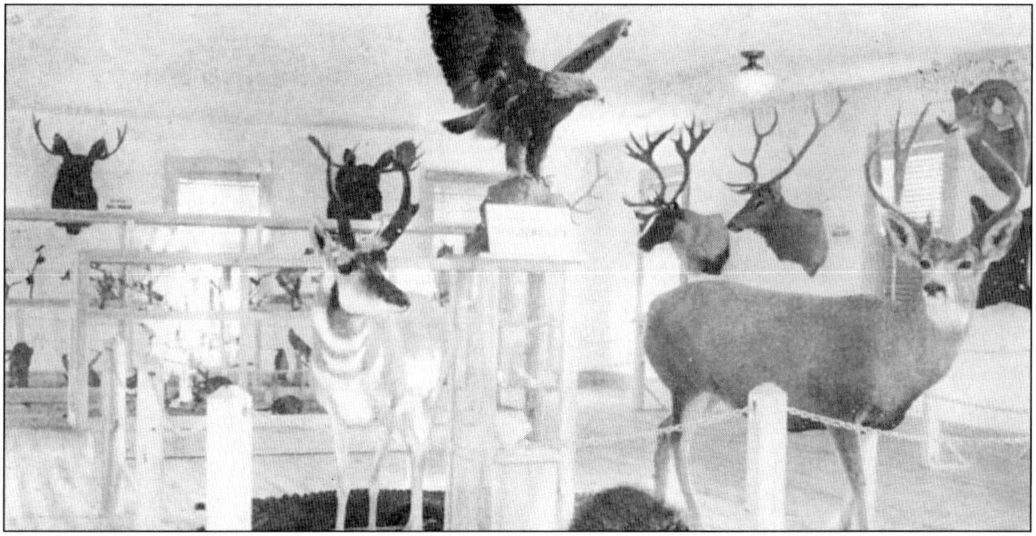

Dr. McDade, who practiced medicine in Burlington, displayed the trophies of numerous safaris in his very own museum. The exhibits were later moved from their original Davis Street location to the building now occupied by the Burlington Recreation and Parks Department. The museum grew to contain far more than the relatively sparsely populated showroom pictured in the postcard above. The author remembers visiting the later location as a small boy, fascinated as he gazed up at the golden eagle and repulsed by various snakes and worms coiled inside large liquid-filled jars. The tusks and feet of elephants also contributed to the static menagerie. Eventually the McDade Museum closed its doors, and the collection was broken up and distributed to other institutions. No one knows the final destination of all the exhibits, but if a visit is paid to the Natural Science Center in Greensboro, it is impossible to escape the sight of a huge, frightening grizzly bear who was formerly a resident of Alamance County. (Courtesy Alamance County Historical Museum, Inc.)

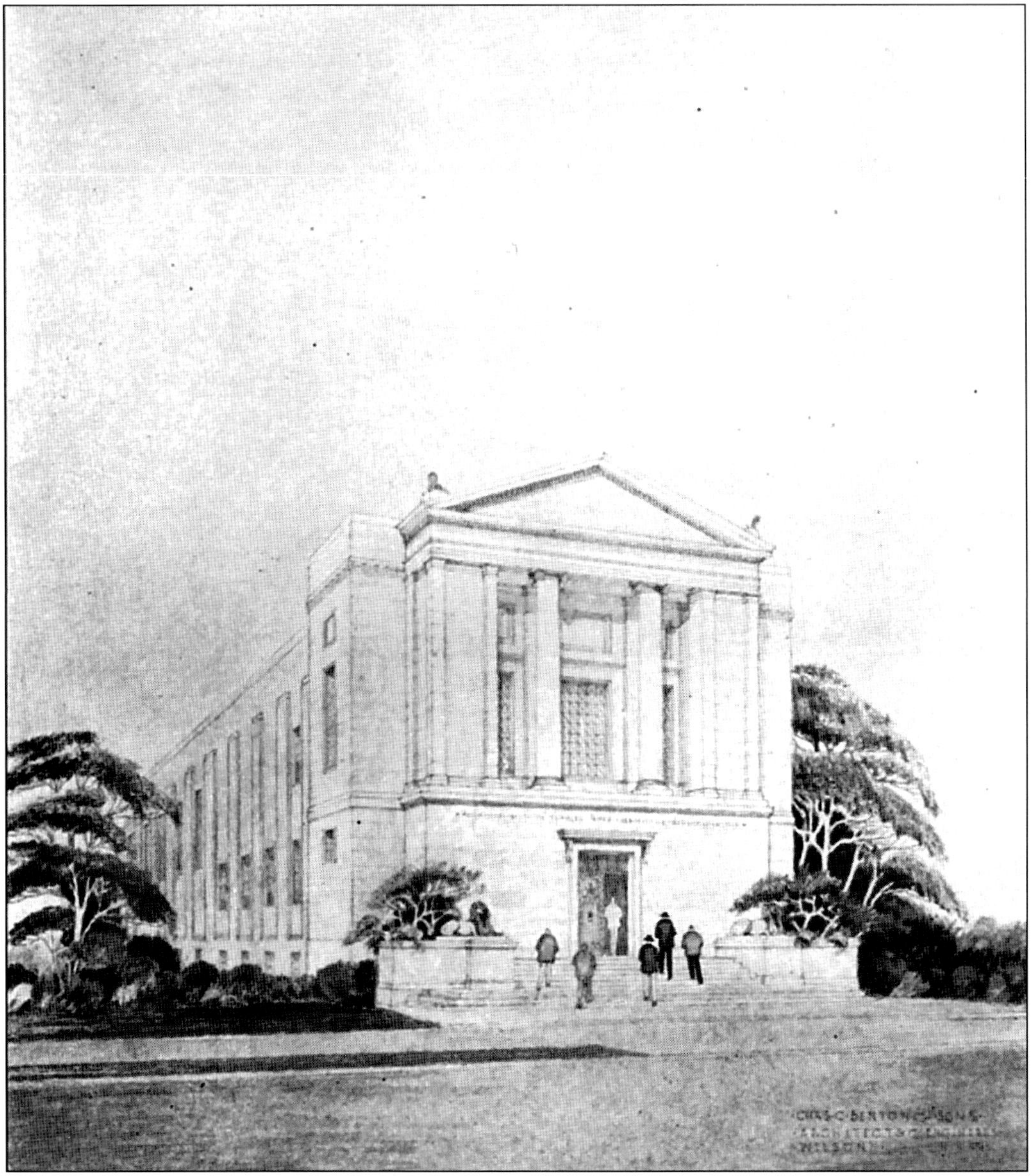

This is an early 1950s artist's conception of Burlington's Masonic Temple, which would be built at 1307 South Main Street. The following is an excerpt from a statement by the building committee: "For the past fifty-seven years Burlington Lodge No. 409 has been paying rent, and today has nothing to show for what has been paid out . . . Burlington is fast taking its place among the larger cities of the state and nation and we as Masons should keep pace with our city and build a Masonic Temple."

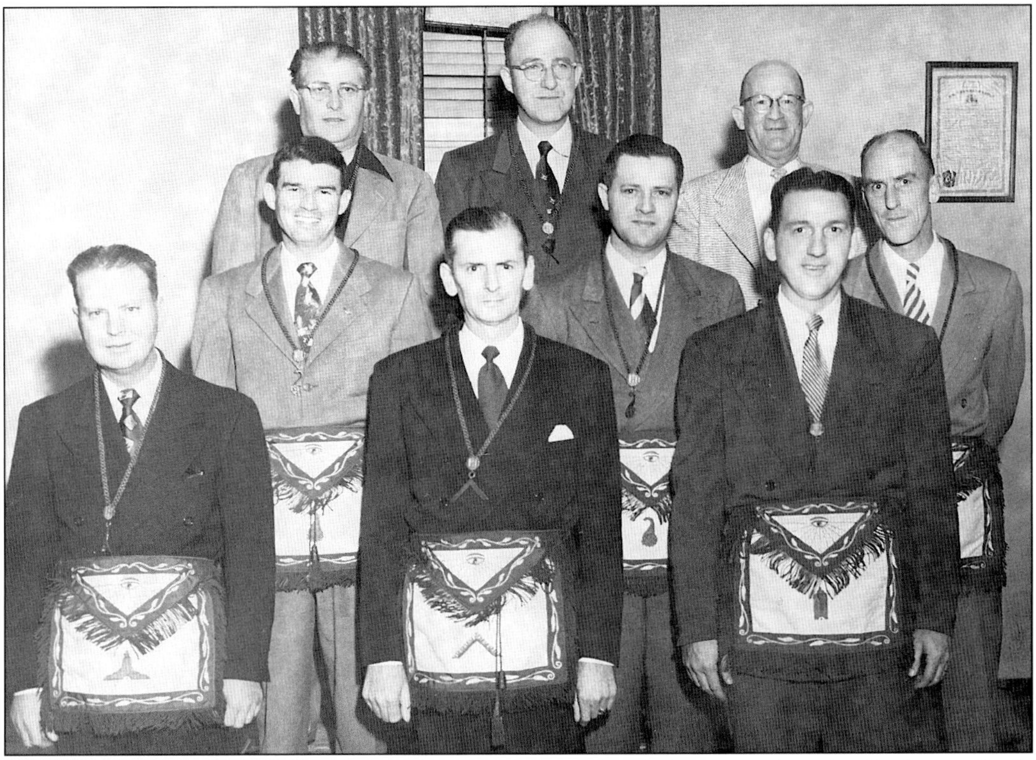

This photograph of new officers for Masonic Bula Lodge 409 appeared in the *Burlington Daily Times-News* on Wednesday, January 16, 1952. Pictured, from left to right, are as follows: (front row) Wayne Beale, senior warden; W.T. Lasley, master; and G.C. Mitchell, junior warden; (middle row) Harold Terrell, senior steward; Gorden Marshall, junior steward; and Marshall Browning, junior deacon; (back row) Jack Wrenn, tyler; W.L. Burke, secretary; and W.S. Owen, treasurer.

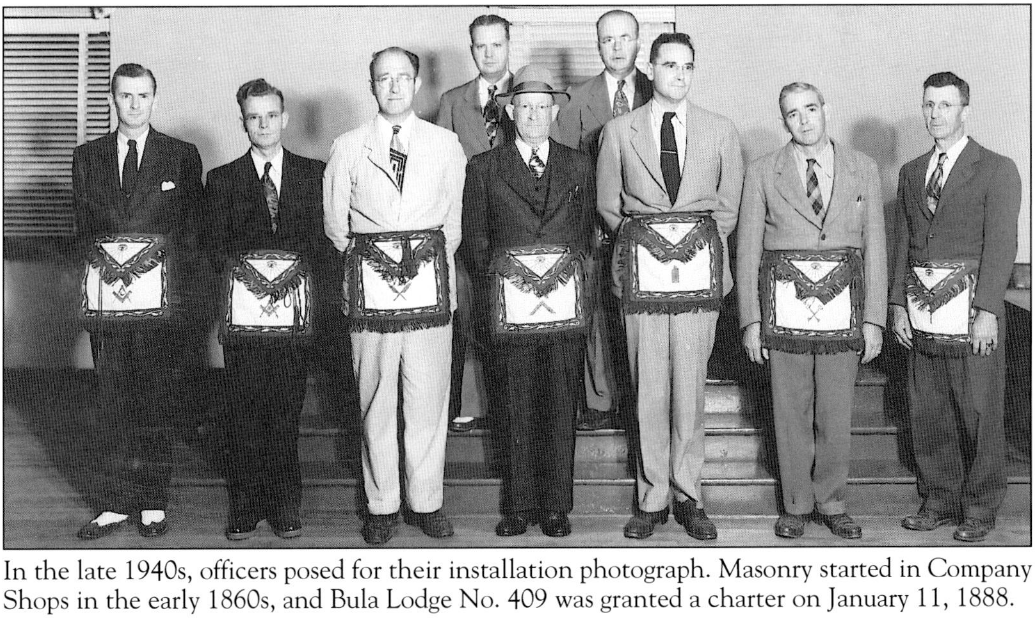

In the late 1940s, officers posed for their installation photograph. Masonry started in Company Shops in the early 1860s, and Bula Lodge No. 409 was granted a charter on January 11, 1888.

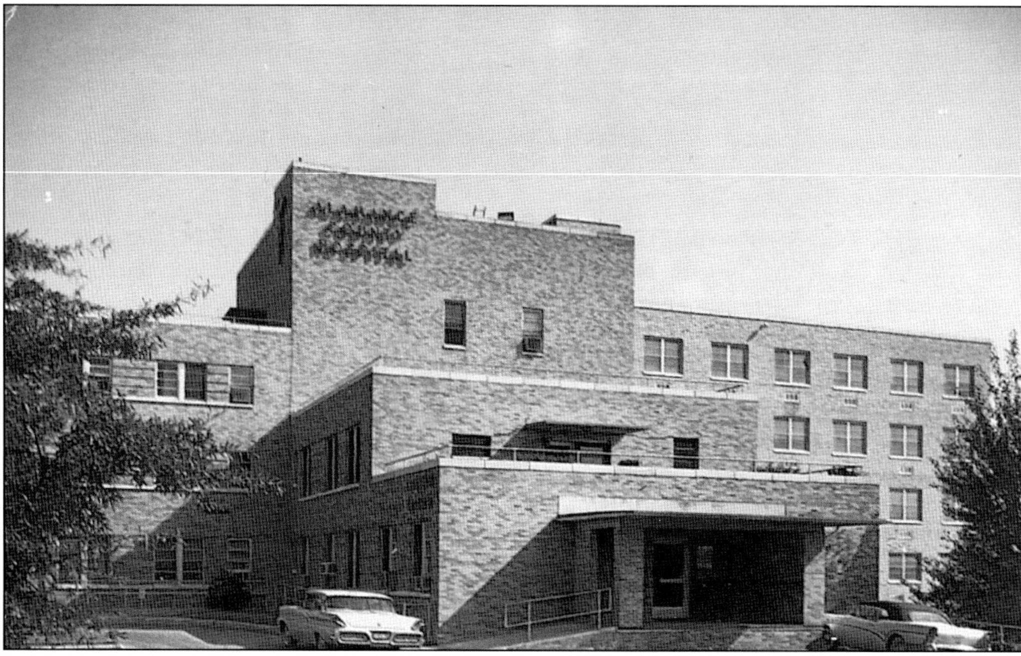

This postcard view of Alamance County Hospital was made on February 22, 1960. The hospital opened in 1951 on Graham-Hopedale Road in Burlington and was a fully accredited, 143-bed institution. (Courtesy Alamance County Historical Museum, Inc.)

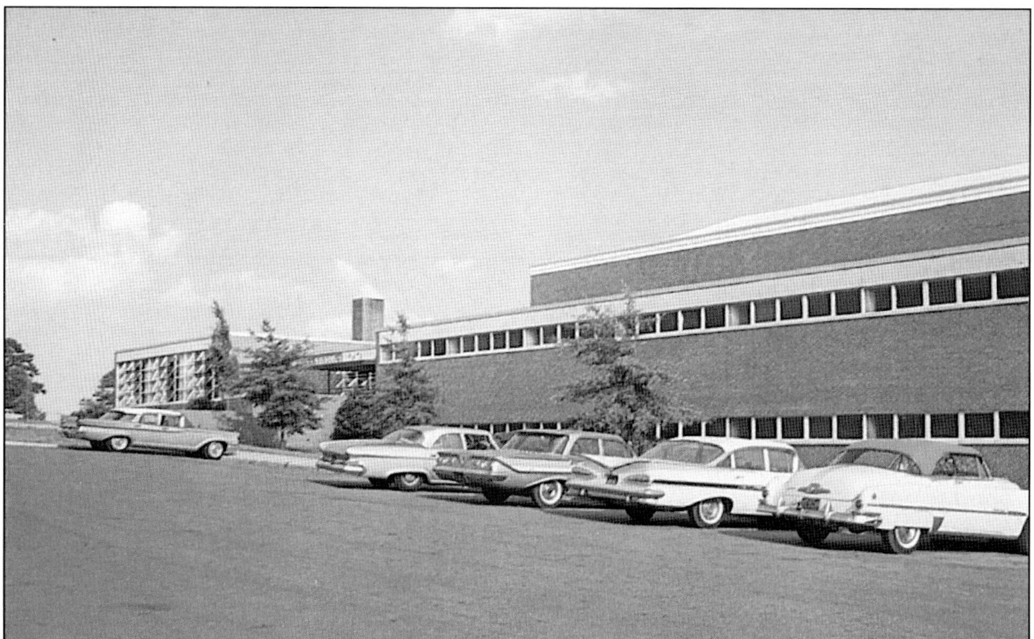

While at the local YMCA, many Alamance County citizens had their very first experience swimming, bowling, playing basketball, and dropping coins into pinball machines and other arcade games. In 1960 this postcard image was made of Burlington's YMCA at 1346 South Main Street, the location where it still functions today.

Four

INDUSTRY

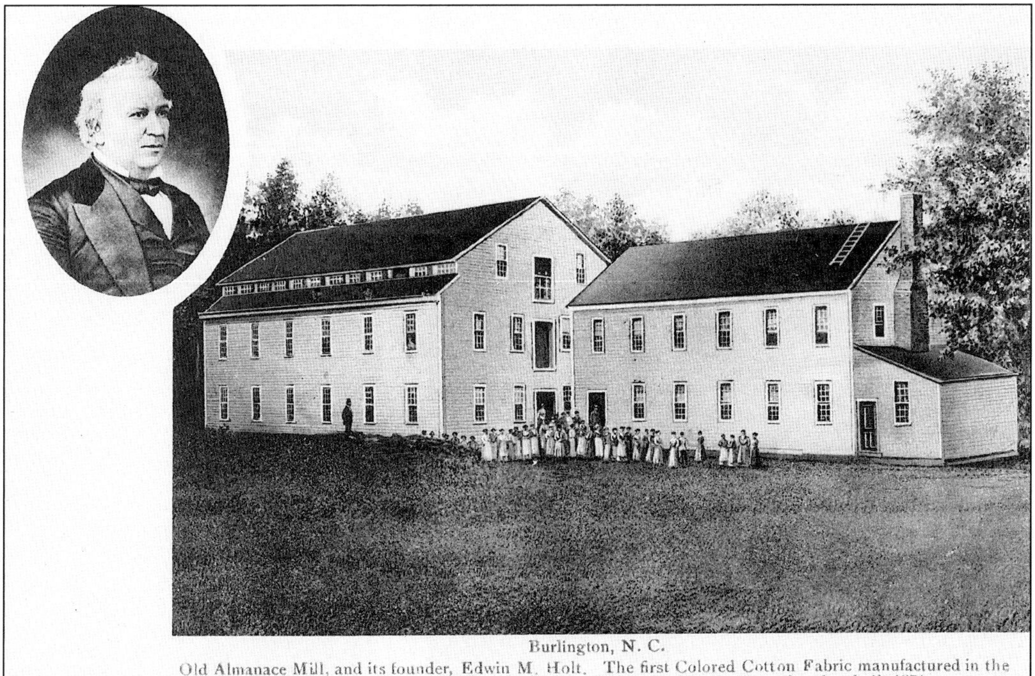

This postcard was designed so that Edwin Michael Holt seems to be presiding over his original cotton mill on Alamance Creek. The factory, built in 1837, was the site where the first colored cotton fabric manufactured in the South was woven. The structure was later destroyed by fire and then re-built in 1871. The image used for this old postcard was probably made about 1851. The Alamance plaids that came out of this mill became nationally famous and began a textile dynasty that is now poised to conquer the third millennium. (Courtesy Alamance County Historical Museum, Inc.)

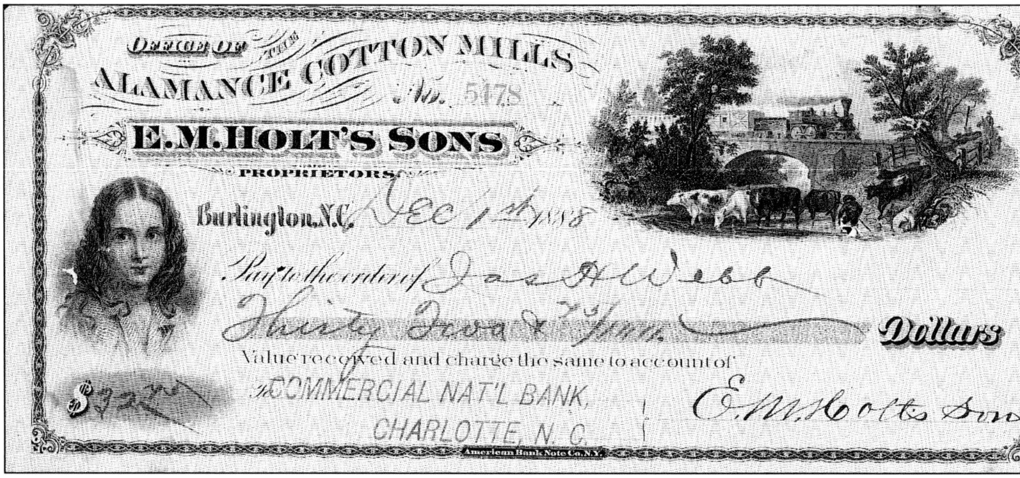

Many checks from Alamance Cotton Mills still exist, such as this one written in 1888.

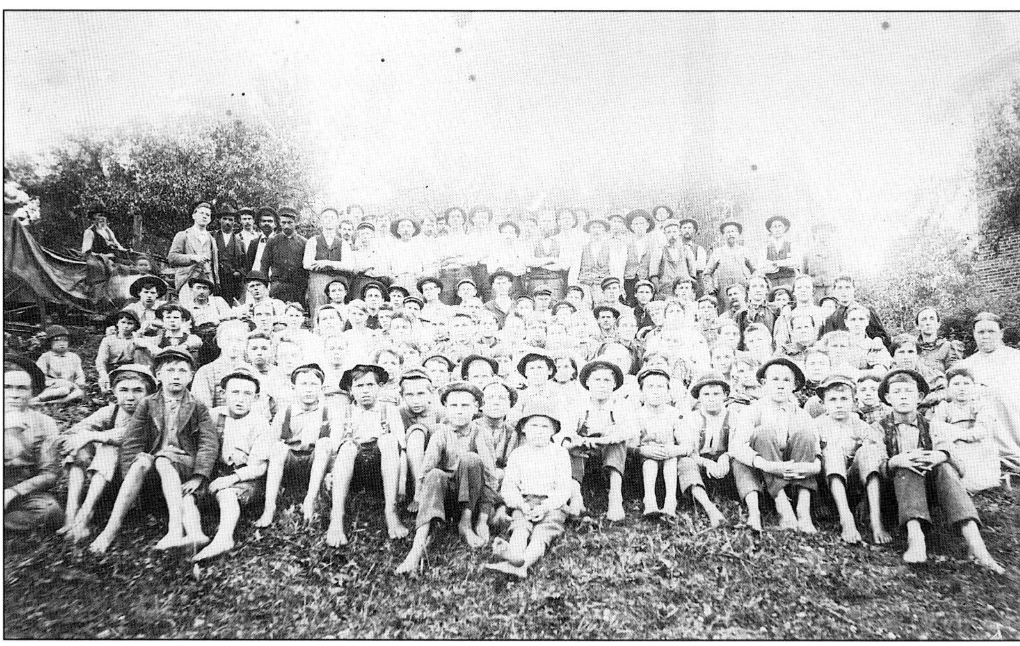

Glencoe Cotton Mill employees pose for a photographer about 1890. The absence of shoes and tool belts suggests a company picnic. In the early 1880s, James and William Holt developed the cotton mill village of Glencoe from an old tobacco processing plant.

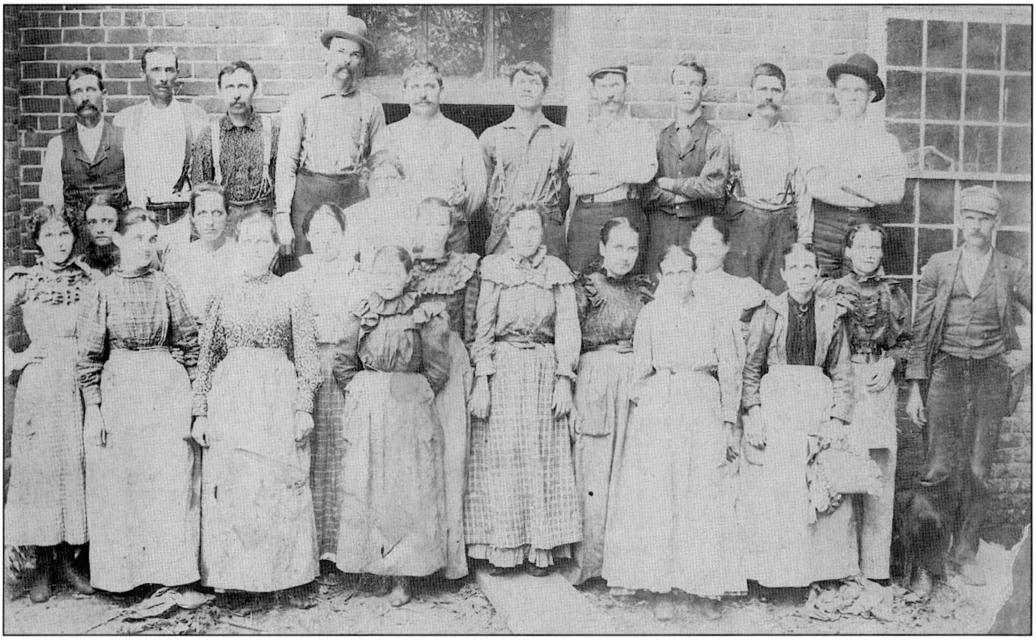

These are employees of Granite Mills on the Haw River, *c.* 1890. Benjamin Trollinger built the cotton mill in 1844. (Courtesy Alamance County Historical Museum, Inc.)

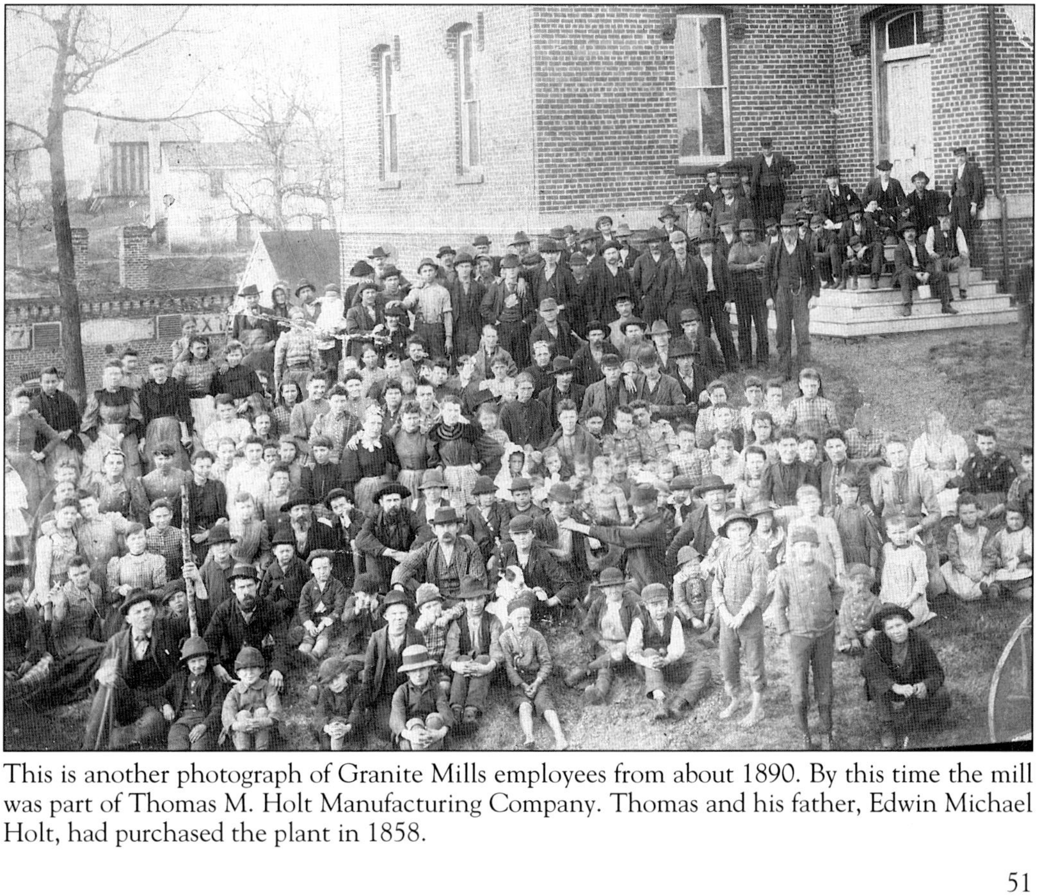

This is another photograph of Granite Mills employees from about 1890. By this time the mill was part of Thomas M. Holt Manufacturing Company. Thomas and his father, Edwin Michael Holt, had purchased the plant in 1858.

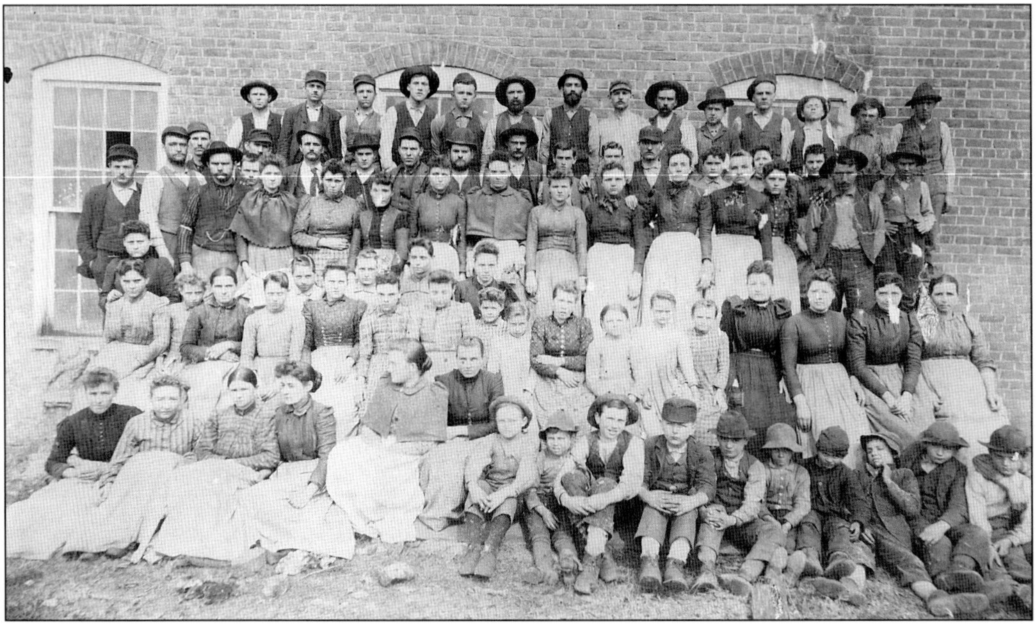

This photograph of workers at the Bellemont Cotton Mill was made between 1890 and 1900. Edwin Michael Holt's cotton-processing business resulted in the establishment of the Village of Bellemont. The mill company built many of the homes in the community. (Courtesy Alamance County Historical Museum, Inc.)

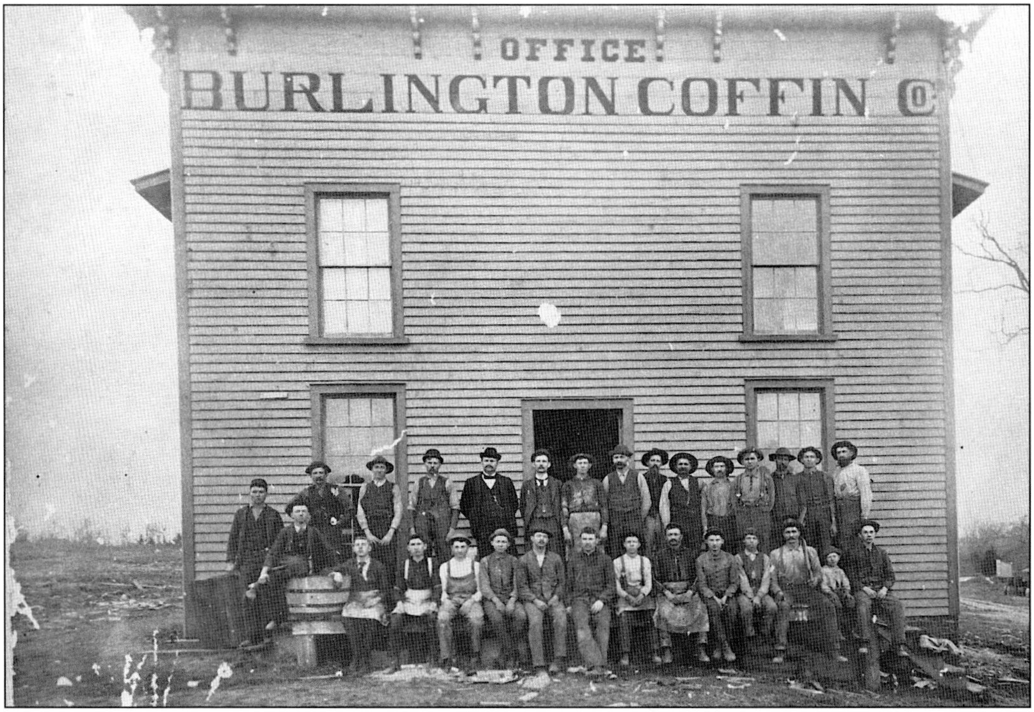

Employees of the Burlington Coffin Company pose for a photograph outside the office building that was erected in 1884 on Maple Avenue and Tucker Street. The structure was destroyed by fire in 1904. (Courtesy Nell Holt Lasley.)

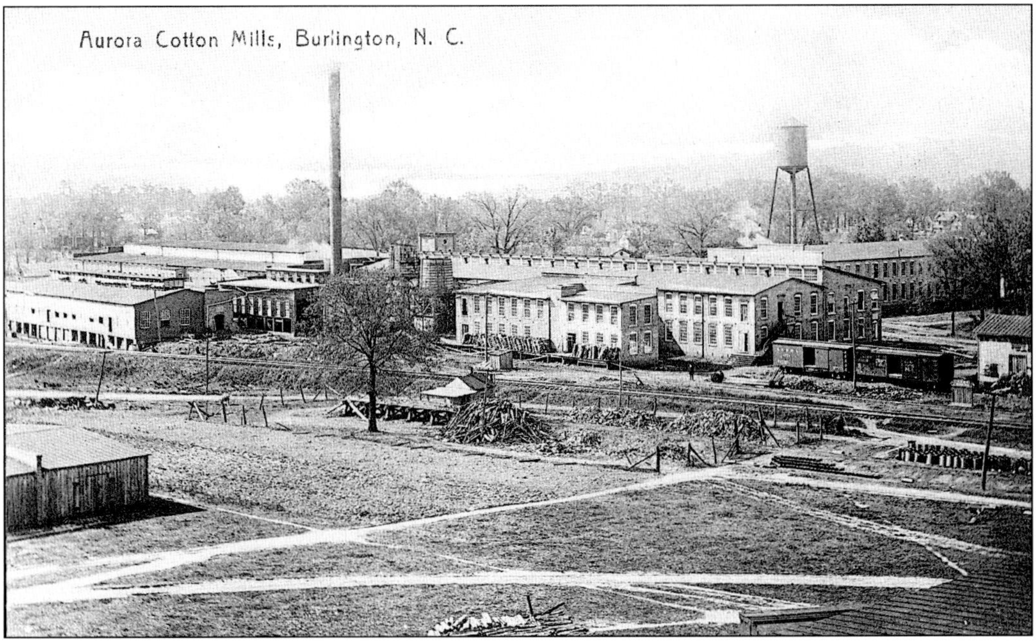

This postcard view shows Burlington's Aurora Cotton Mills near Webb Avenue. After the railroad shops closed, textile mills became the main industry in Burlington. The Aurora mill later became the site of Standard Hosiery Mill's dyeing and finishing processes.

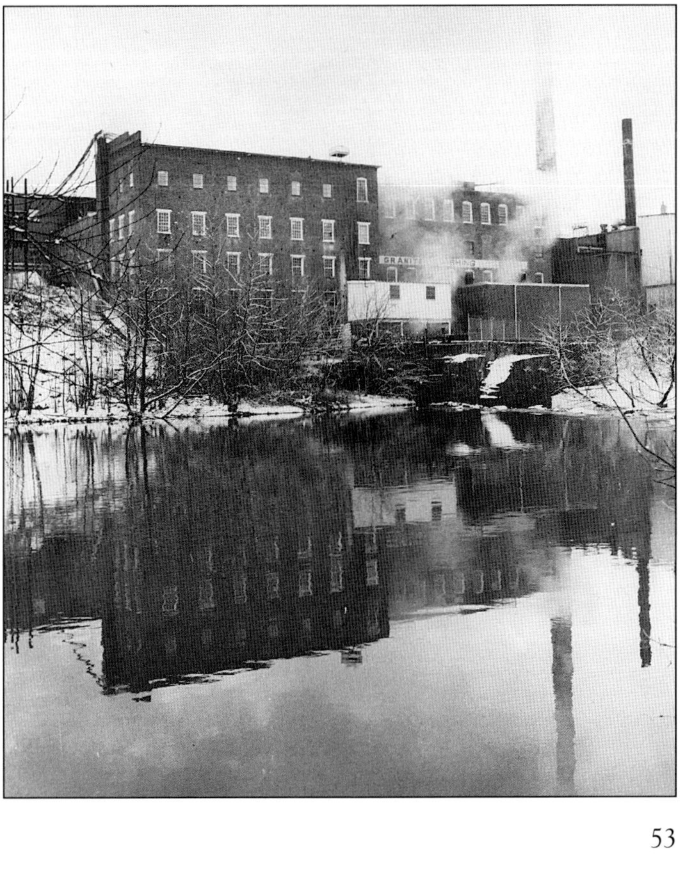

In this beautiful image, the old Granite Finishing plant stands majestically on snow-covered banks, overlooking its reflection in the Haw River while steam or smoke issues skyward. (Given by Don Bolden to Haw River Historical Association Museum.)

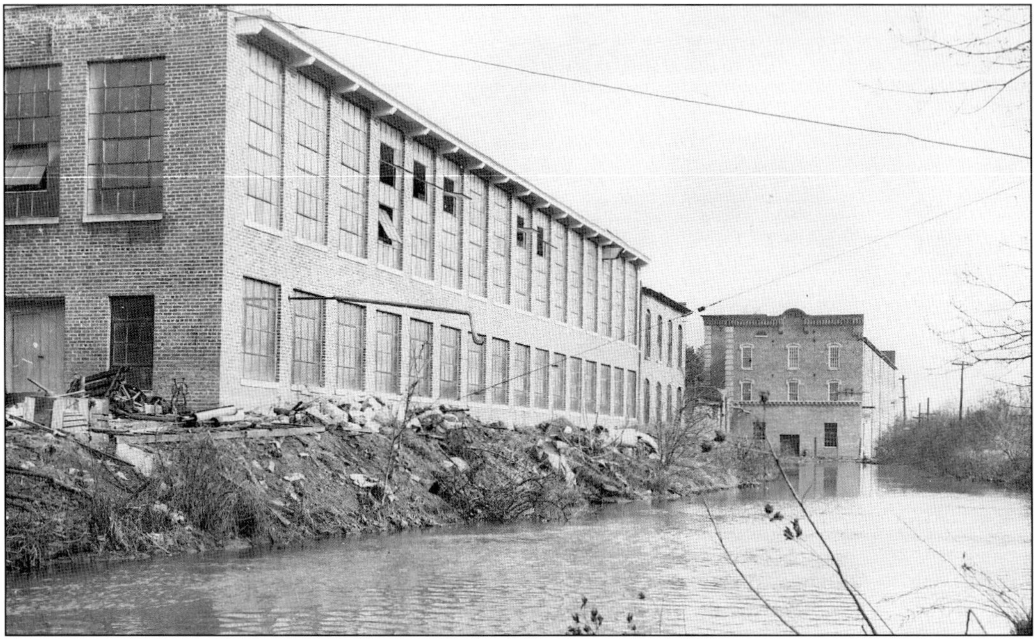

In 1942 this nicely composed image was made of Glencoe Mills. James and William Holt acquired the original building in 1879. (Courtesy Alamance County Planner Steve M. Hundley.)

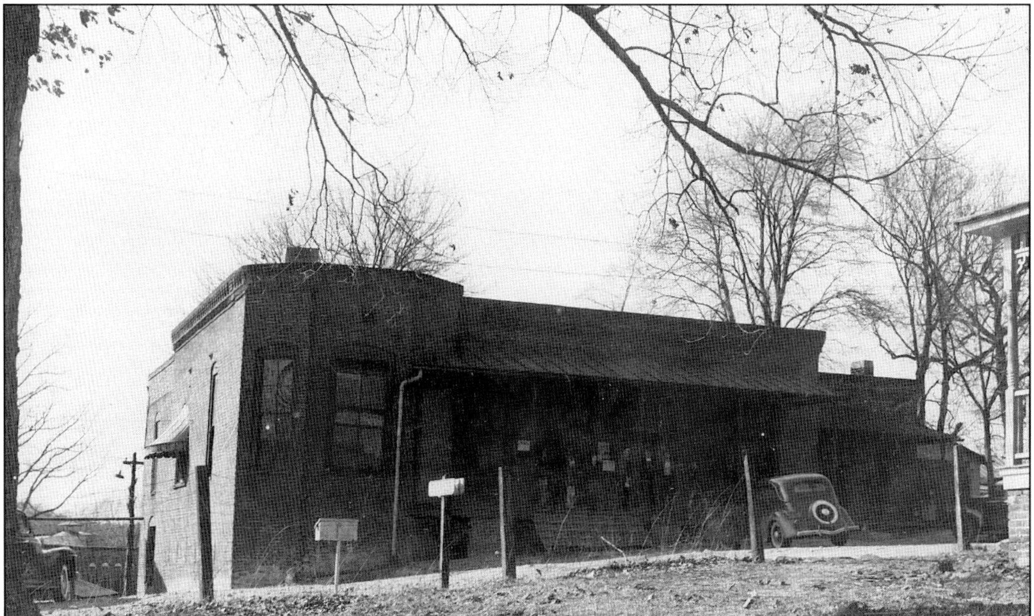

This is the way the Glencoe Mill office looked in 1942. By this time, the mill's main product was shirting flannels. (Courtesy Alamance County Planner Steve M. Hundley.)

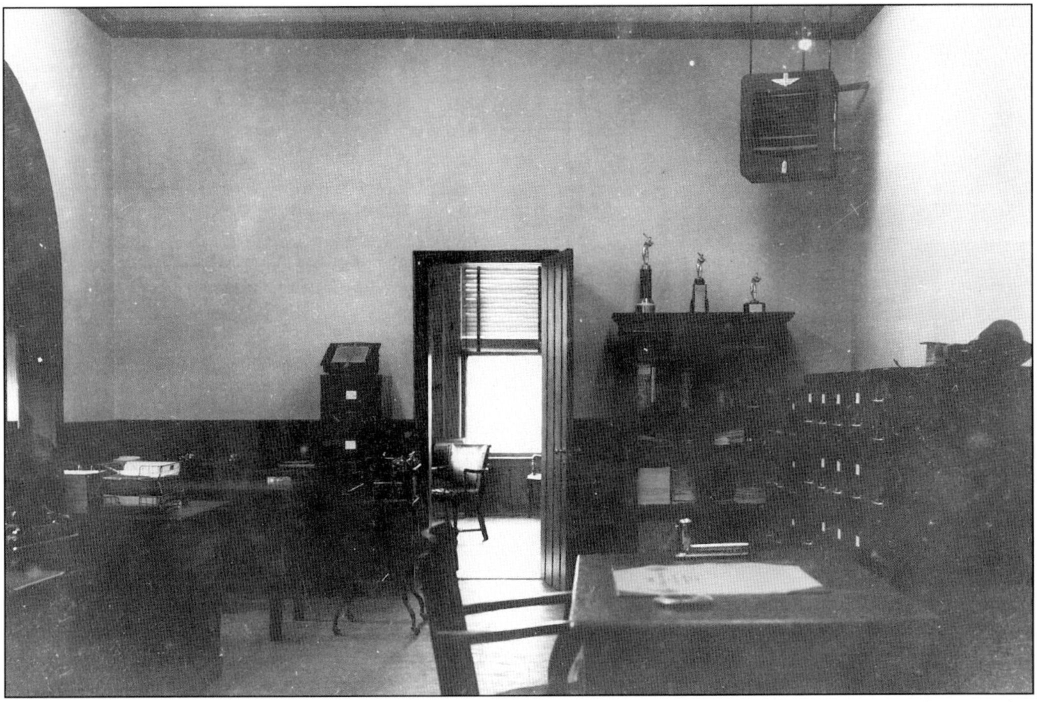

The interior of the Glencoe Mill office, in 1942, presents itself as quite functional despite the display of baseball trophies. (Courtesy Alamance County Planner Steve M. Hundley.)

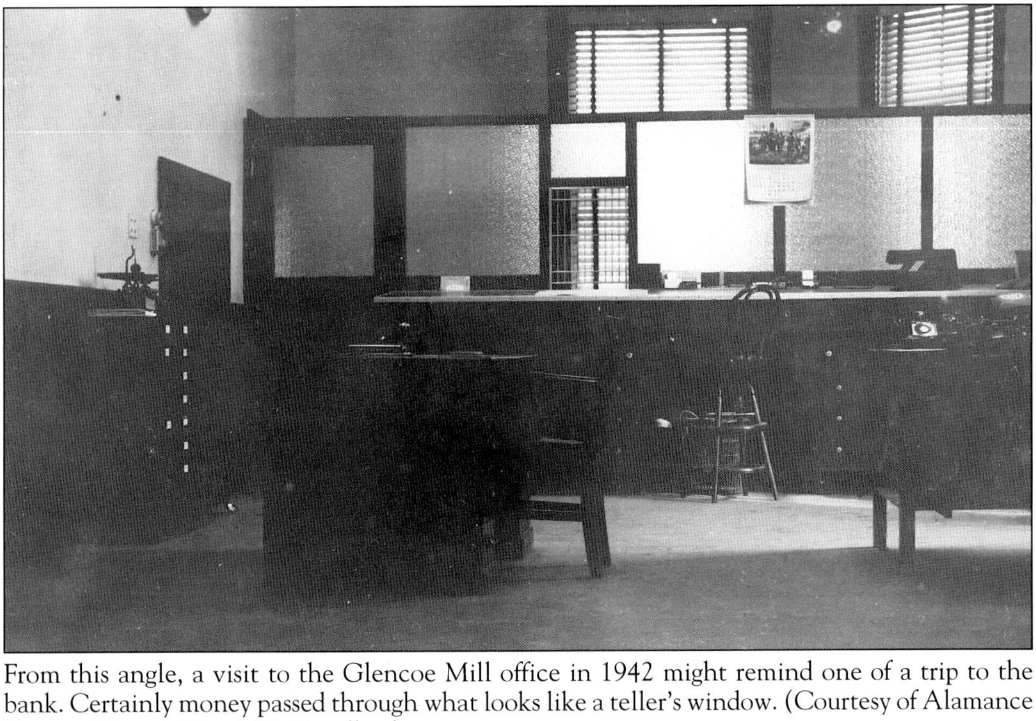

From this angle, a visit to the Glencoe Mill office in 1942 might remind one of a trip to the bank. Certainly money passed through what looks like a teller's window. (Courtesy of Alamance County Planner Steve M. Hundley.)

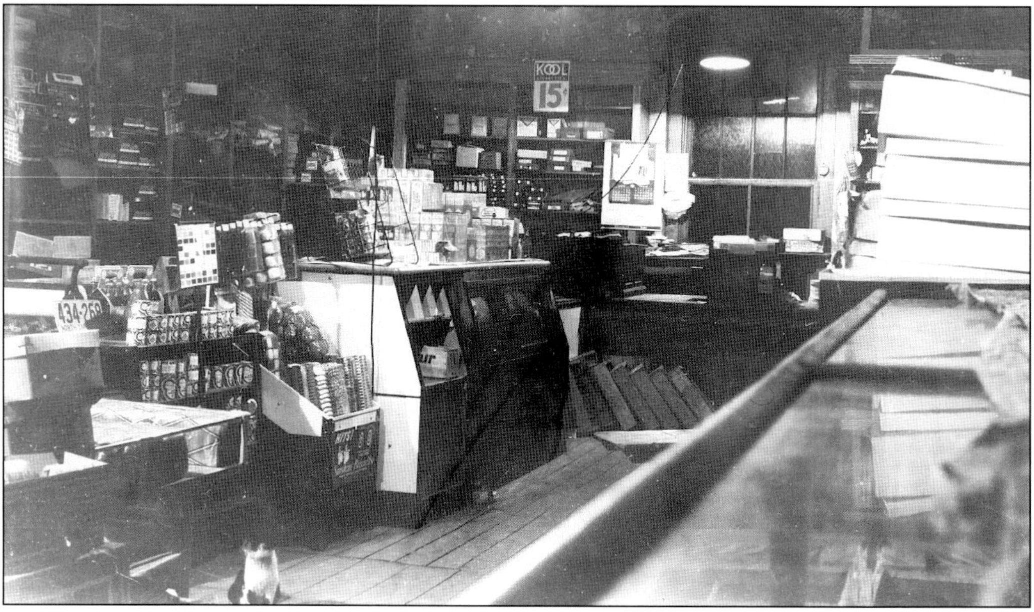

A cat seems to be the only customer in the Glencoe Mill Store. Could it be contemplating the outrageous price of 15¢ for a pack of Kool cigarettes in 1942? (Courtesy Alamance County Planner Steve M. Hundley.)

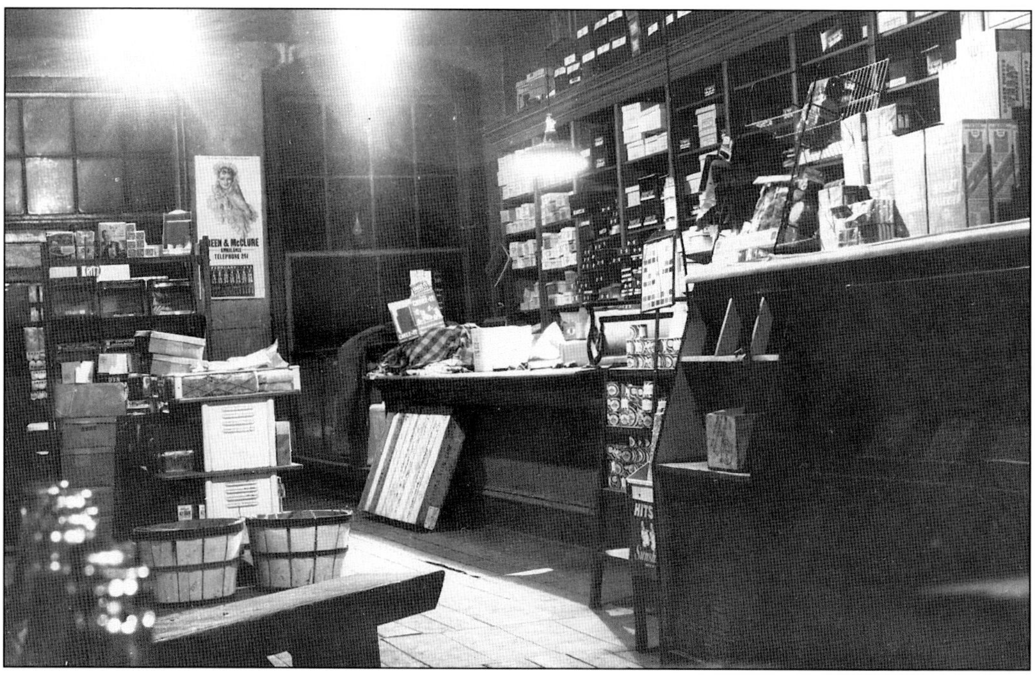

The store in the mill village of Glencoe was well stocked. An advertisement on a calendar serves as a reminder that in 1942, a desired party could usually be reached by telephone after dialing only three digits. (Courtesy Alamance County Planner Steve M. Hundley.)

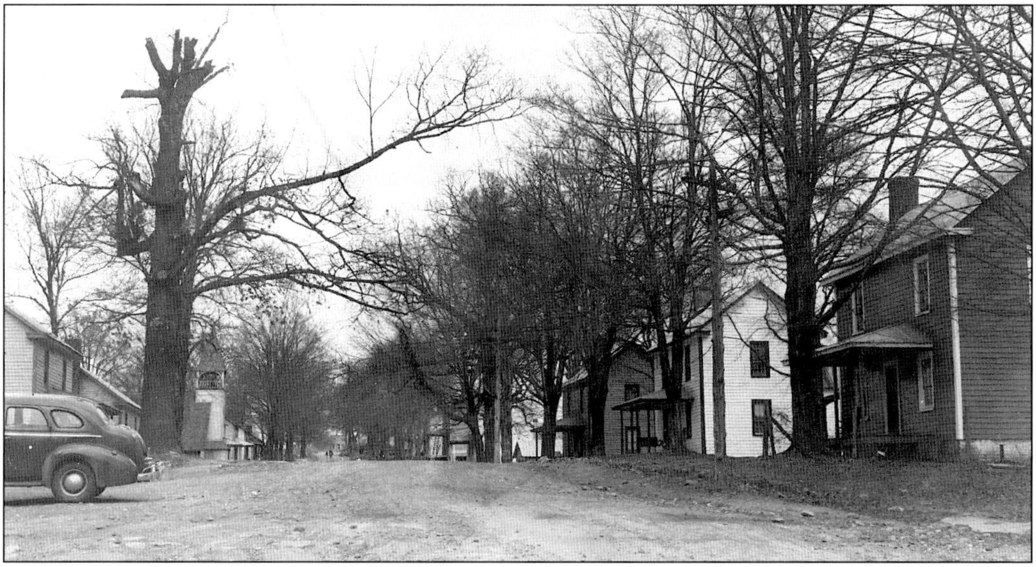

This is another image in the comprehensive 1942 photo session that took place in the mill village of Glencoe. The tenement houses and company store were built between 1879 and 1880. The name, "Glencoe," comes from Scotland. (Courtesy Alamance County Planner Steve M. Hundley.)

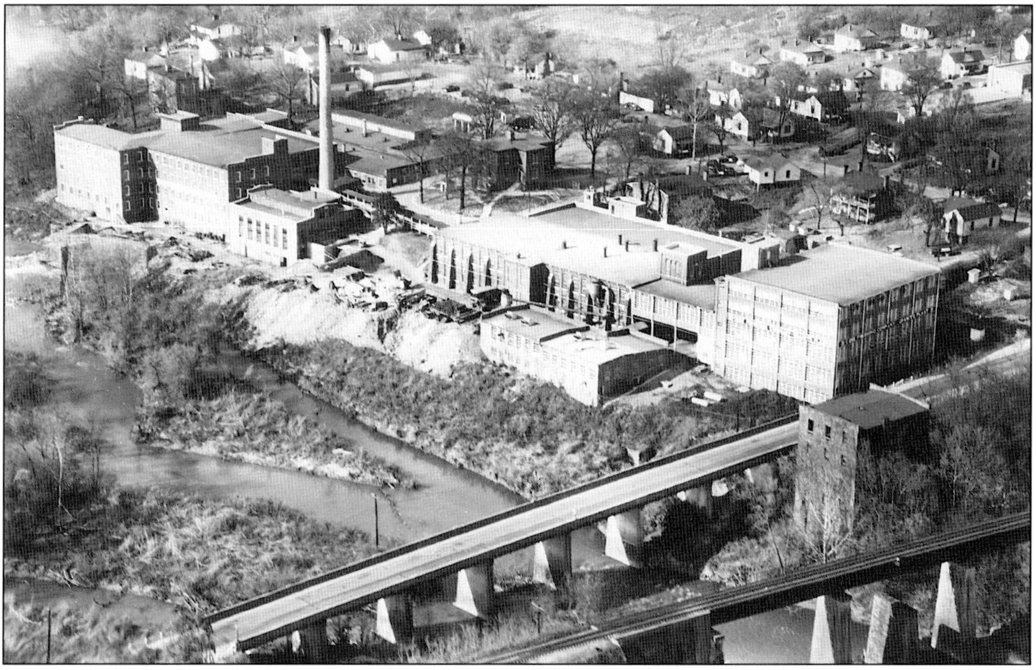

Much of the history of Haw River can be read from this 1951 aerial view. A Trollinger gristmill, built in 1838, can be seen, as well as the Granite Cotton Mill Building, constructed by General Benjamin Trollinger in 1844. The area of houses in the upper portion of the picture is known as "Old Town." By the time this photograph was made, the entire complex had passed out of the hands of the Holt family and was now known as Cone Mills Corporation. (Courtesy Haw River Historical Association Museum.)

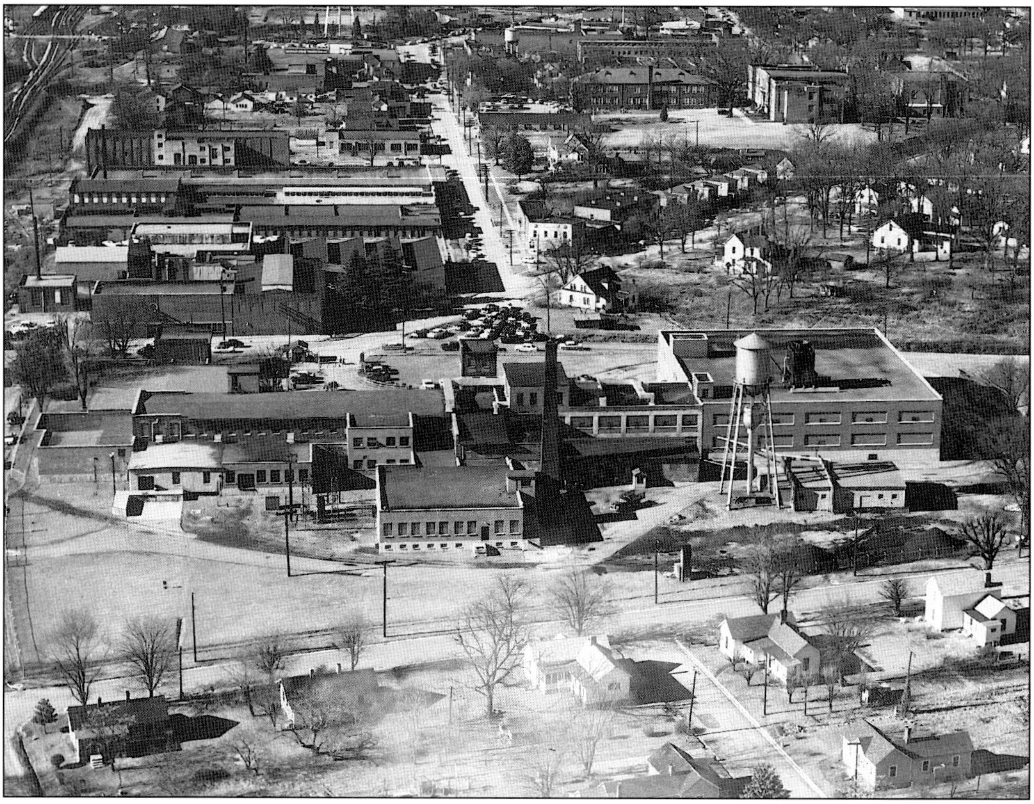

This view of Burlington's Celanese Corporation on Ireland Street is from 1959. The plant was originally built in 1890 as Windsor Cotton Mills and later became King Cotton Mills. Since becoming part of the Celanese Corporation in 1941, it has produced many millions of pounds of yarn and has been a major employer.

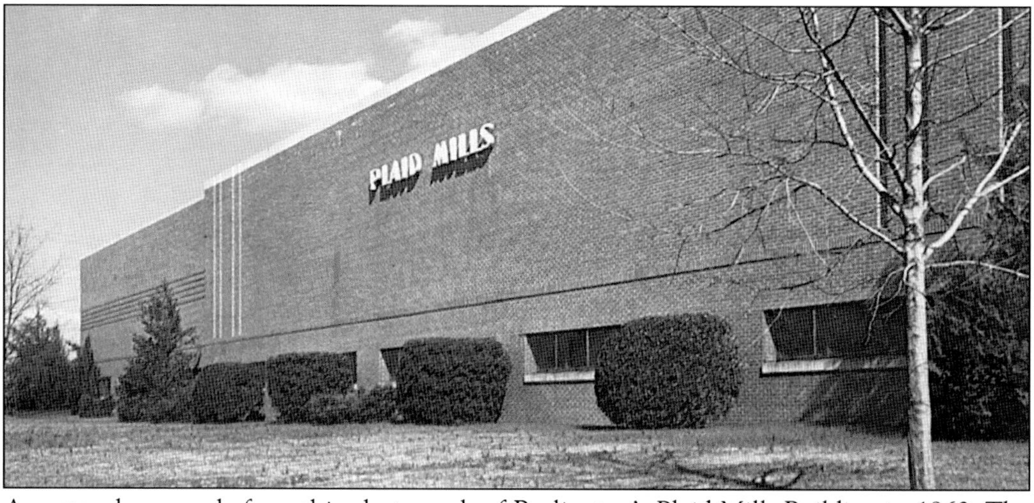

A postcard was made from this photograph of Burlington's Plaid Mills Building in 1960. The plant was a unit of world-renowned Burlington Industries and was an example of cutting-edge industrial architecture in the South. (Courtesy Alamance County Historical Museum, Inc.)

Five

HOMES

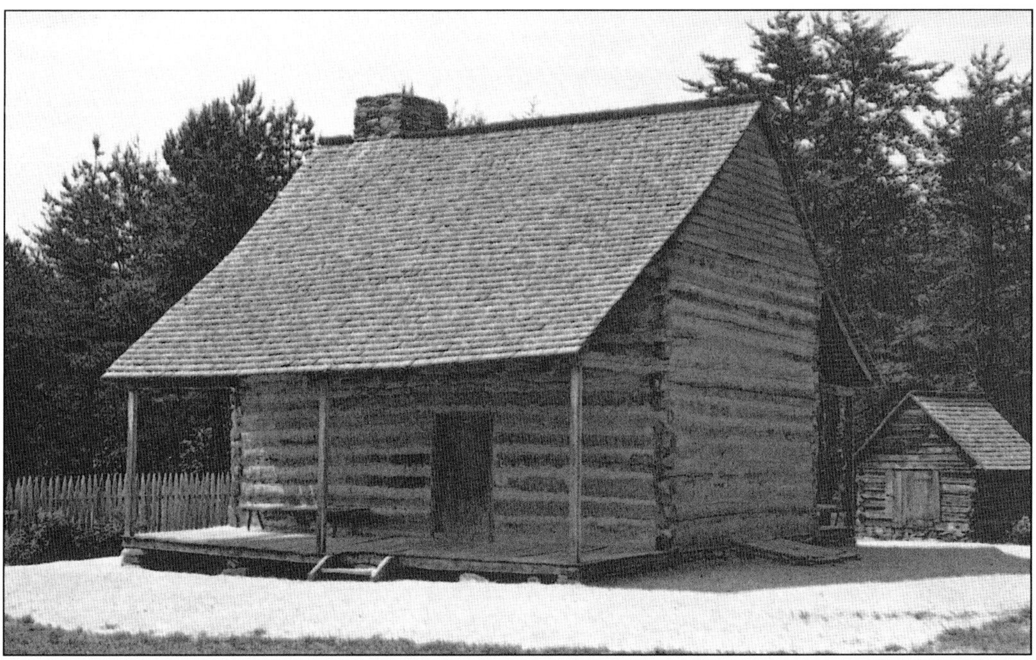

In 1782 a pioneer-type log cabin, now known as the John Allen House, was built in Snow Camp. In 1967 it was restored after being moved to Alamance Battleground State Historic Site. Displayed containing many of its original eighteenth-century furnishings, the Allen House is probably the oldest home still standing in the county.

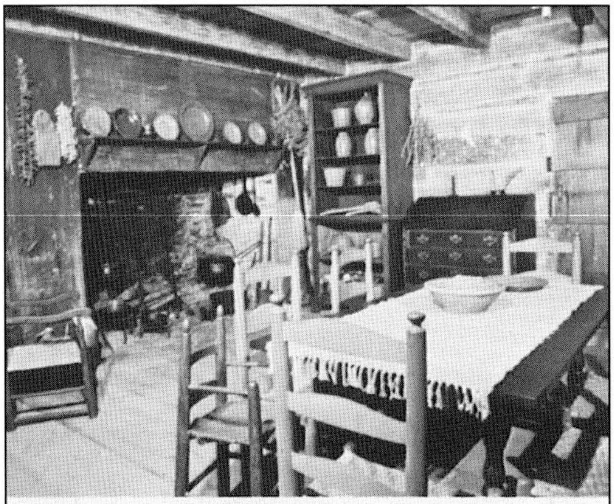

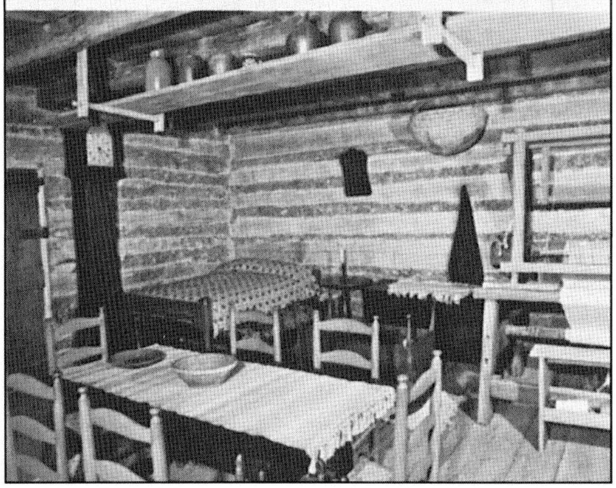

These two interior views of Alamance Battleground's John Allen House provide a typical example of the lifestyle of the period.

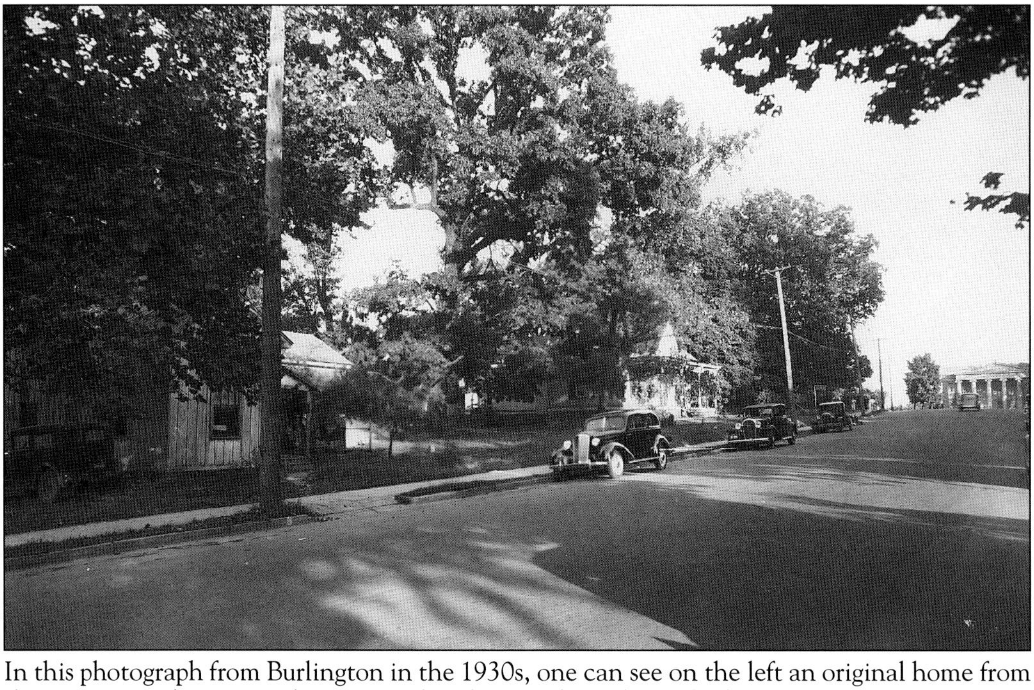

In this photograph from Burlington in the 1930s, one can see on the left an original home from the Company Shops era. The Baptist church is on the right in the background.

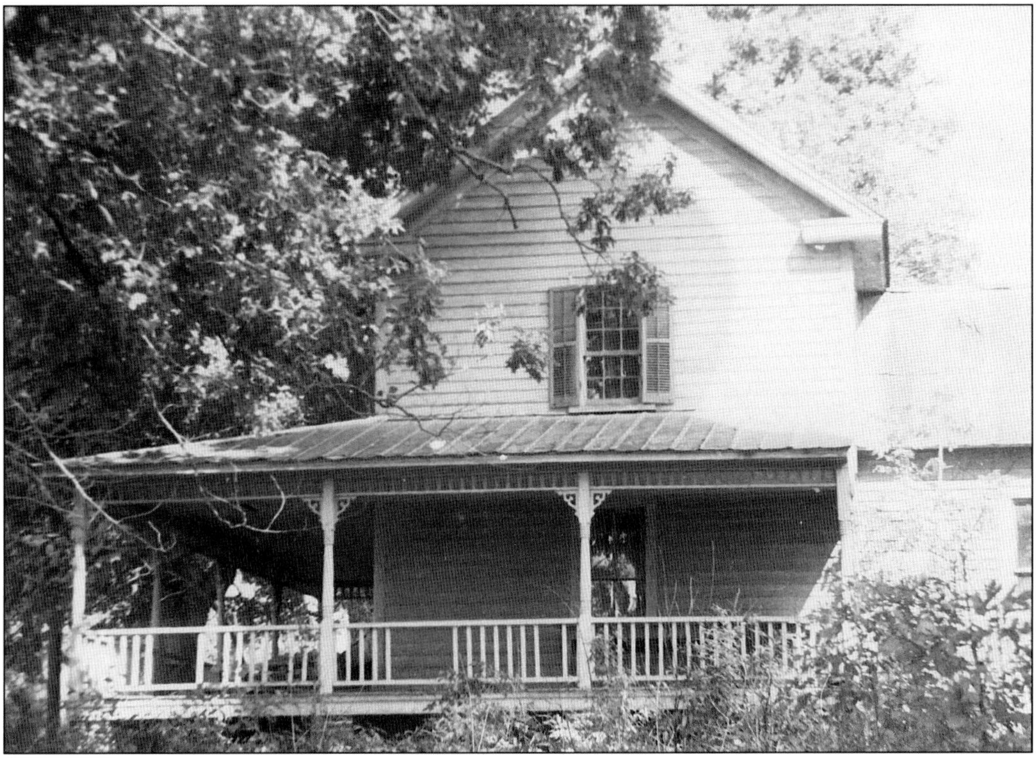

In 1942 a photographer snapped this shot of the Glencoe Mills superintendent's house. The large porch distinguished it from most other homes in the mill village. (Courtesy Alamance County Planner Steve M. Hundley.)

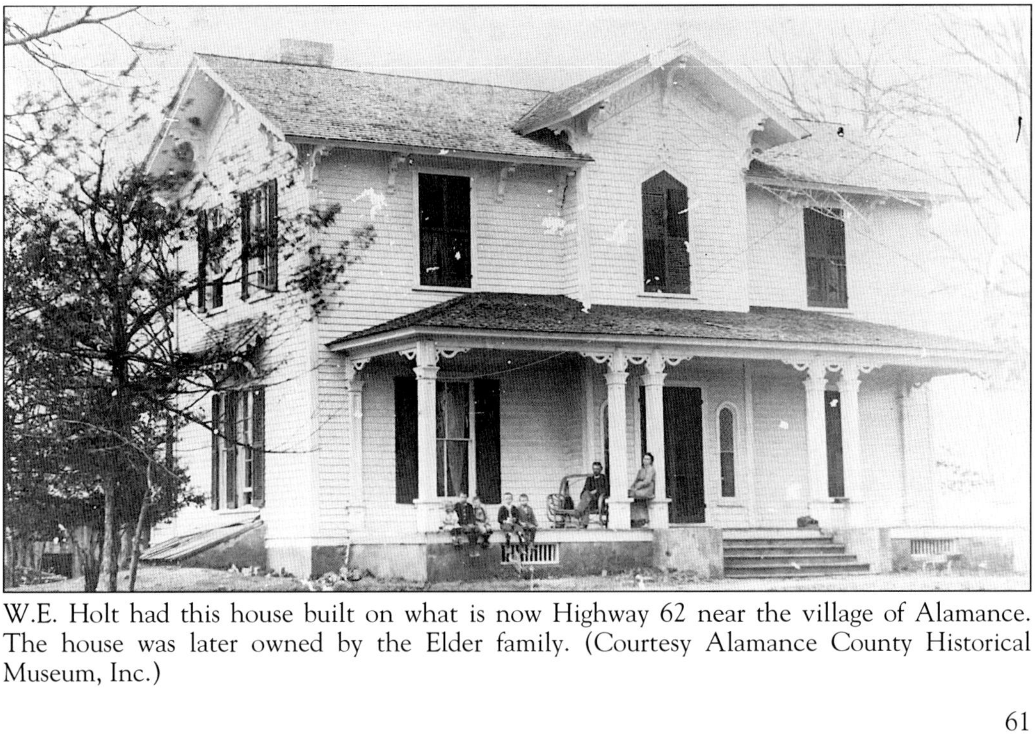

W.E. Holt had this house built on what is now Highway 62 near the village of Alamance. The house was later owned by the Elder family. (Courtesy Alamance County Historical Museum, Inc.)

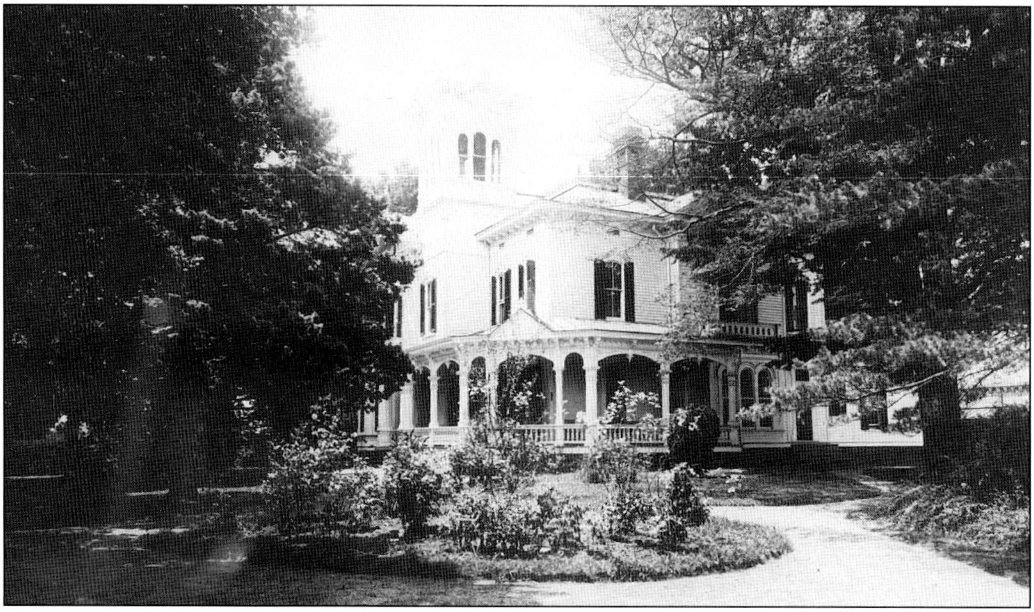

This beautiful photograph from Graham shows off the home of Lynn Banks Holt (1842–1920). L. Banks Holt was one of the sons of Edwin Michael Holt, and after his father's retirement in 1866, he became co-owner of the Alamance Mill. (Courtesy Austin Holt McCormick.)

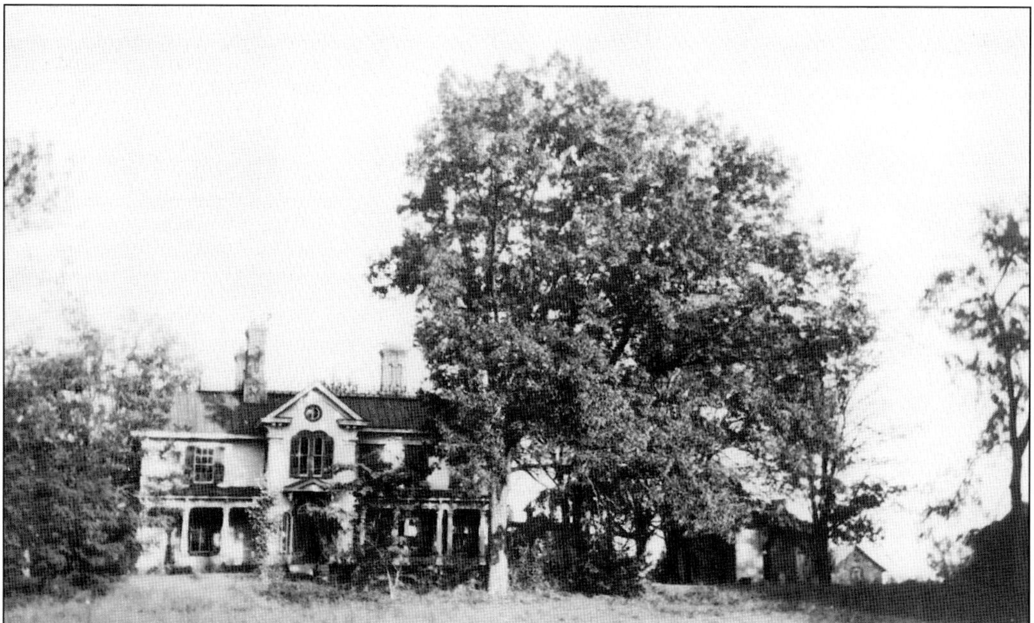

Visitors to Haw River could, in times past, behold the home of Governor Thomas M. Holt. The house was demolished in 1940. (Courtesy Haw River Historical Association Museum.)

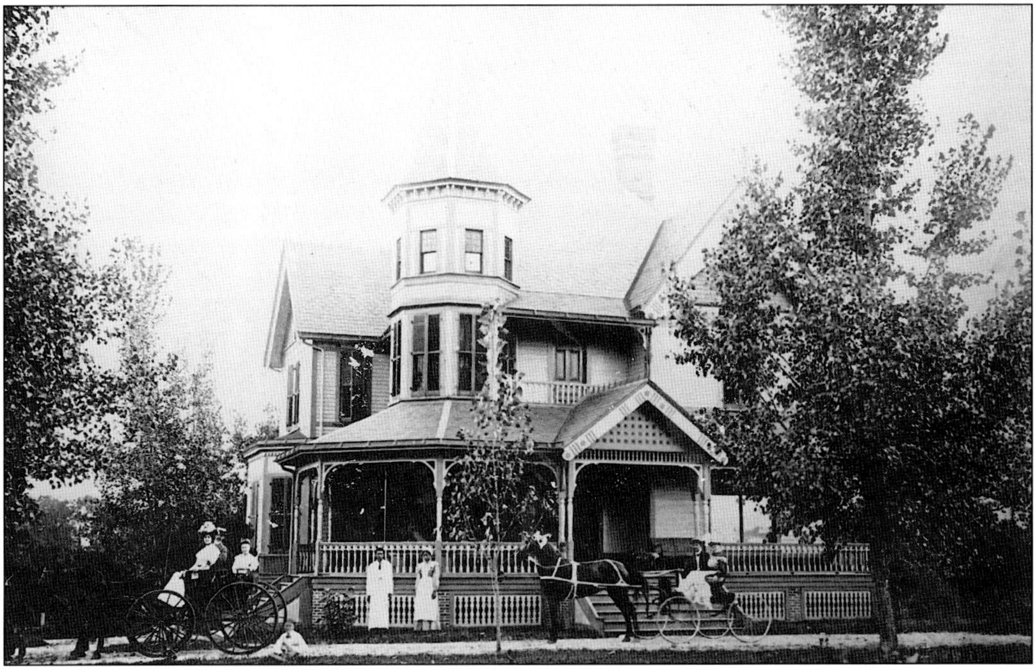

In this pleasant image, the home of Colonel Jim Holt on West Davis Street in Burlington is complemented by passenger-filled, horse-drawn carriages and attendants in waiting. (Courtesy Nell Holt Lasley.)

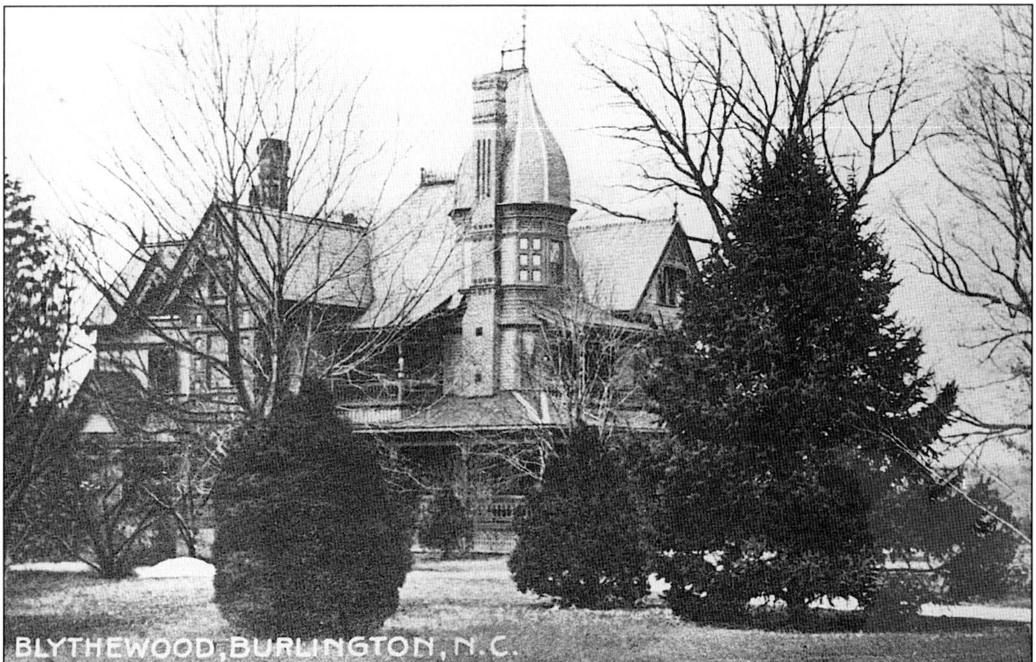

Lawrence Holt Sr. dwelled in a magnificent Victorian mansion that was known as "Blythewood."

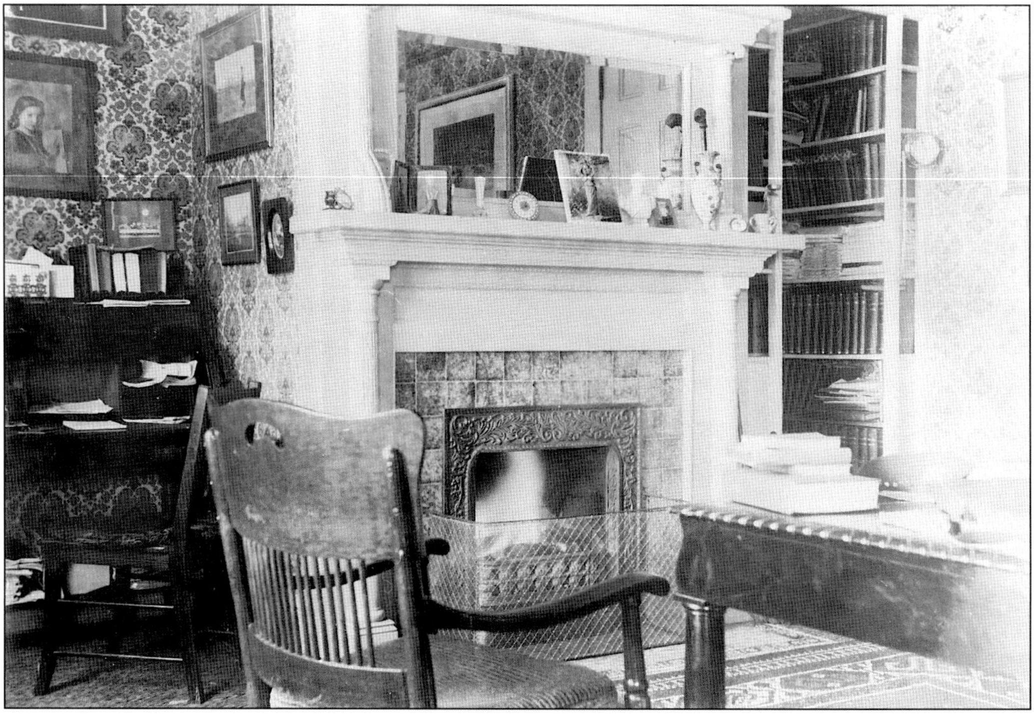

The pictures on this page and the next offer a rare glimpse inside a fine turn-of-the-century home. Above is the library of the Charles Thomas Holt house in Haw River. (Courtesy Alamance County Historical Museum, Inc.)

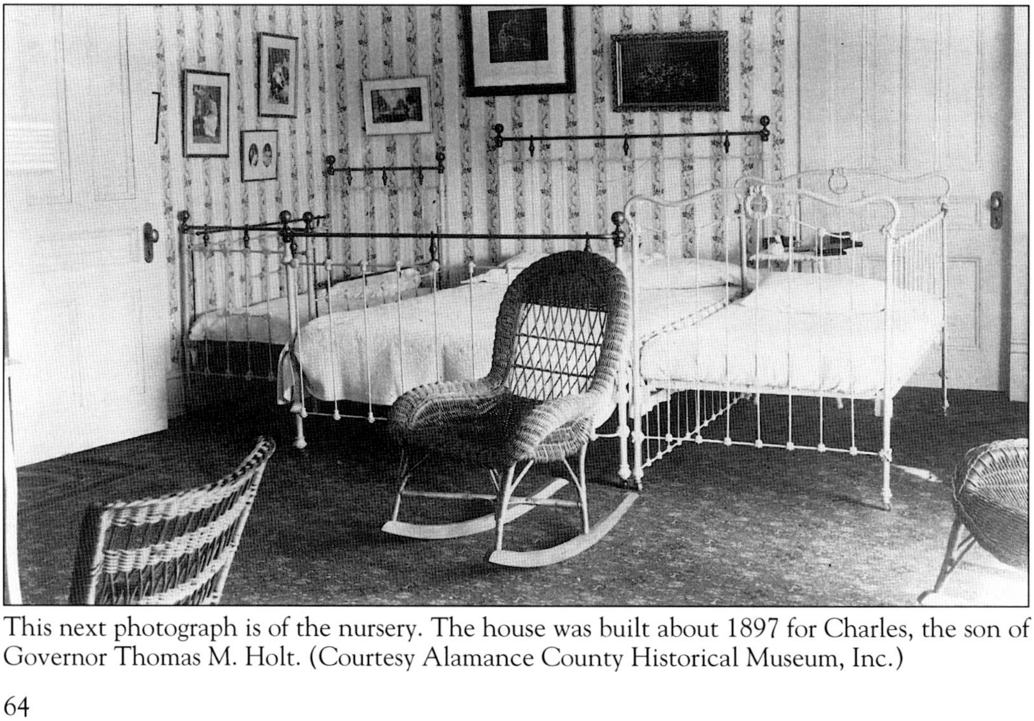

This next photograph is of the nursery. The house was built about 1897 for Charles, the son of Governor Thomas M. Holt. (Courtesy Alamance County Historical Museum, Inc.)

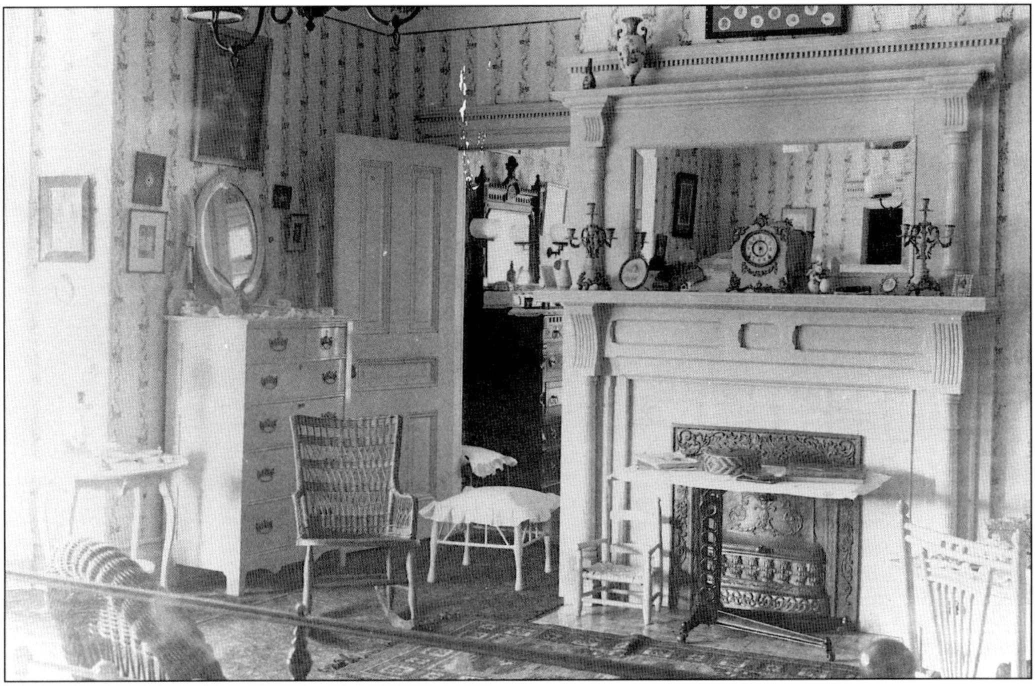

This view shows the opposite side of the nursery. Charles had been left to run Thomas M. Holt Manufacturing Company after his father died in 1896. From its vantage point, the house overlooked the entire mill operation. (Courtesy Alamance County Historical Museum, Inc.)

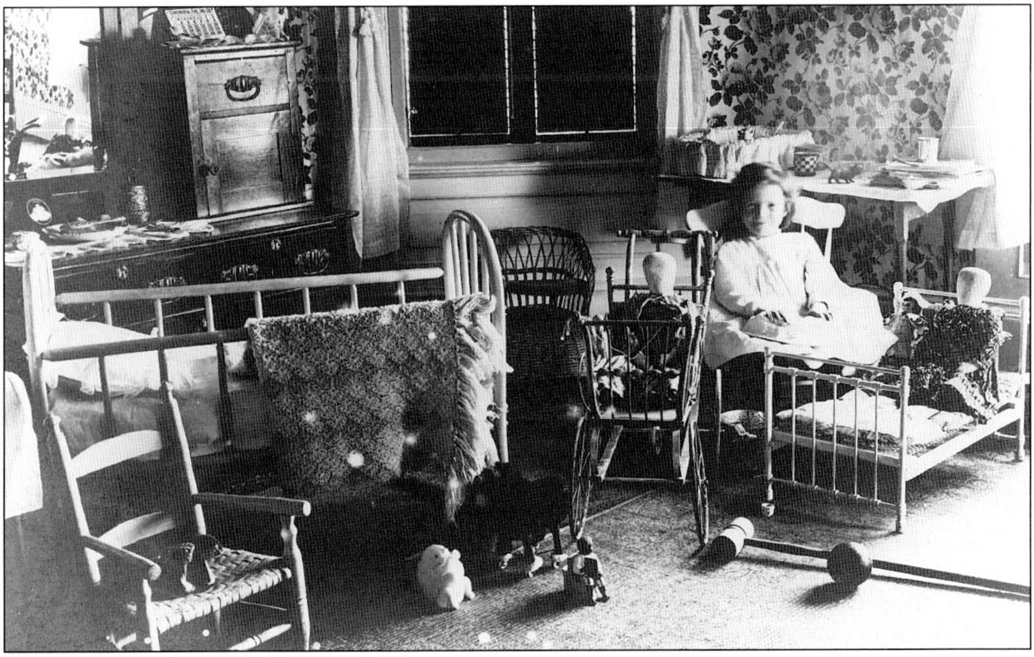

In this fantastic image, Louise Moore Holt (1899–1938) happily poses in her wonderful room of toys. The house still stands in Haw River and is one of Alamance County's greatest examples of Victorian-era architecture. (Courtesy Alamance County Historical Museum, Inc.)

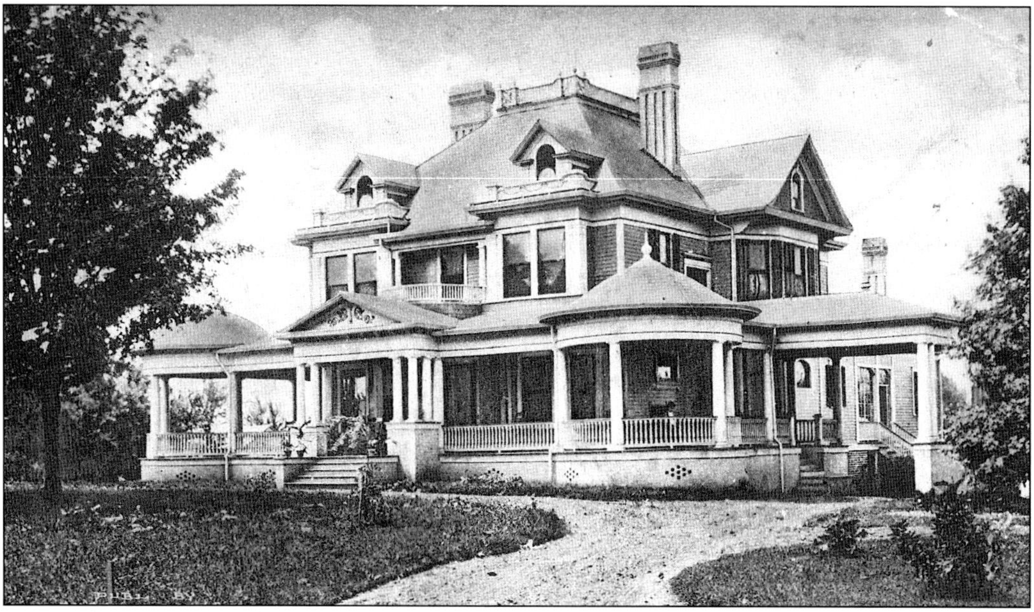

Pictured in this postcard is the residence of Colonel Eugene Holt on Davis Street in Burlington. One of many postcards of the city published by C.V. Sellers Art Store, it was postmarked 2 a.m., April 15, 1910, and sent to Creedmoor after someone affixed a 1¢ stamp.

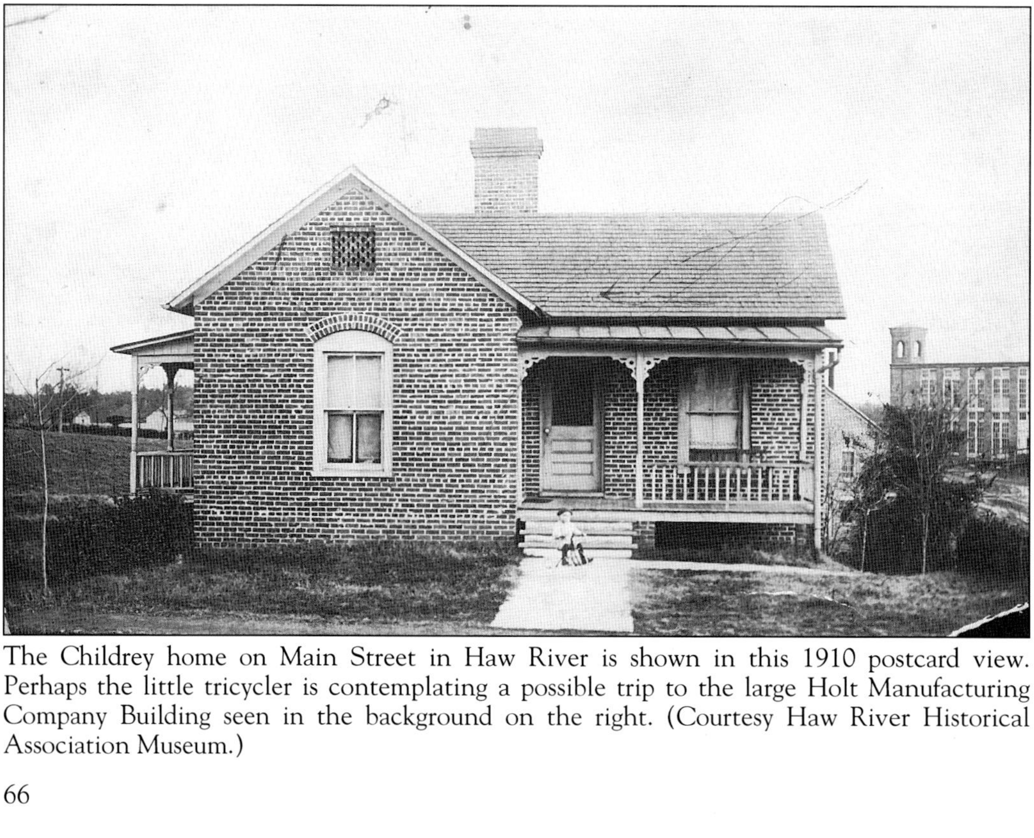

The Childrey home on Main Street in Haw River is shown in this 1910 postcard view. Perhaps the little tricycler is contemplating a possible trip to the large Holt Manufacturing Company Building seen in the background on the right. (Courtesy Haw River Historical Association Museum.)

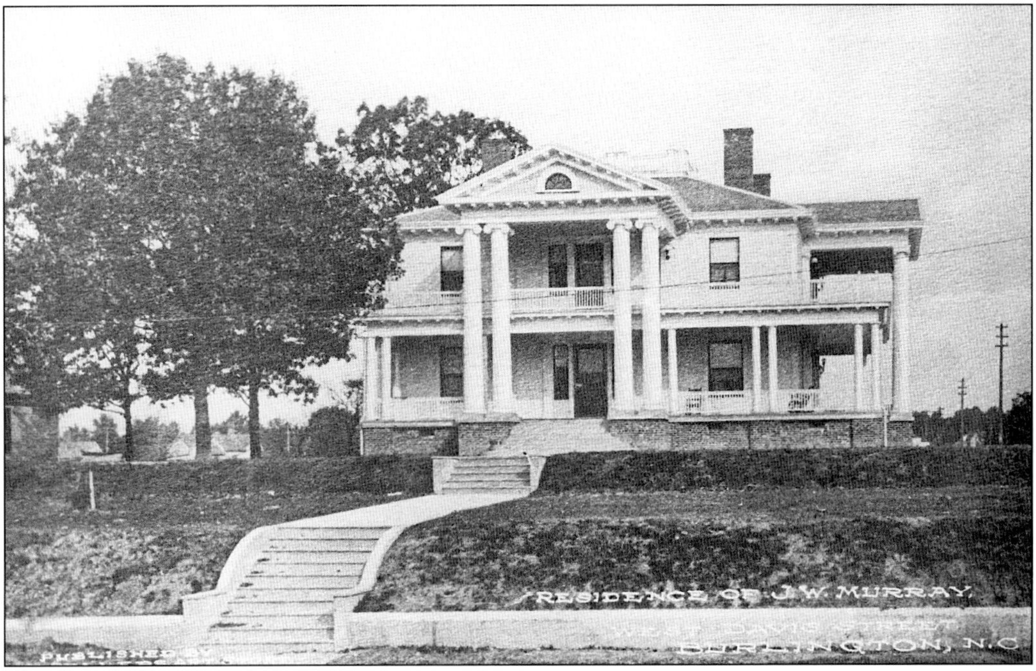

This house on West Davis Street in Burlington was the residence of J.W. Murray in the early part of the twentieth century. The home stands today as one of the city's most recognizable landmarks.

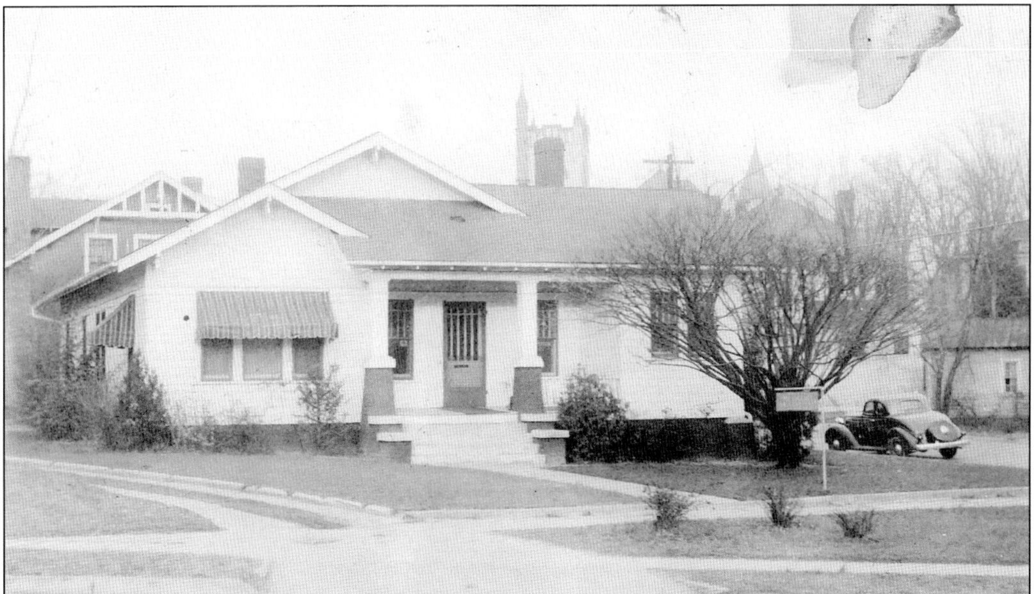

The home seen in this postcard from the 1930s is typical of many houses situated in the towns and cities of Alamance County during the time.

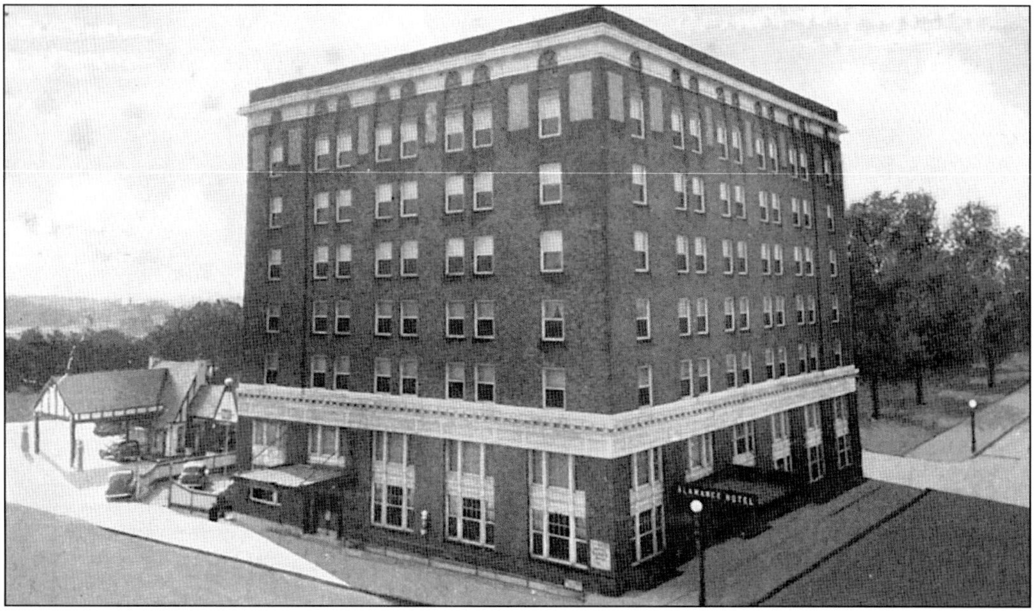

The Alamance Hotel, shown in this postcard picture, was constructed in the 1920s at the corner of Main Street and Maple Avenue in Burlington. The hotel became the scene of banquets, civic club meetings, dances, and parties. (Courtesy Alamance County Historical Museum, Inc.)

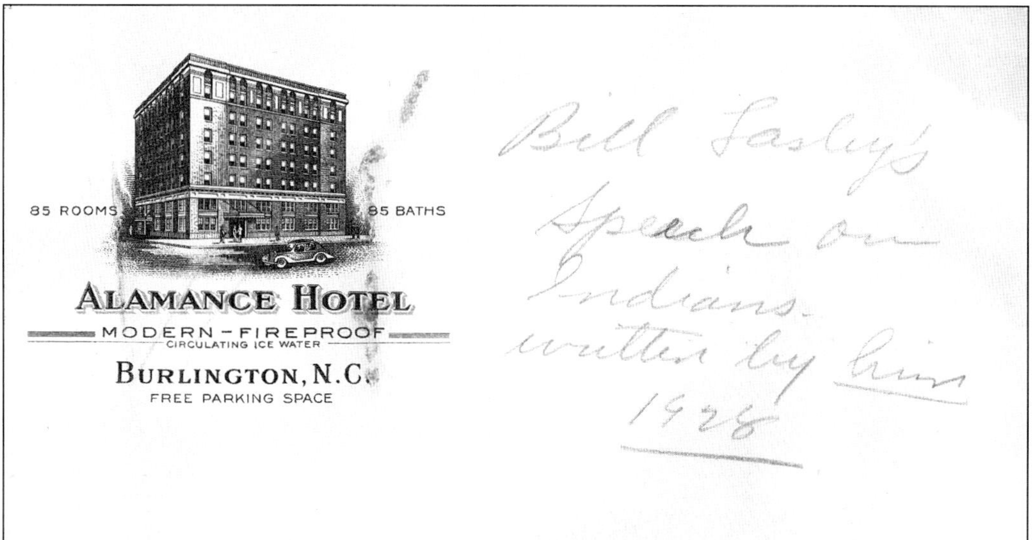

An official stationery envelope from the hotel provides some vital statistics. The Alamance Hotel was modern and claimed to be fireproof. It contained 85 rooms, each with a bath, offered free parking spaces, and boasted of circulating ice water. Printing on the envelope flap reads, "Burlington, N.C. The Hosiery Center of the South." Eventually, motels along the interstate helped close down the business. The building is in use today as Alamance Plaza, a home for the elderly.

Six

BUSINESS

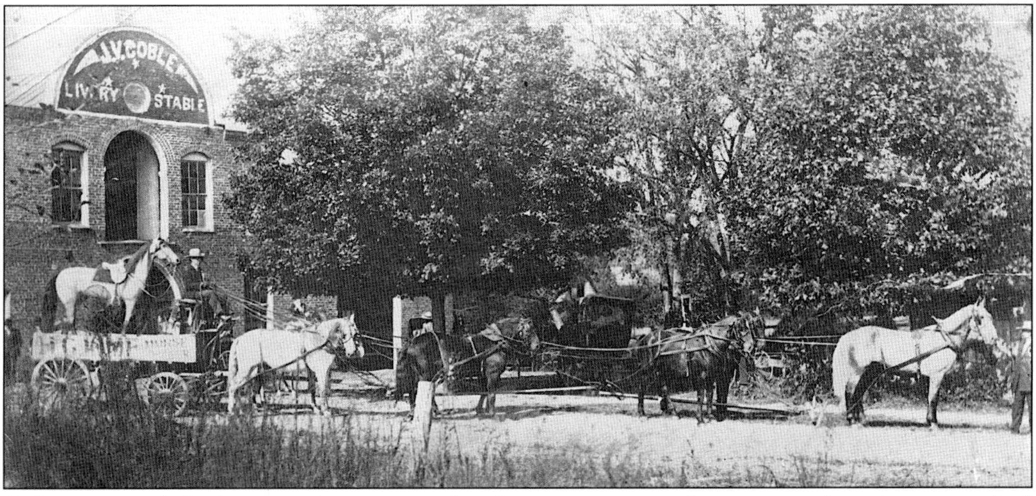

Before automobiles became the main mode of transportation, almost every American town had at least one livery stable. This was a place where horses and carriages were available for hire or where horses were kept and fed for a fixed charge. Here, outside J.V. Coble Livery Stable, a large team of horses is hitched to a wagon. Their cargo is another horse. The man at the reins is Eugene S. Patterson.

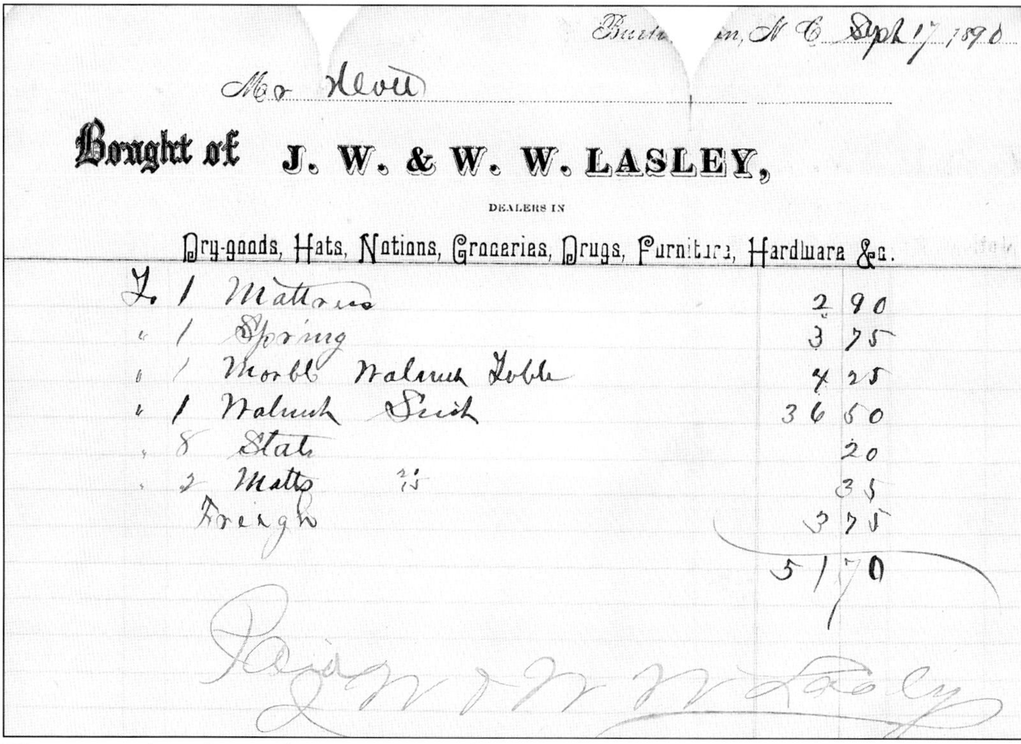

Burl… n, N C Sept 17 1890

Mr Holt

Bought of J. W. & W. W. LASLEY,

DEALERS IN

Dry-goods, Hats, Notions, Groceries, Drugs, Furniture, Hardware &c.

To 1 Mattress	2 90
" 1 Spring	3 75
" 1 Marble Walnut Table	4 25
" 1 Walnut Suit	36 50
" 8 Slats	20
" 2 Matts	35
Freight	3 75
	51 70

Paid J W & W W Lasley

This receipt from September 17, 1890, is for a typical retail transaction of the time. By May 1882, Dr. John Wayne Lasley Sr. and his brother William Winslow Lasley had established a mercantile business on West Front Street in Burlington. According to the receipt, a Mr. Holt purchased a walnut bedroom suite that included a marble-top table. The entire purchase, with freight charge added, totaled $51.70.

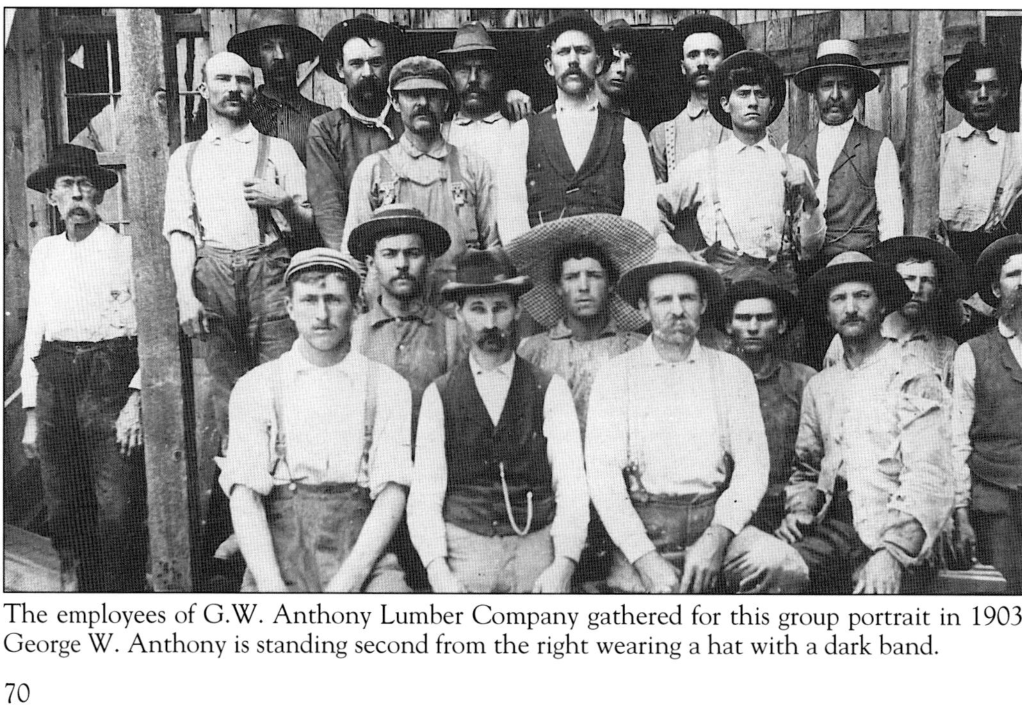

The employees of G.W. Anthony Lumber Company gathered for this group portrait in 1903. George W. Anthony is standing second from the right wearing a hat with a dark band.

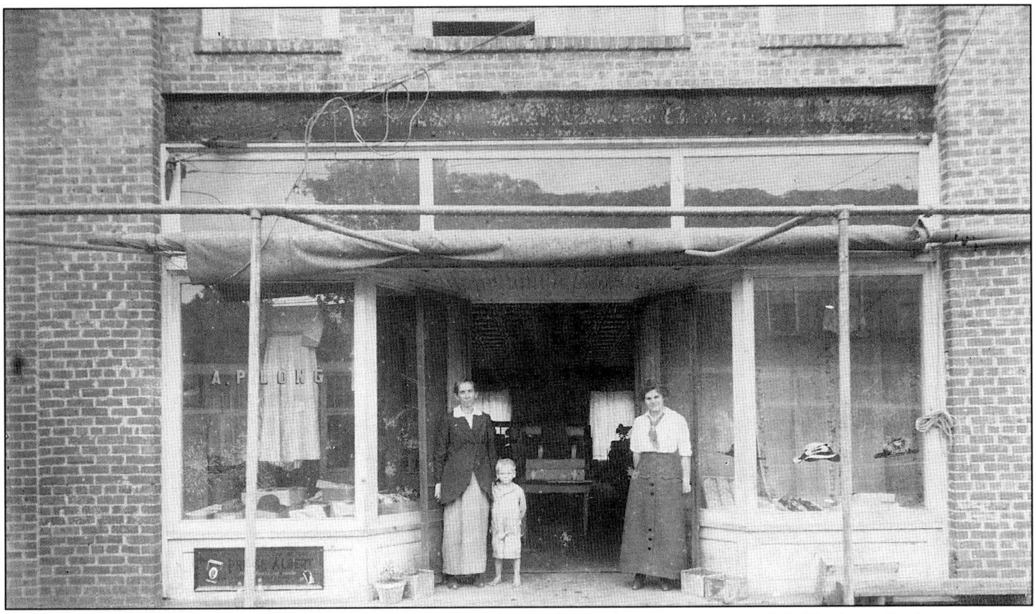

The term "department store" was in wide use by 1887. This is a view of A.P. Long's department store in Mebane. (Courtesy Alamance County Historical Museum, Inc.)

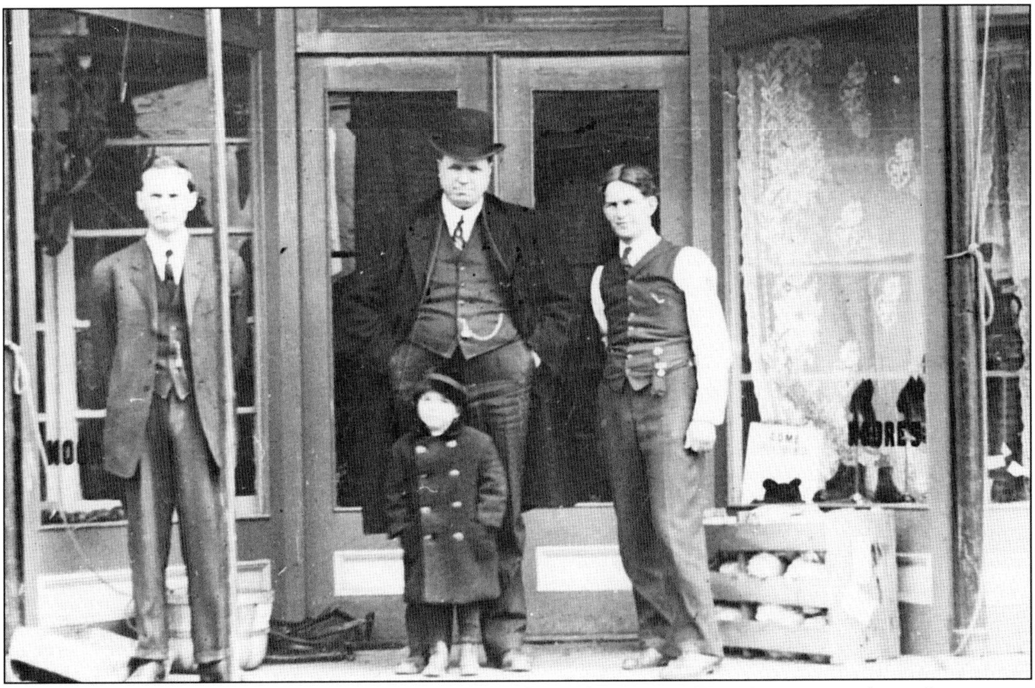

James Black, John A. Hill, with son Linwood, and Grover D. Moore stand in downtown Burlington, *c*. 1912. Moore owned and operated a wholesale grocery on North Main Street.

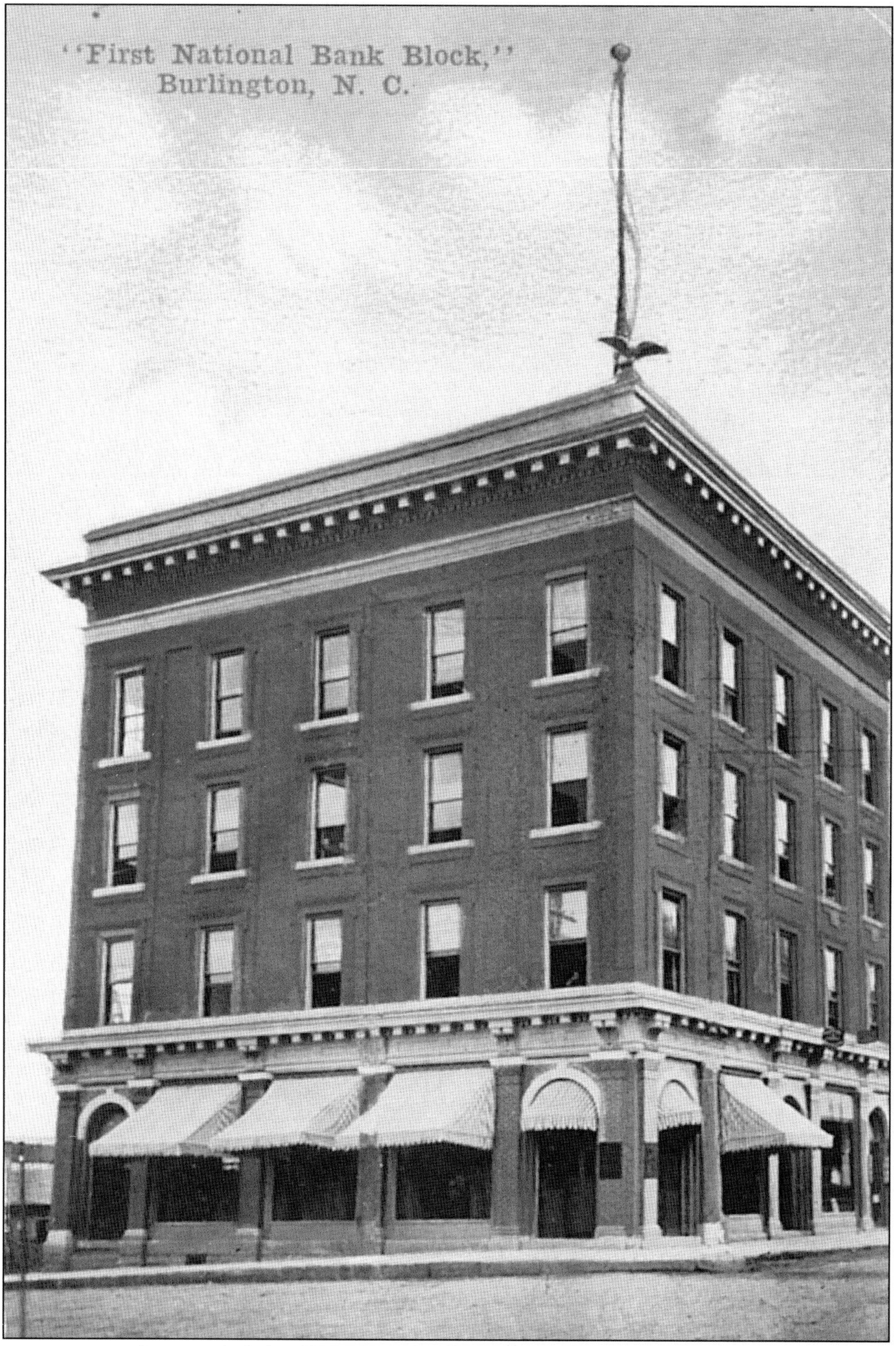

This is a postcard image of the First National Bank Building in Burlington. Having been originally founded earlier as the People's Bank, it later became First National Bank of Burlington. It closed in 1932 but re-opened as the National Bank of Burlington. Later, the bank merged with Wachovia Bank and Trust Company. (Courtesy Alamance County Historical Museum, Inc.)

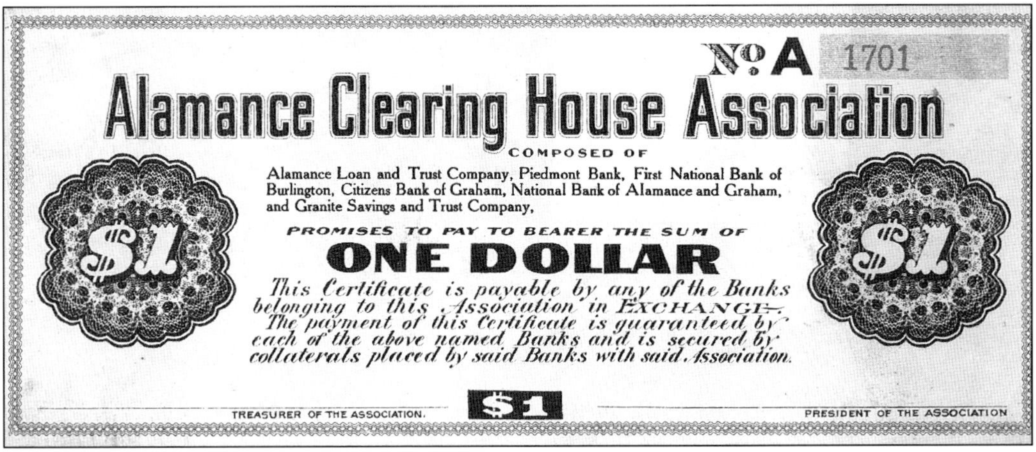
No. A 1701

Alamance Clearing House Association

COMPOSED OF

Alamance Loan and Trust Company, Piedmont Bank, First National Bank of Burlington, Citizens Bank of Graham, National Bank of Alamance and Graham, and Granite Savings and Trust Company,

PROMISES TO PAY TO BEARER THE SUM OF

ONE DOLLAR

This Certificate is payable by any of the Banks belonging to this Association in EXCHANGE. The payment of this Certificate is guaranteed by each of the above named Banks and is secured by collaterals placed by said Banks with said Association.

$1 $1 $1

TREASURER OF THE ASSOCIATION. PRESIDENT OF THE ASSOCIATION

The First National Bank of Burlington (see previous page), among other savings and loan institutions, was a member of the Alamance Clearing House Association. Certificates such as this could be redeemed at any member location.

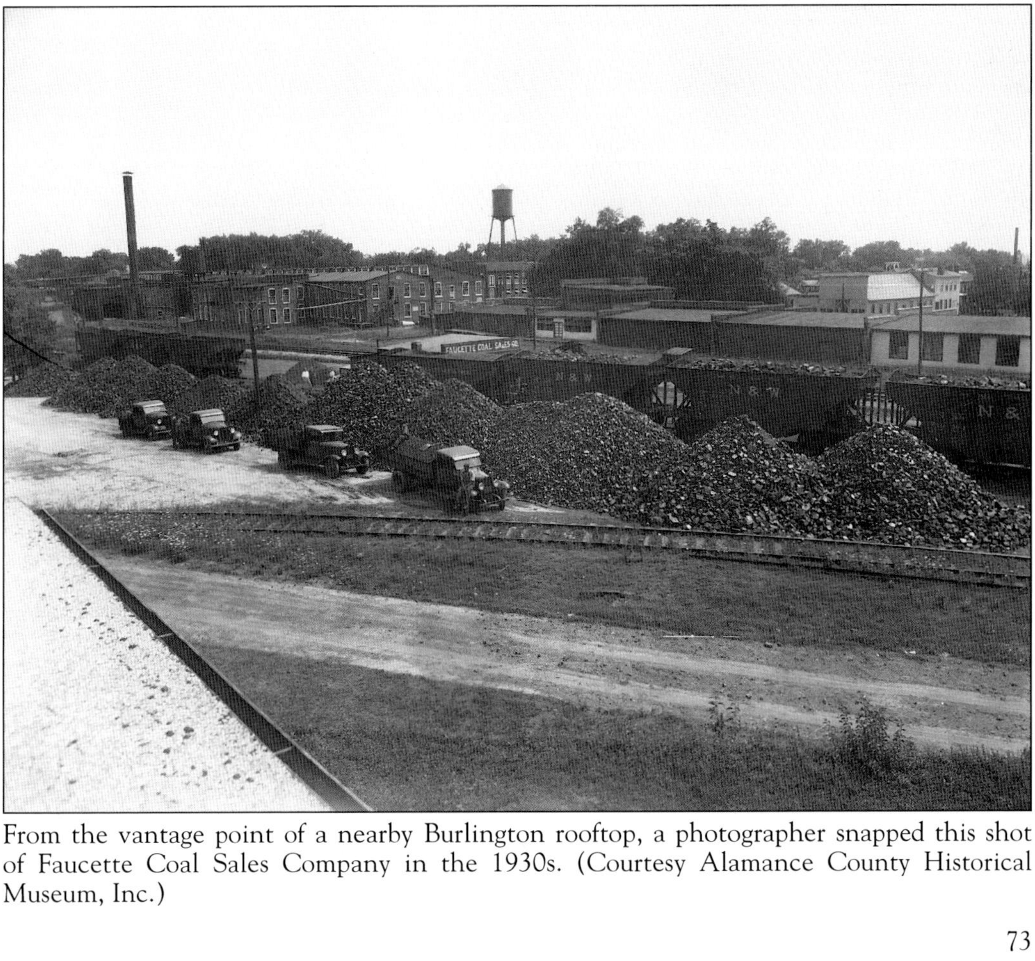

From the vantage point of a nearby Burlington rooftop, a photographer snapped this shot of Faucette Coal Sales Company in the 1930s. (Courtesy Alamance County Historical Museum, Inc.)

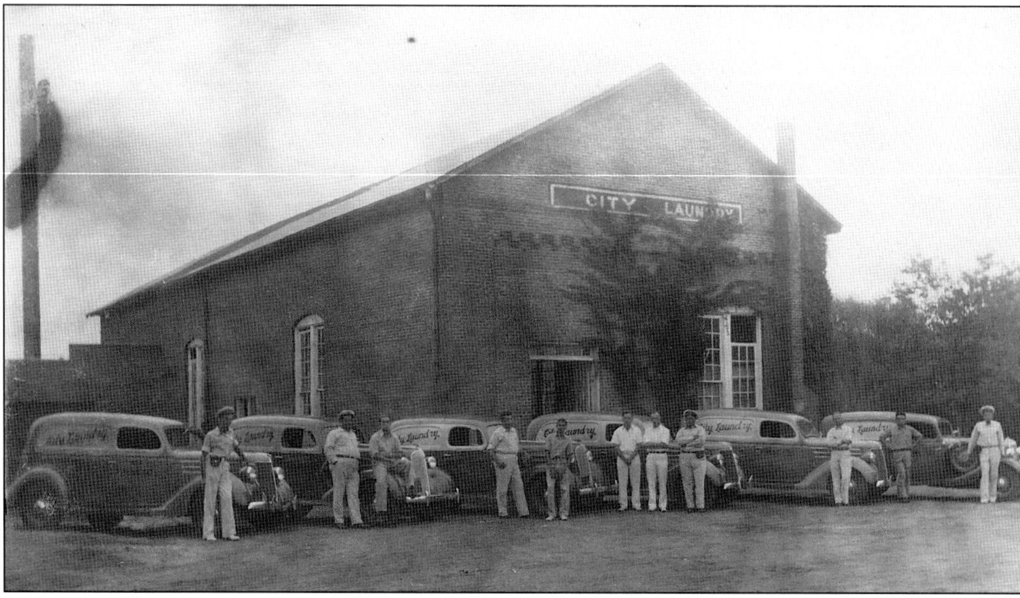

By the early 1940s, City Laundry in Burlington had a fleet of six cars to employ in the transport of the community's dirty clothes. Uniformed employees such as Otis Hedgepath, who had a route in the Beaumont Avenue area, would regularly provide pick up and delivery services to one's home. Cleaned laundry would be returned wrapped in brown paper. The original location on Rainey Street, pictured here, later burned. (Courtesy Haw River Historical Association Museum.)

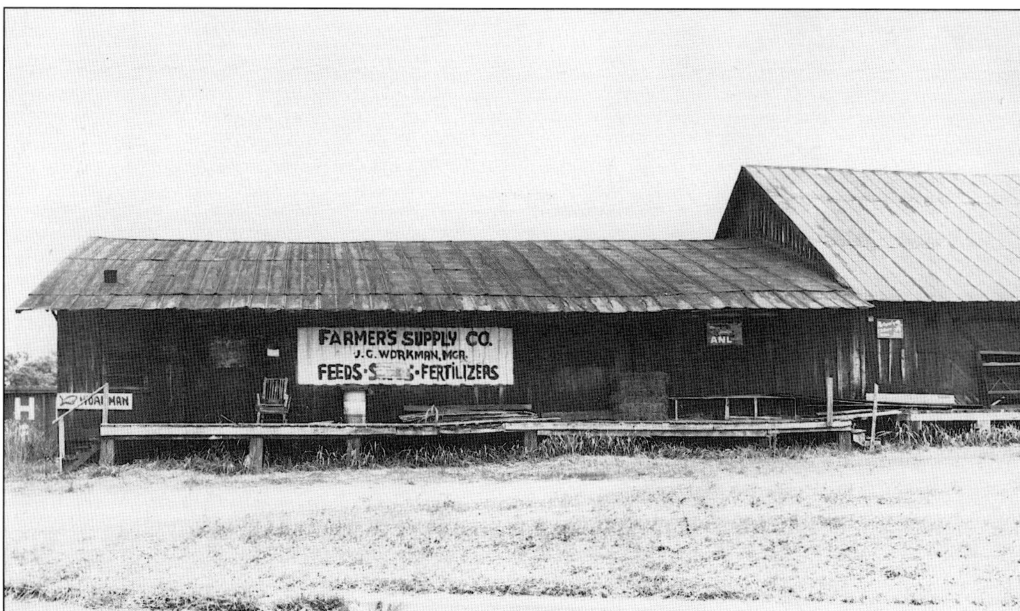

The 1940s saw the heyday of Farmers Supply Company near downtown Burlington. J.G. Workman was the manager, providing feeds and fertilizers to area residents. One sign on the building reads, "You'll really ring the profit bell when you use Arcadian ANL." Another sign advertises Natural Chilean Soda.

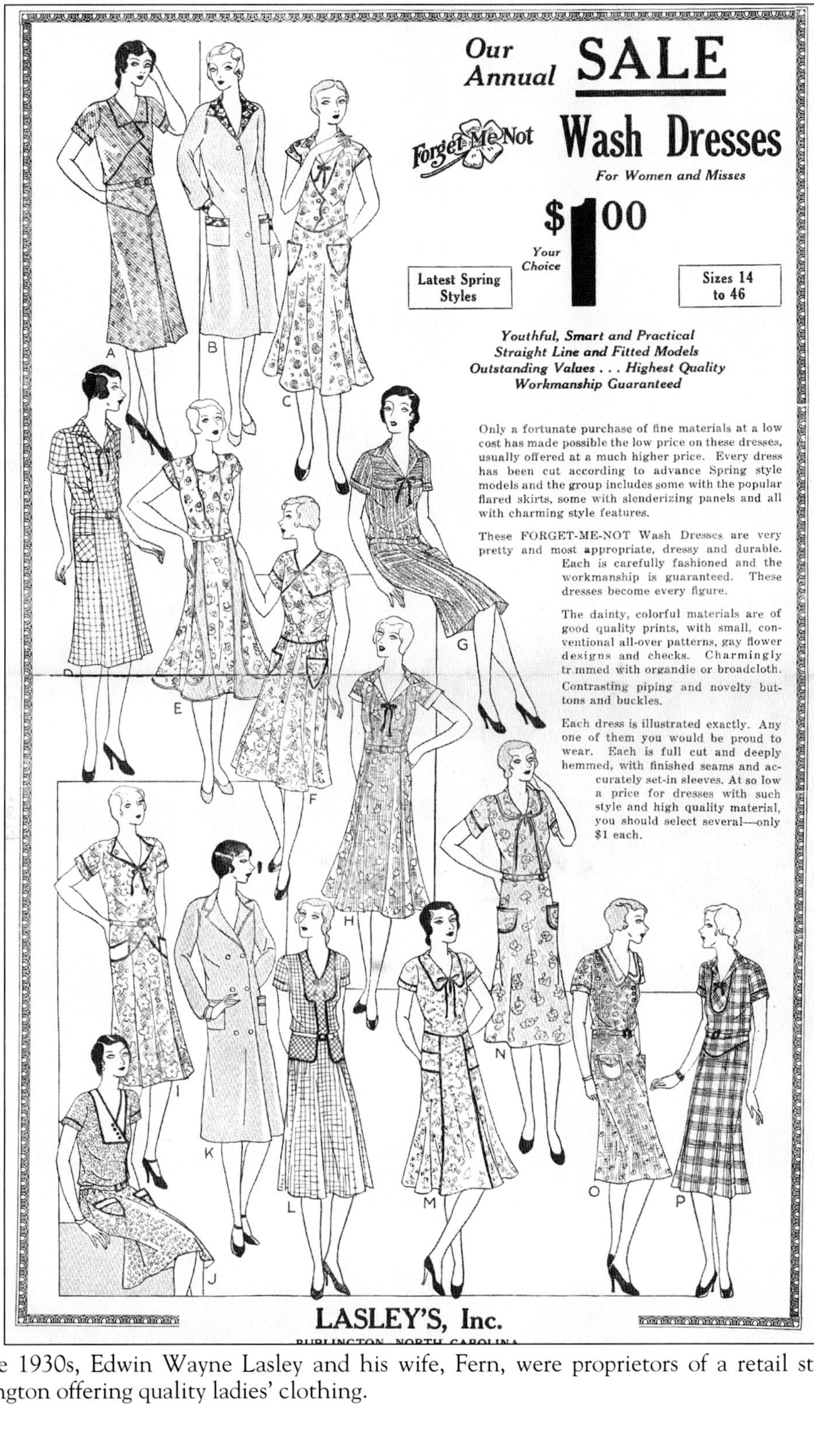

In the 1930s, Edwin Wayne Lasley and his wife, Fern, were proprietors of a retail store in Burlington offering quality ladies' clothing.

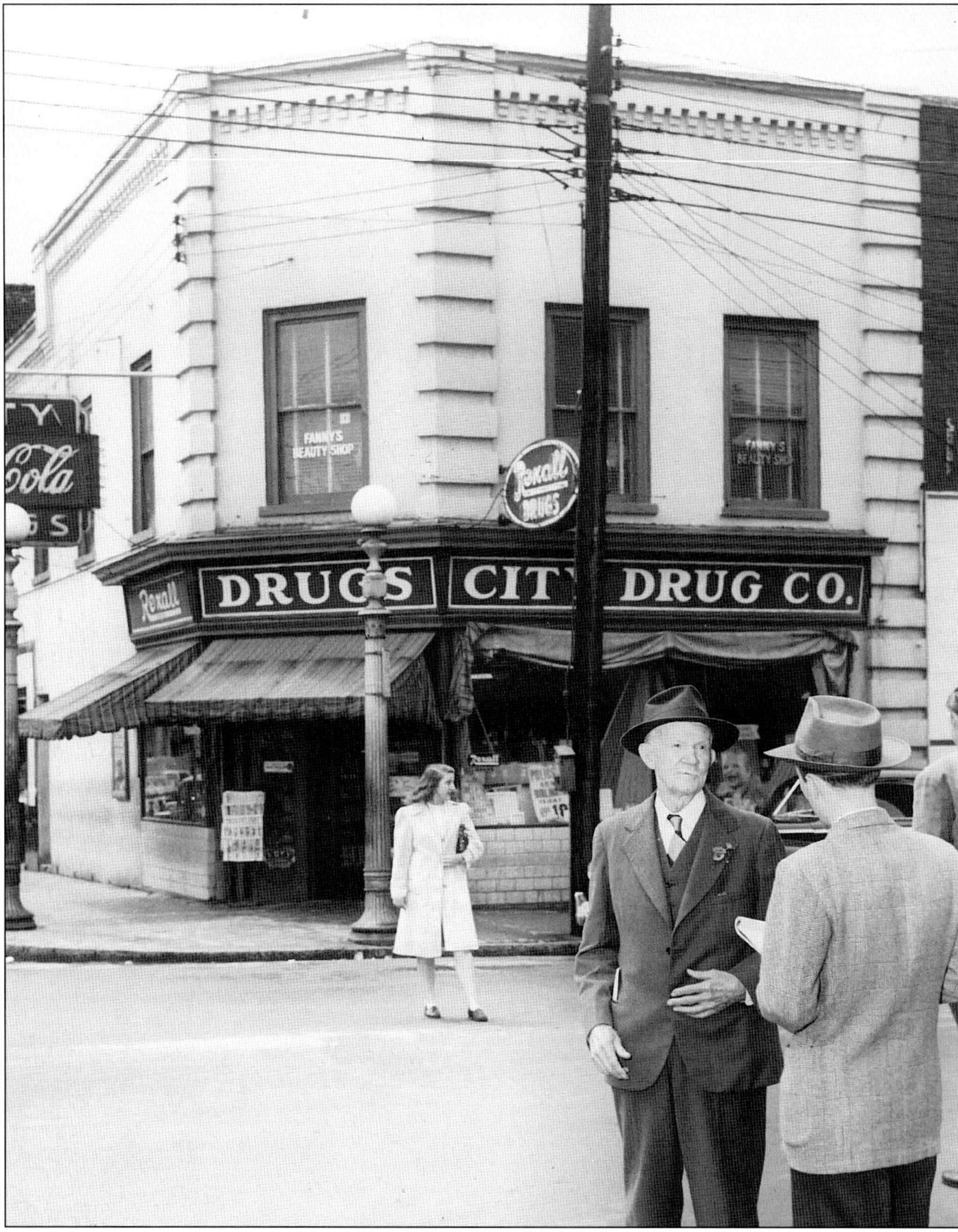

In this photograph from 1947, Dr. W.S. Long stands in front of City Drug Company. The business was located in the first brick building that was constructed within the corporate limits of Burlington. (Courtesy Nell Holt Lasley.)

B.A. Sellars and Sons was situated on Main Street in Burlington. In 1887 Dr. B.A. Sellars served on the committee that chose the new name for the town of Company Shops.

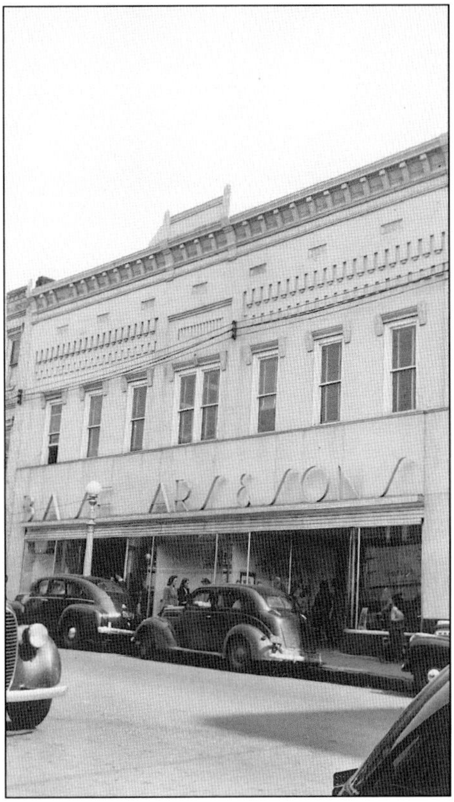

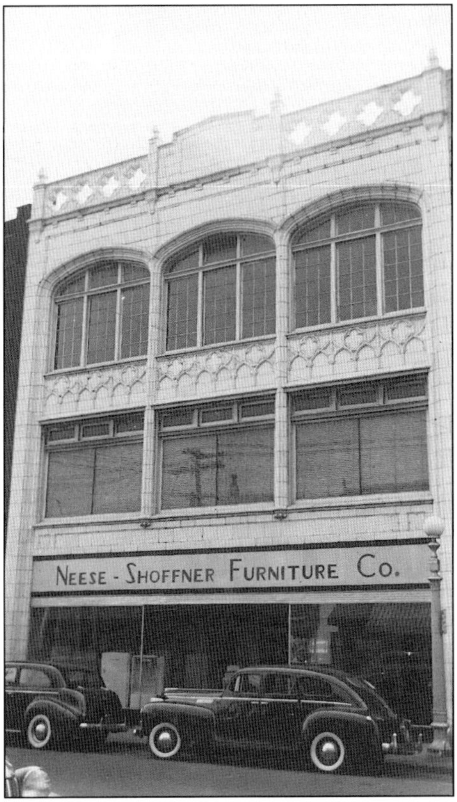

In the 1940s, this photograph was taken of Neese-Shoffner Furniture Company on Davis Street in Burlington.

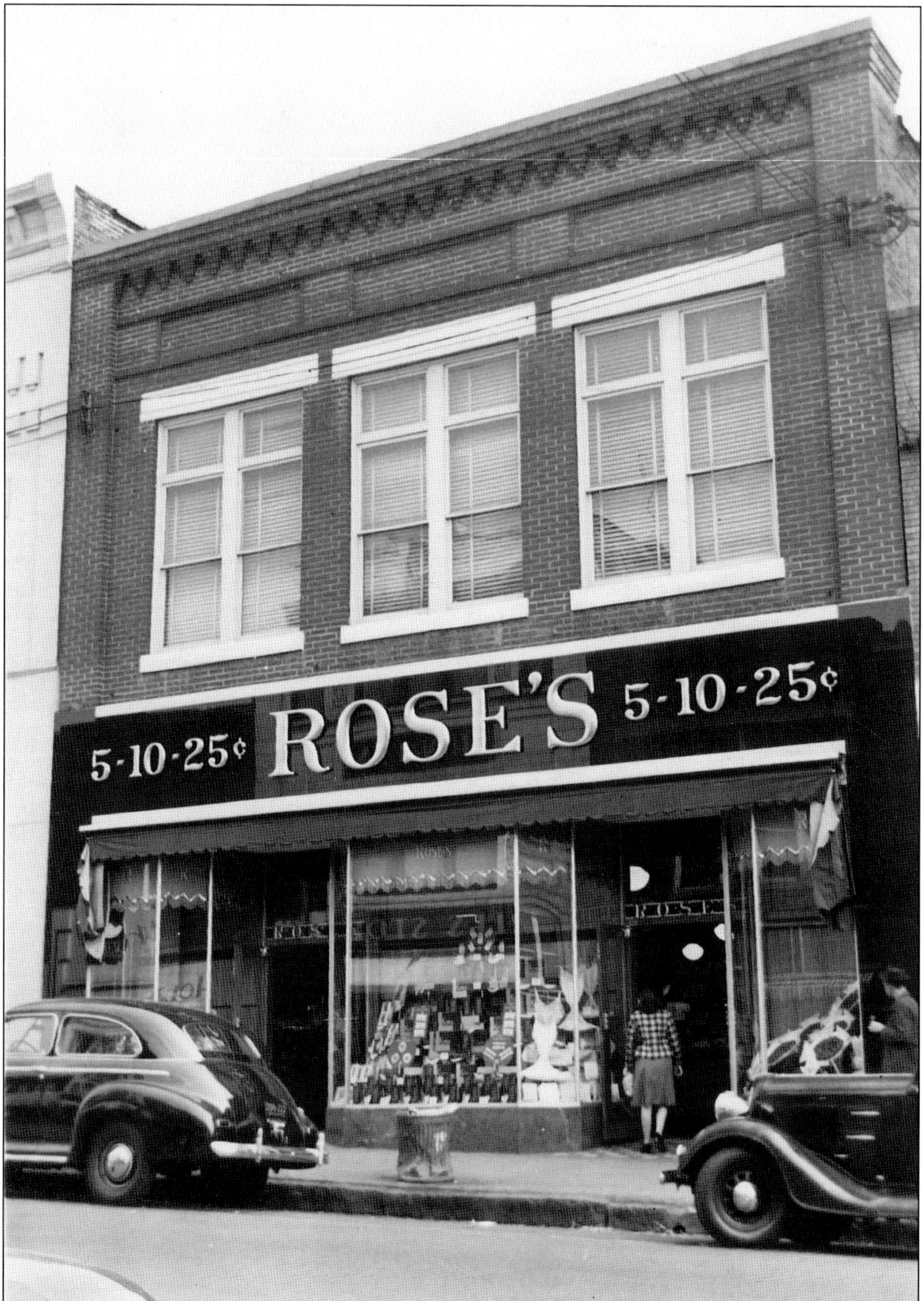

Regional department store chains were once more common than they are now. For decades there was a Rose's location on Main Street in Burlington.

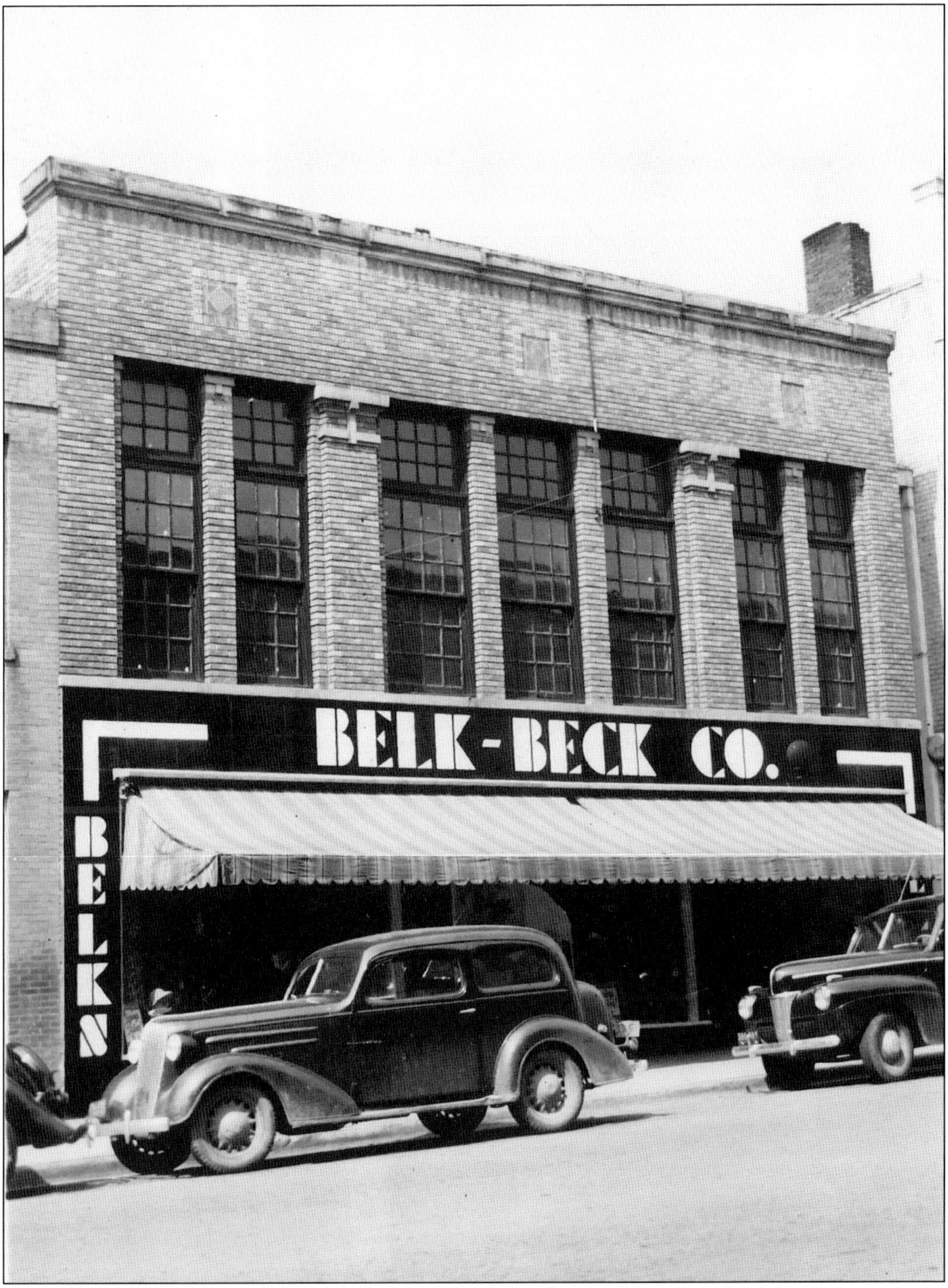

Before shopping malls diverted the flow of customers, downtown sections of communities were home to businesses like Belk-Beck on Main Street in Burlington.

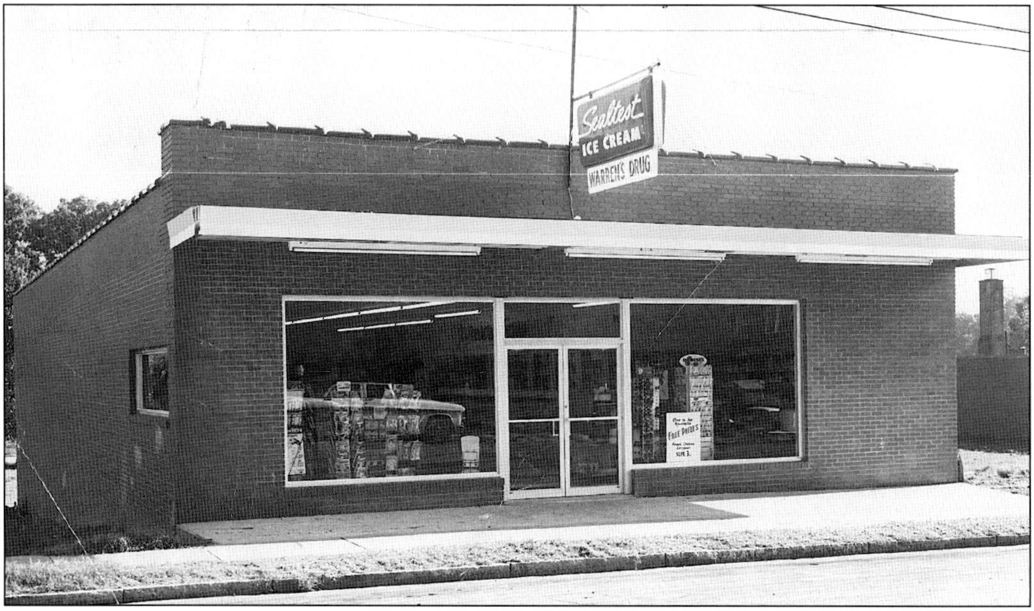

This view of Warren's Drugstore in Mebane was taken in August of 1960. Owners Virgil Warren and Calvin Oakley planned their formal opening for September 3 of that same year. Free prizes were given away to registrants. Through one window, a rack of comic books is topped off with the once common, "Hey Kids Comics" sign. One of the publications is titled *Spooky*. Sunglasses and products from a "Dr. West" were also on display. (Courtesy Town of Mebane.)

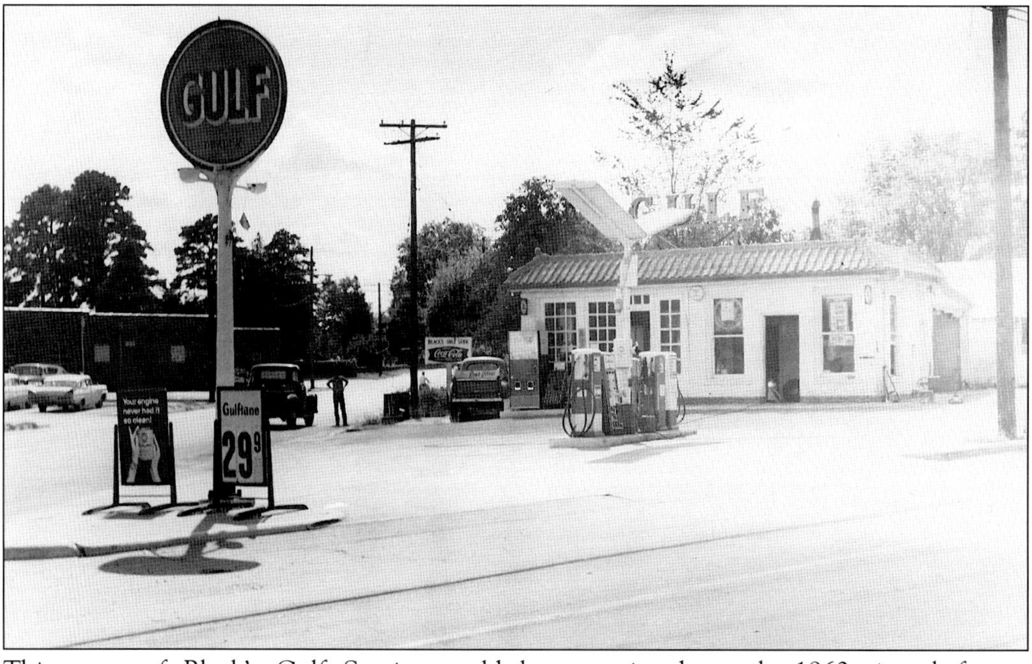

This scene of Black's Gulf Service could be seen in the early 1960s just before a major renovation.

Seven

EDUCATION

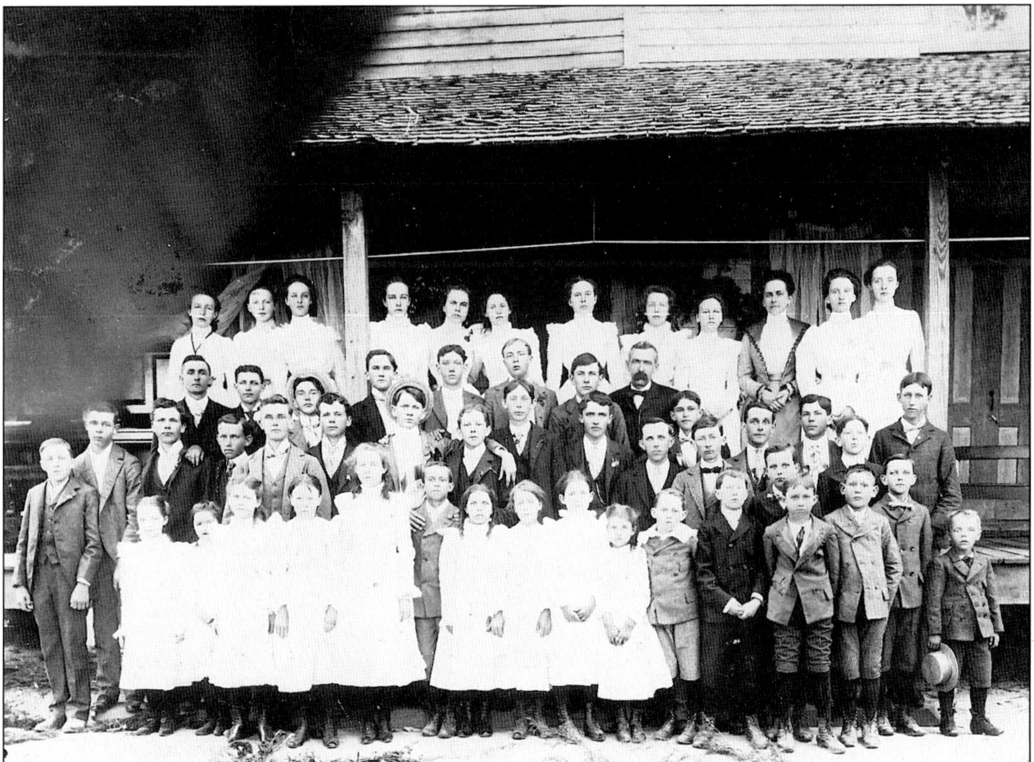

Union Academy was founded in 1839 at Union Ridge. Parents who could afford it sent their children to this private boarding school. The academy was one of Alamance County's leading educational institutions during the second half of the nineteenth century. The exact year of the photograph is unknown. (Courtesy Alamance County Historical Museum, Inc.)

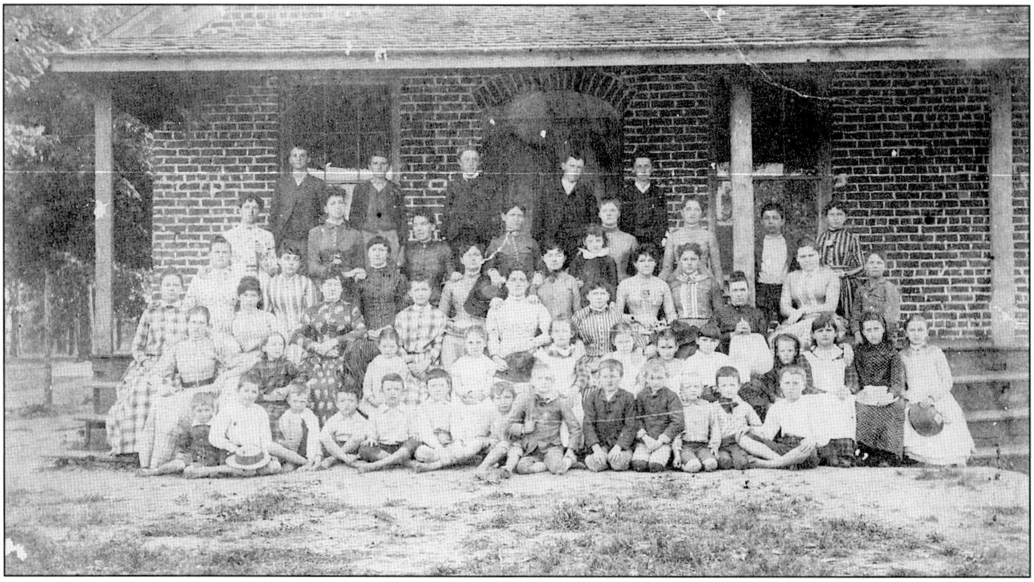

This image shows an assemblage of Mrs. Witherspoon's school in Burlington. (Courtesy Alamance County Historical Museum, Inc.)

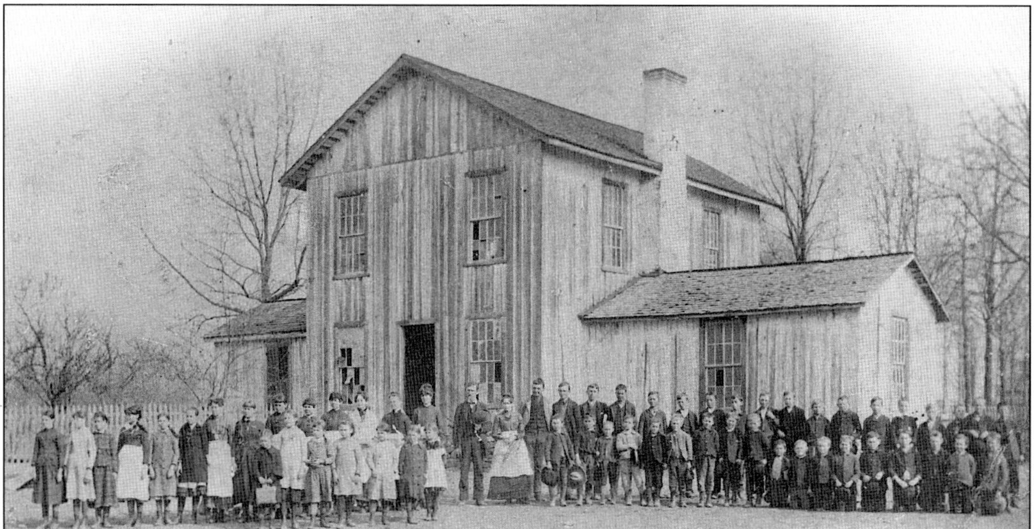

The first school in Burlington was also the town's first house of worship. The North Carolina Railroad Company erected this building, which was used as both a schoolhouse and as a meeting place for churches of different denominations. The photograph was probably made during the 1890–91 school year. Dora Teague and John Washington Ellis Fonville were the teachers. (Courtesy Alamance County Historical Museum, Inc.)

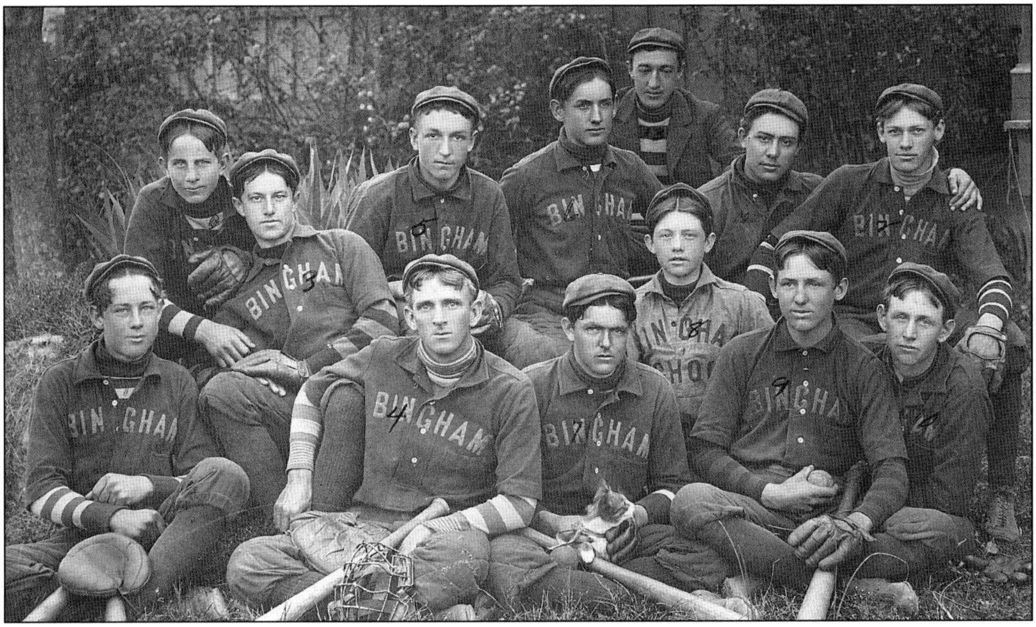

After Bingham Academy was moved to Asheville in 1891, the Mebane school continued for a time as a Presbyterian church school. Pictured above is the 1901 baseball team, from left to right, as follows: (front row) Simpson (first base), Crowder (catcher), Cooper (apparently keeper of feline mascot), Crump, Wynne (pitcher), and Peden (shortstop); (back row) Harris (right field), Clark, Heath (captain and second base), Green (left field), Mangum (manager), McDonald (pitcher), and Davant (third base).

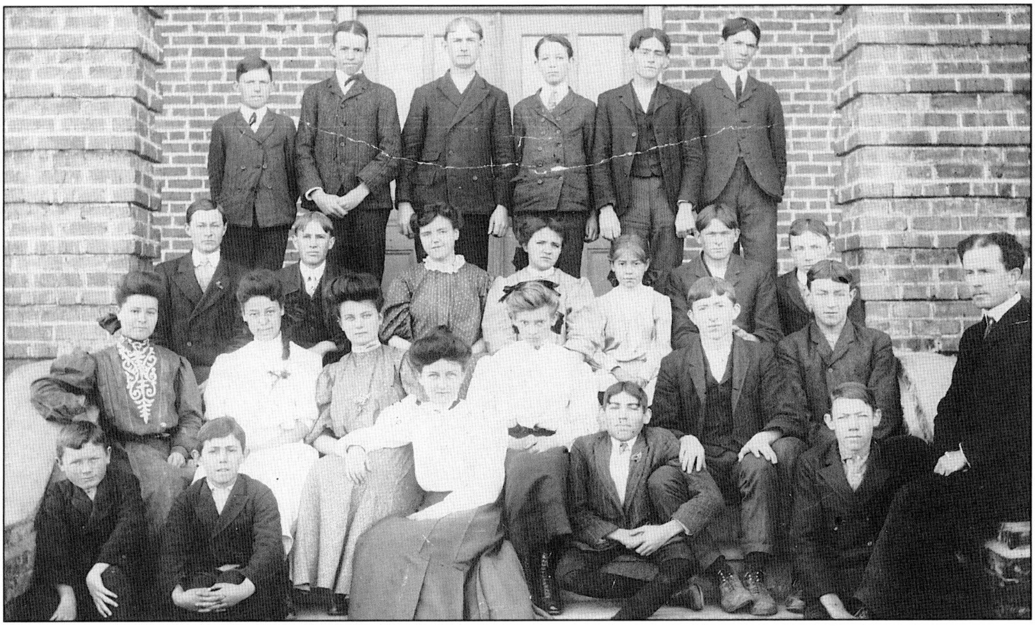

The fifth and sixth grades of Aycock Graded School in Haw River posed for this picture in 1906. Miss Mary Maynard (bottom center) was the teacher, and Mr. J.A. McLean (far right) served as superintendent. The institution opened in 1904 as the first graded school in Alamance County. (Courtesy Haw River Historical Association Museum.)

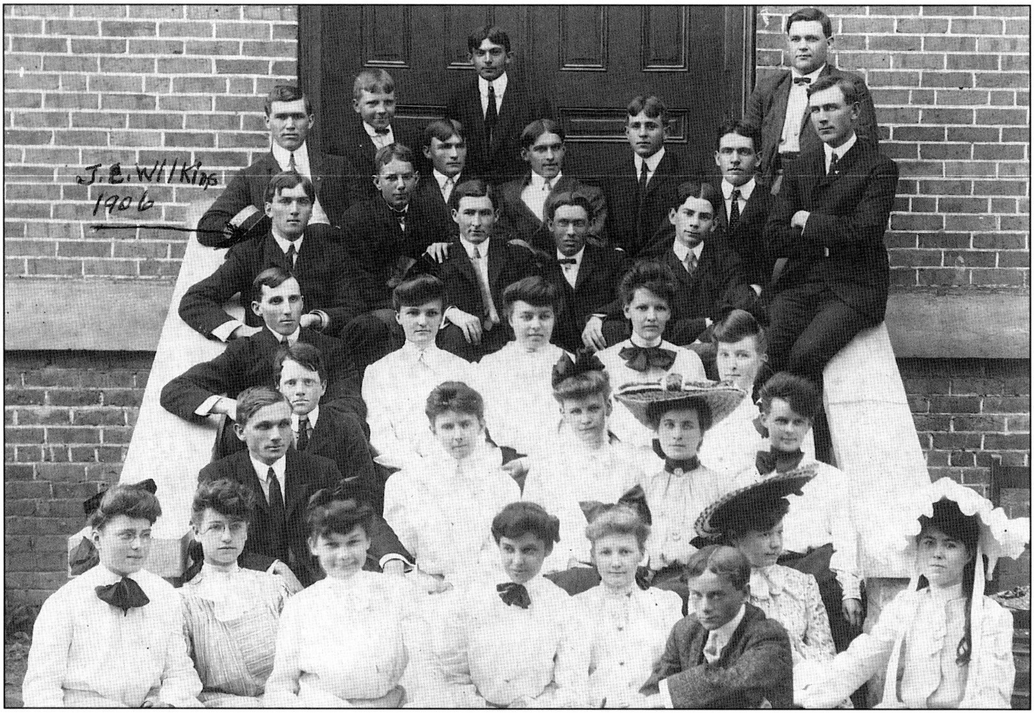

This photograph of the senior class at Elon College was made during the 1906–07 school year. The college was established by the Christian Church and opened on September 14, 1890. (Courtesy Haw River Historical Association Museum.)

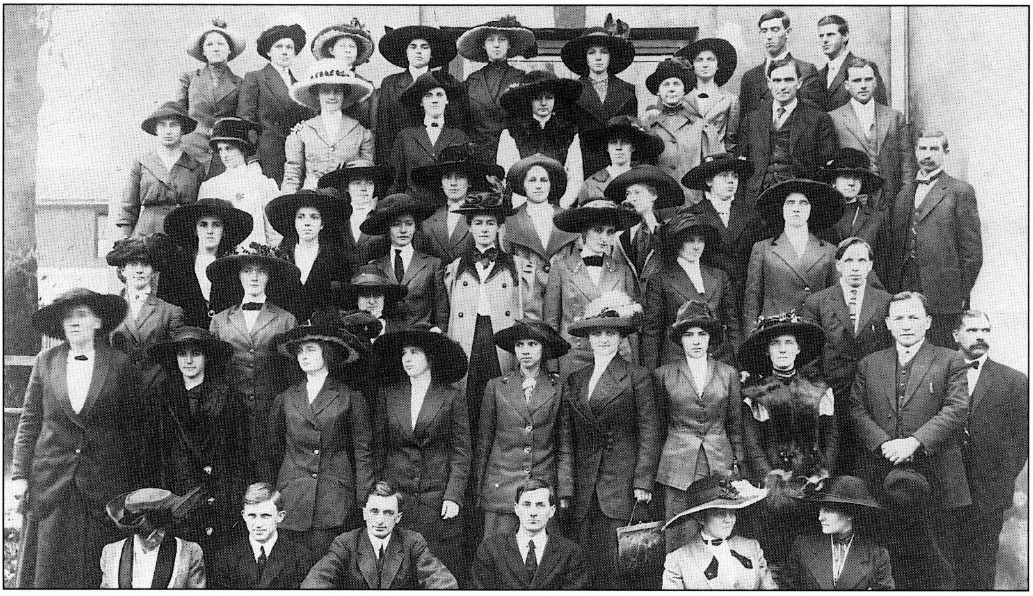

The Alamance County public schoolteachers gathered in Graham for this picture in 1910. By 1908, subjects taught in the county's high schools included English, grammar, composition and rhetoric, English literature, advanced arithmetic, algebra, English history, ancient history, American history, North Carolina history, Latin, and physical geography. (Courtesy Alamance County Historical Museum, Inc.)

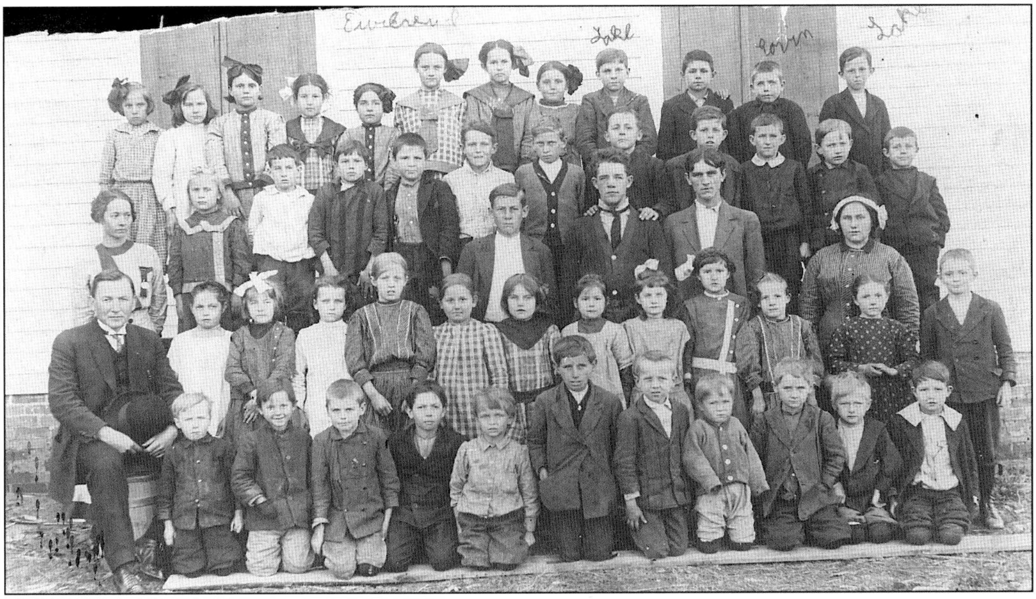

The students at Glenwood School posed for this 1913 image. (Courtesy Alamance County Historical Museum, Inc.)

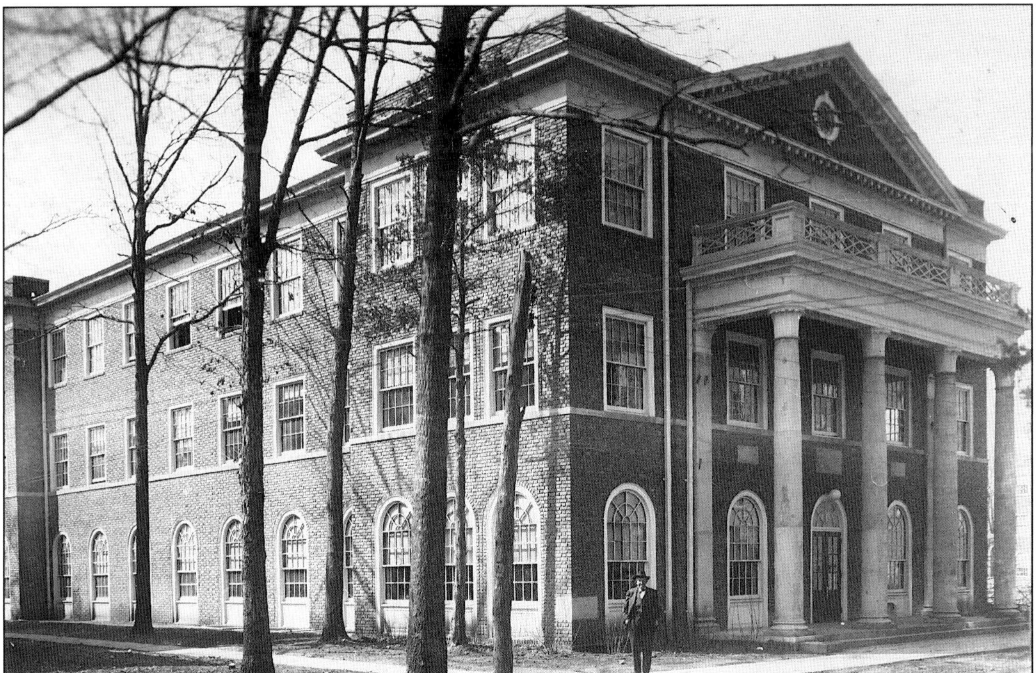

The Duke Building, on the campus of Elon College, was newly dedicated when Artelia Roney Duke's youngest brother, Amos Kendall Roney, stood before it for this photograph. The college's many oak trees inspired its name. The Hebrew word for oak is "elon." (Courtesy Haw River Historical Association Museum.)

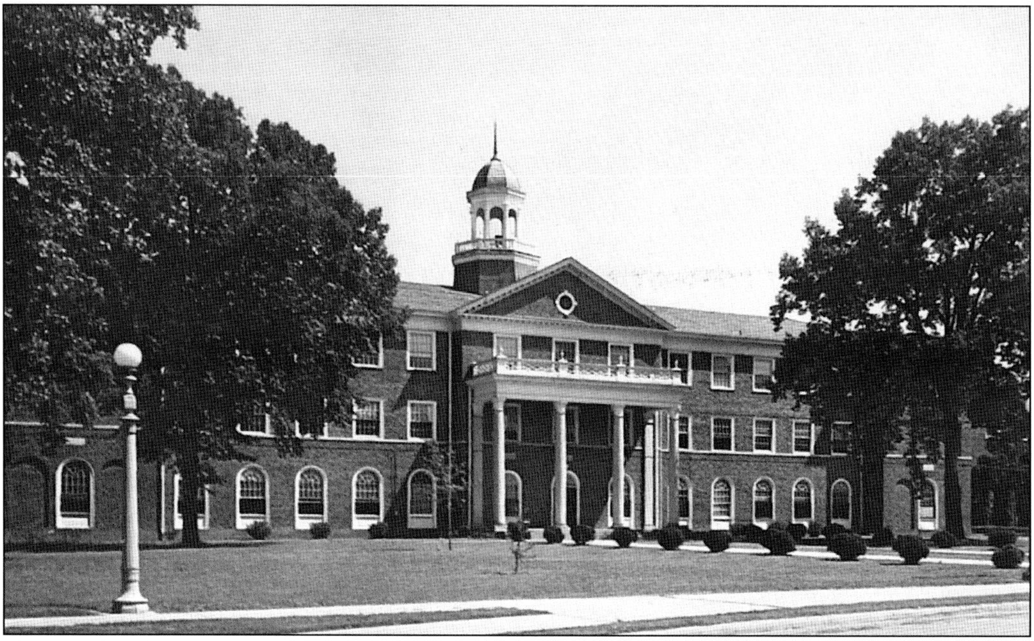

Elon College's Alamance Building is seen in this postcard view from about 1960. Formerly known as Mill Point, the town of Elon College was incorporated on April 7, 1893. (Courtesy Alamance County Historical Museum, Inc.)

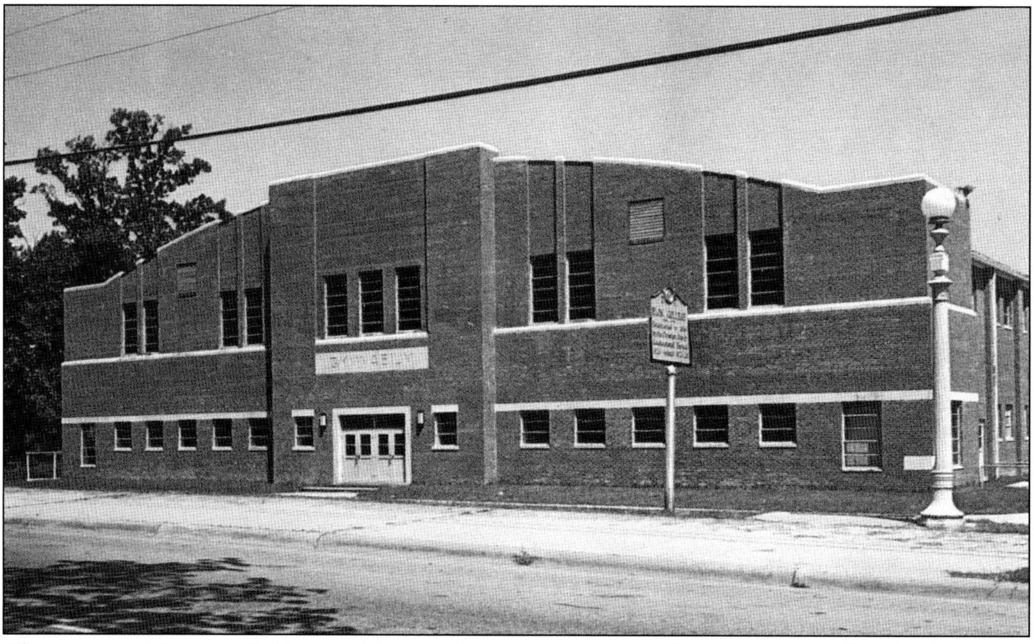

This postcard image of Alumni Memorial Gymnasium, on the campus of Elon College, was made during a February 22, 1960 photo session. The college would later add many newer athletic facilities. (Alamance County Historical Museum, Inc.)

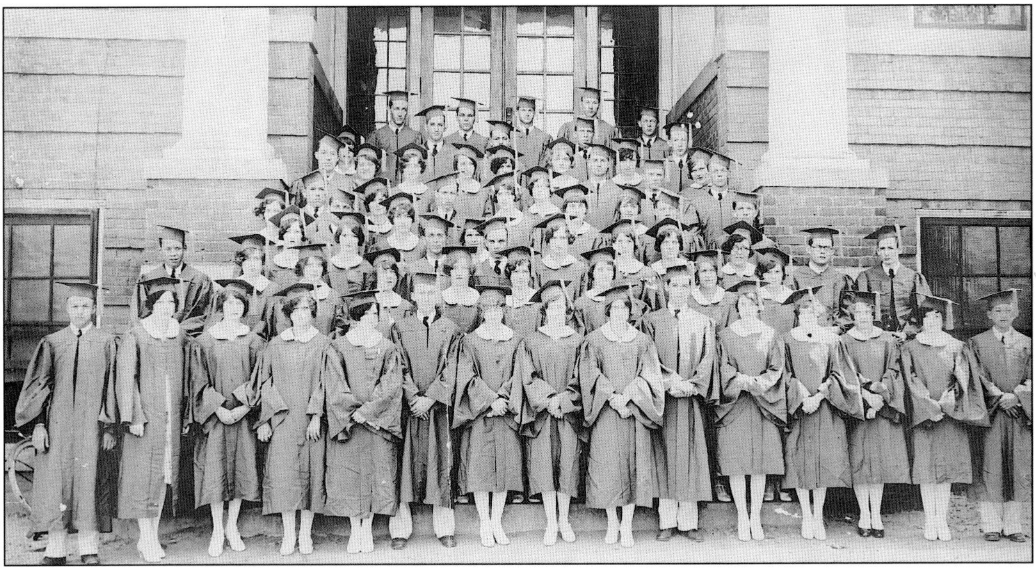

Members of Burlington High School's Class of 1928 stand regally in cap and gown. The building behind was constructed in 1916 on Broad Street. (Courtesy Nell Holt Lasley.)

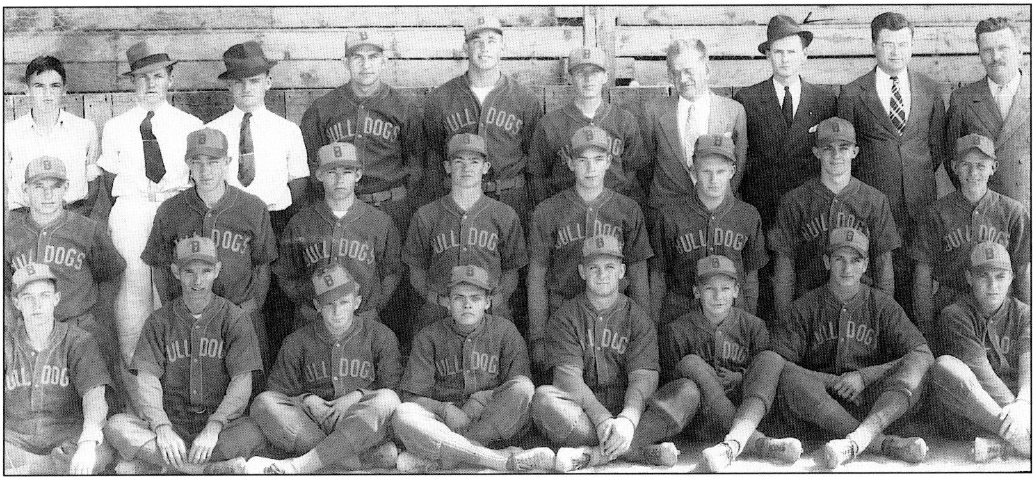

On May 14, 1936, the Burlington High School Bulldogs baseball team won the state championship. From left to right are as follows: (bottom row) George Hickey, Elmo Covington, Virgin Hodgin, George Hardie, Ralph Goins, Calvin Walker, Burman Bare, and Ed Ketner; (middle row) J.B. Williams, Adolphus Sorrell, Herman Nunnery, Jimmy Cross, Vestle Johnson, Charlie Steward, Bob Gammon, and Clarence "Sonny" Vaughn; (top row) Howard Walker, Willard Wagoner and Kenneth Boland (managers), John Reiber (assistant coach), Kendall Moran (captain), John O. Reynolds (coach), E.C. Leonard (principal), and *Daily Times-News* team advisory committee members W.T. Lasley, R. M. Hodges, and Ray J. Nally.

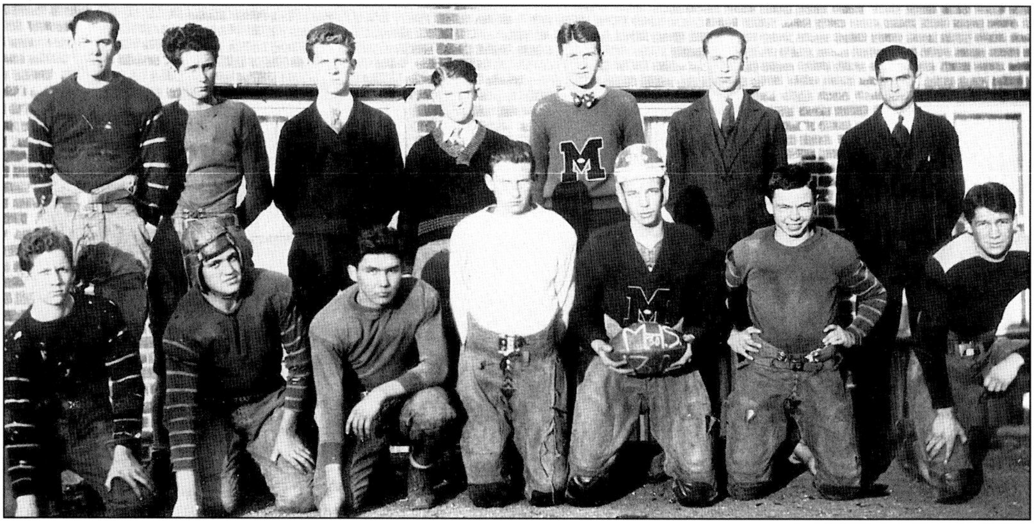

These young men were members of the Mebane High School football team in 1930. From left to right are as follows: (bottom row) Dick Graves, Floyd Moore, Bill LeGrand, Tom Pettigrew, Cliff Rascoe, Dick Hupman, and Vern Williams; (top row) John Fox, Oct Farrell, Edward Graves, Marcus Allred, Joe Mason, Harlen McCauley, and coach J.O. Saunders. Team members not present for this picture were Bill York, J.C. James, Earl Oakley, and Lynch Hamby. (Courtesy Town of Mebane.)

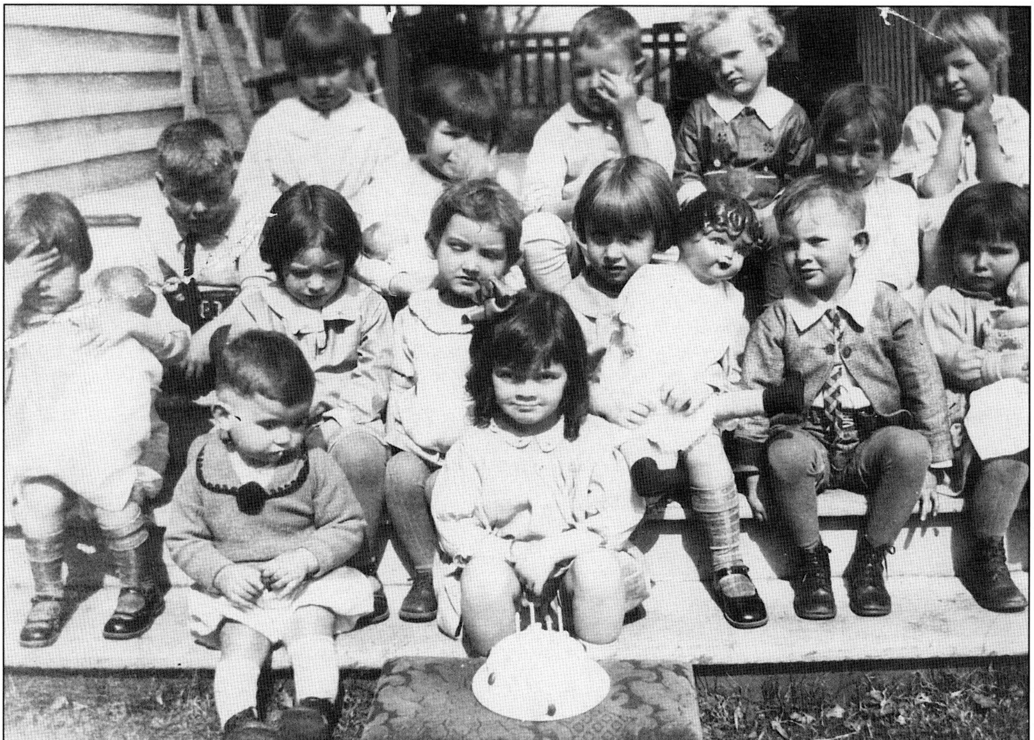

In 1928 Barbara Simpson celebrated her fourth birthday with a party at Miss Nell's kindergarten in Haw River. (Courtesy Haw River Historical Association Museum.)

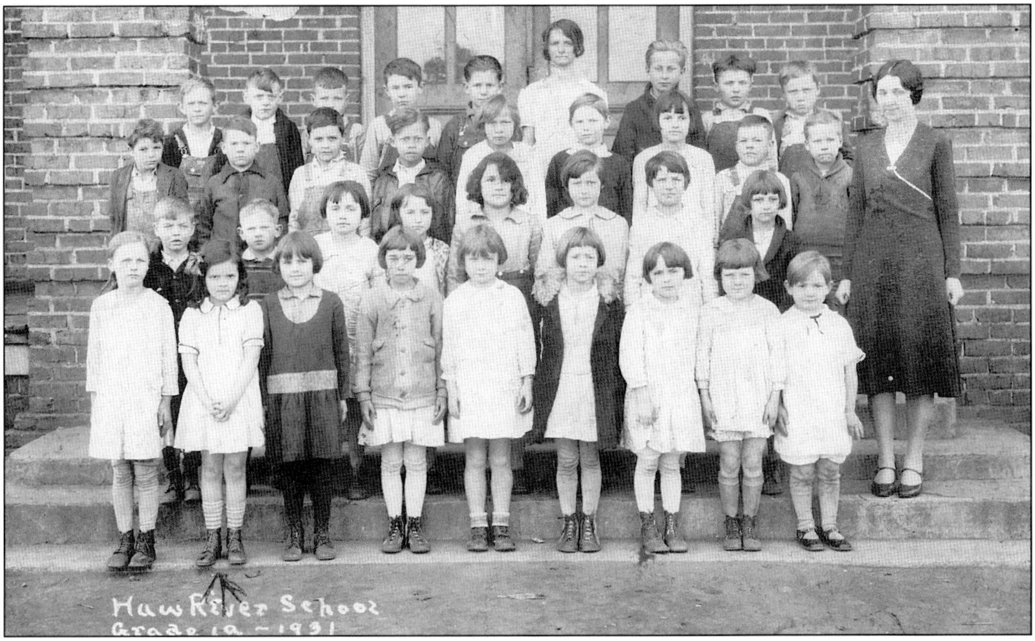

This postcard shows Mrs. Nell Simpson and her first grade students at Haw River School in 1931. The school first opened in 1904. (Courtesy Haw River Historical Association Museum.)

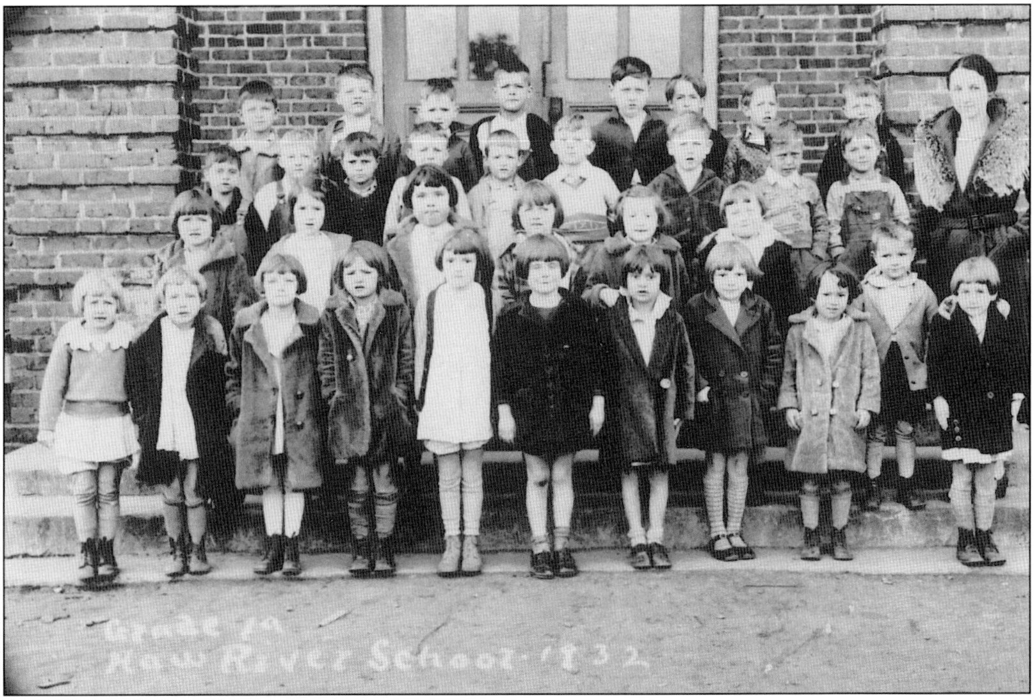

In 1932 first grade students at Haw River School could still be taught by Mrs. Nell Simpson. (Courtesy Haw River Historical Association Museum.)

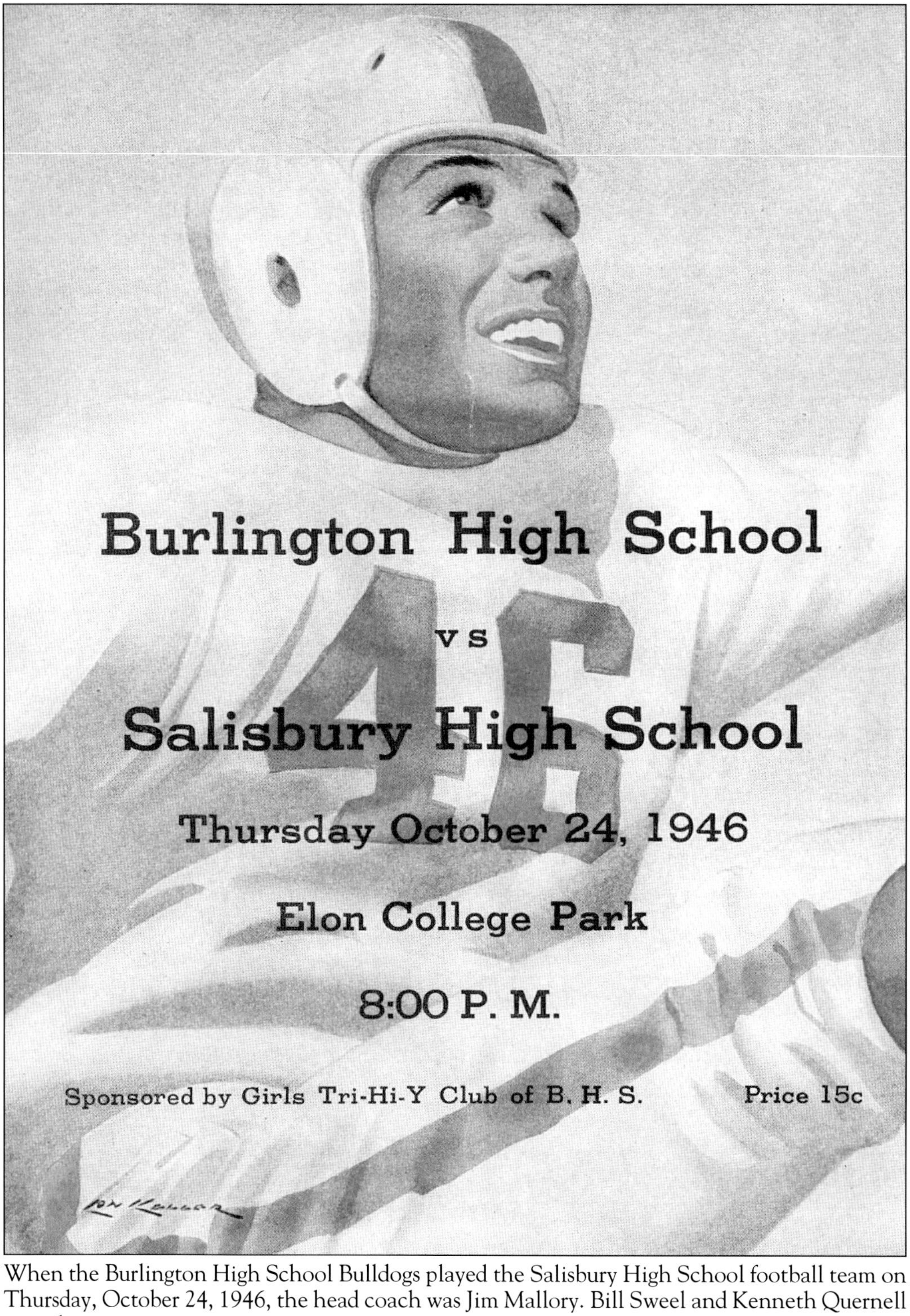

When the Burlington High School Bulldogs played the Salisbury High School football team on Thursday, October 24, 1946, the head coach was Jim Mallory. Bill Sweel and Kenneth Quernell served as assistants.

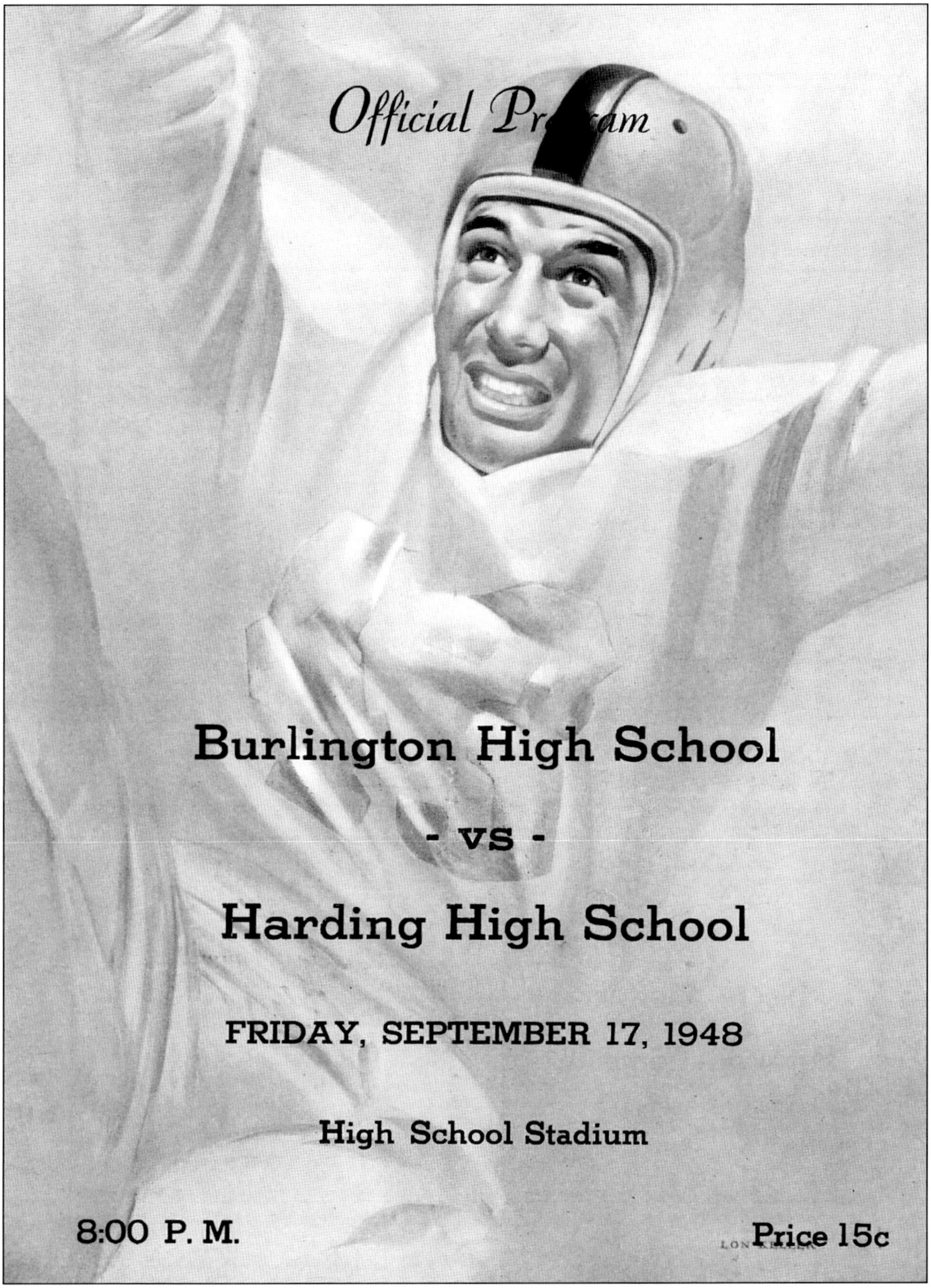

By 1948 most of Burlington High School's football games were scheduled to be played on Friday nights, a practice that continued for many years.

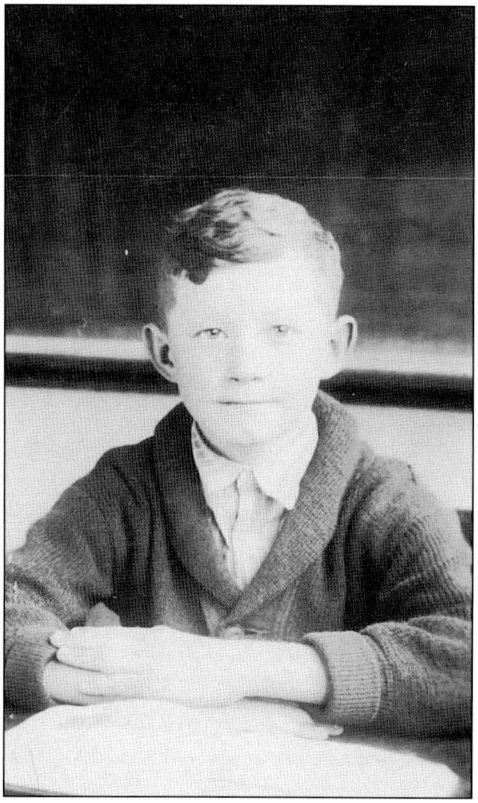

After leaving Haw River School, where this snapshot was made, Max Wilson went on to become a major league baseball player. (Courtesy Haw River Historical Association Museum.)

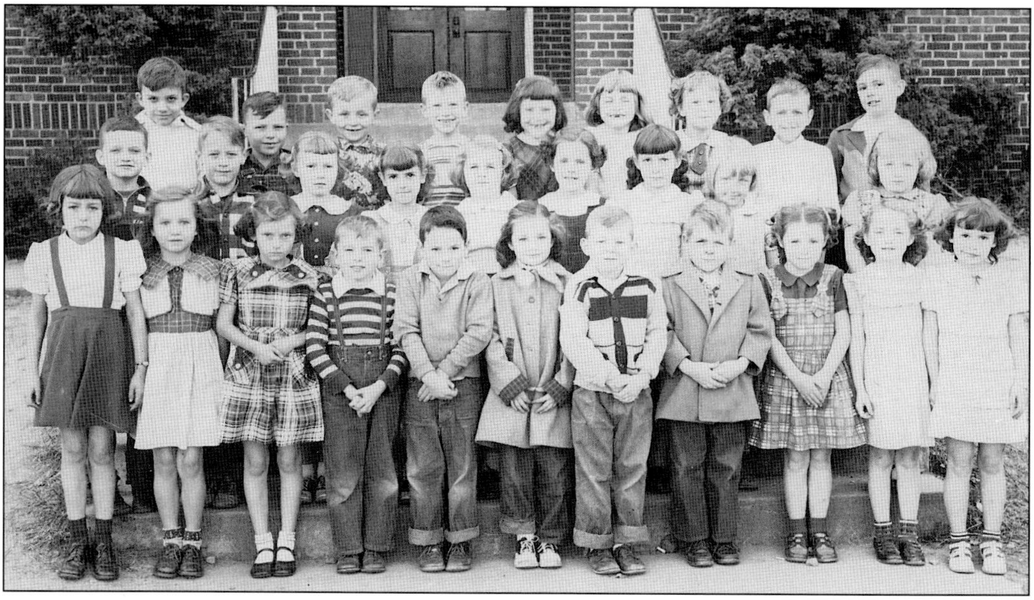

Haw River School had been in operation for about 45 years when these second graders were photographed, *c.* 1950. The school closed in 1962.

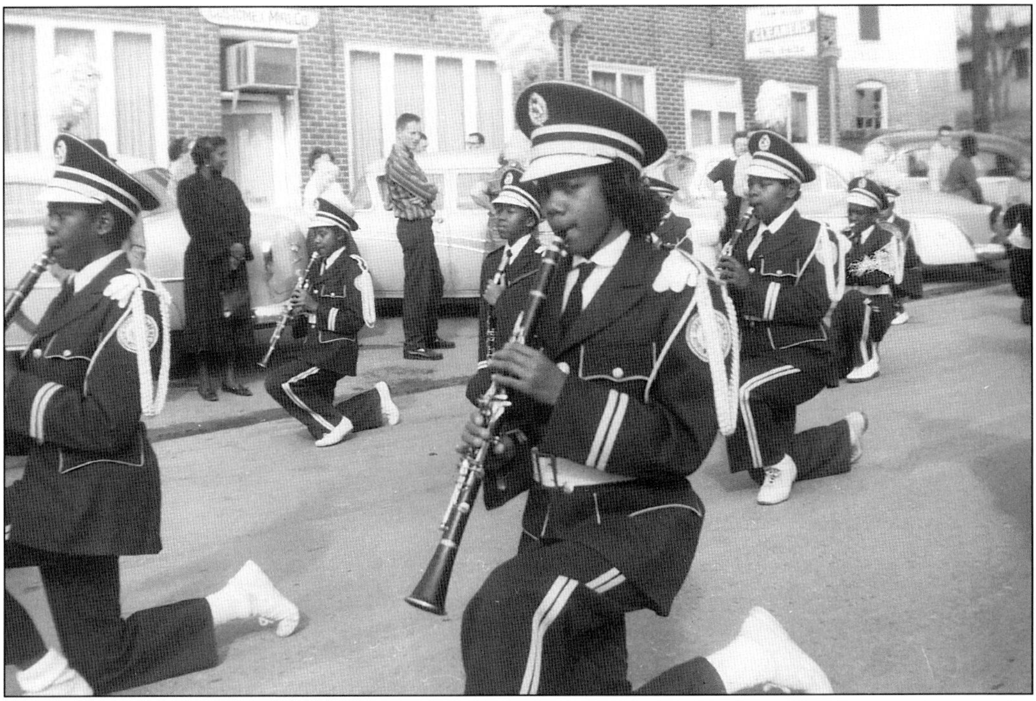

In Burlington, members of the Jordan Sellers High School Marching Band were famous for their performances in local parades, as in this December 1958 image.

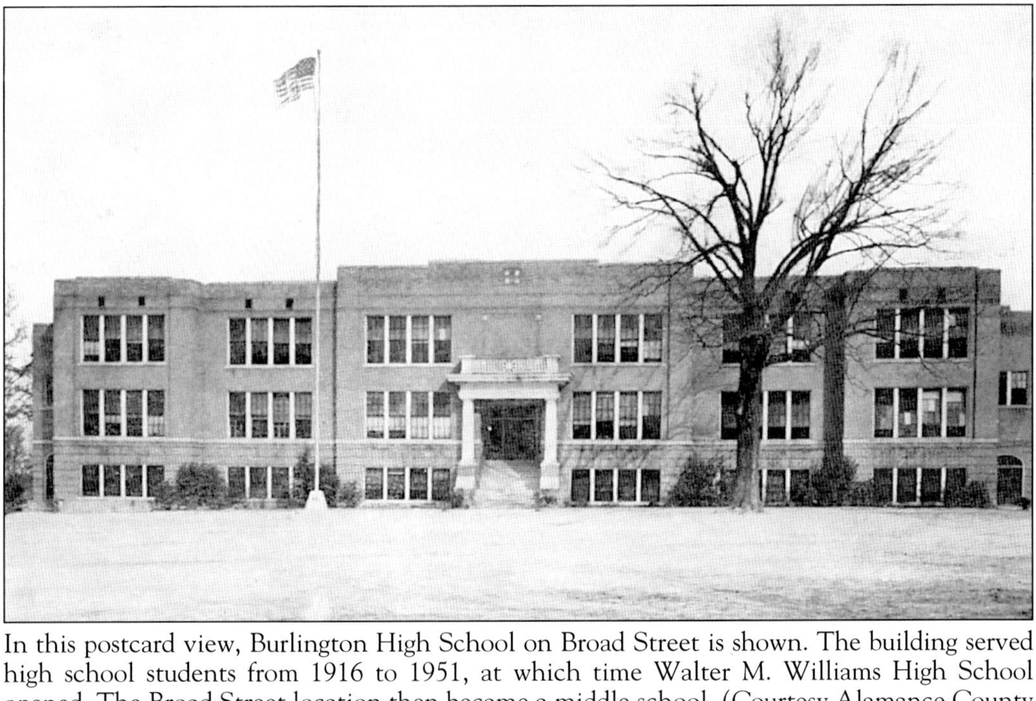

In this postcard view, Burlington High School on Broad Street is shown. The building served high school students from 1916 to 1951, at which time Walter M. Williams High School opened. The Broad Street location then became a middle school. (Courtesy Alamance County Historical Museum, Inc.)

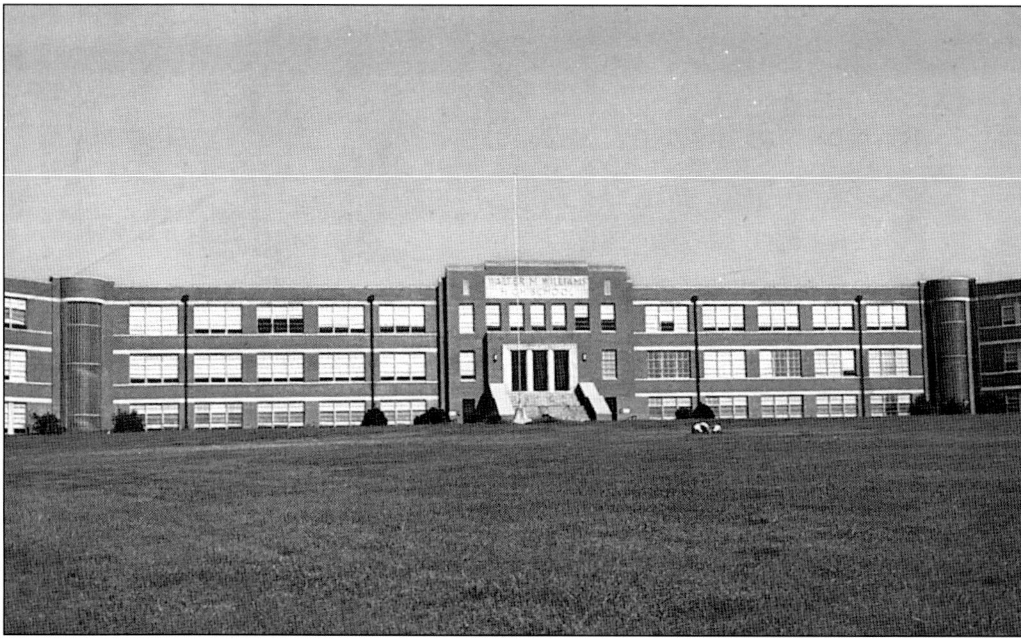

Walter M. Williams High School is the subject of this postcard made on February 22, 1960. The school opened in 1951 and, as of the turn of the millennium, was still functioning as one of Burlington's two high schools, along with Hugh M. Cumming High School. (Courtesy Alamance County Historical Museum, Inc.)

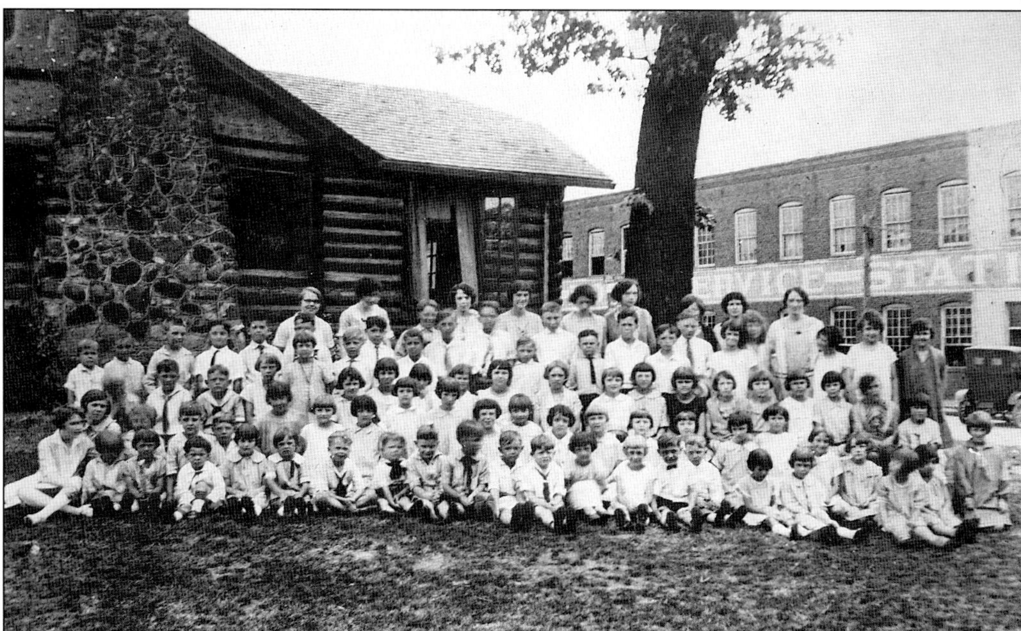

Perhaps the service station in the background will provide a clue as to the identity of the school class pictured here. The mystery photo was taken somewhere in Alamance County, probably in the 1920s. (Courtesy Austin Holt McCormick.)

Eight

Houses of Worship

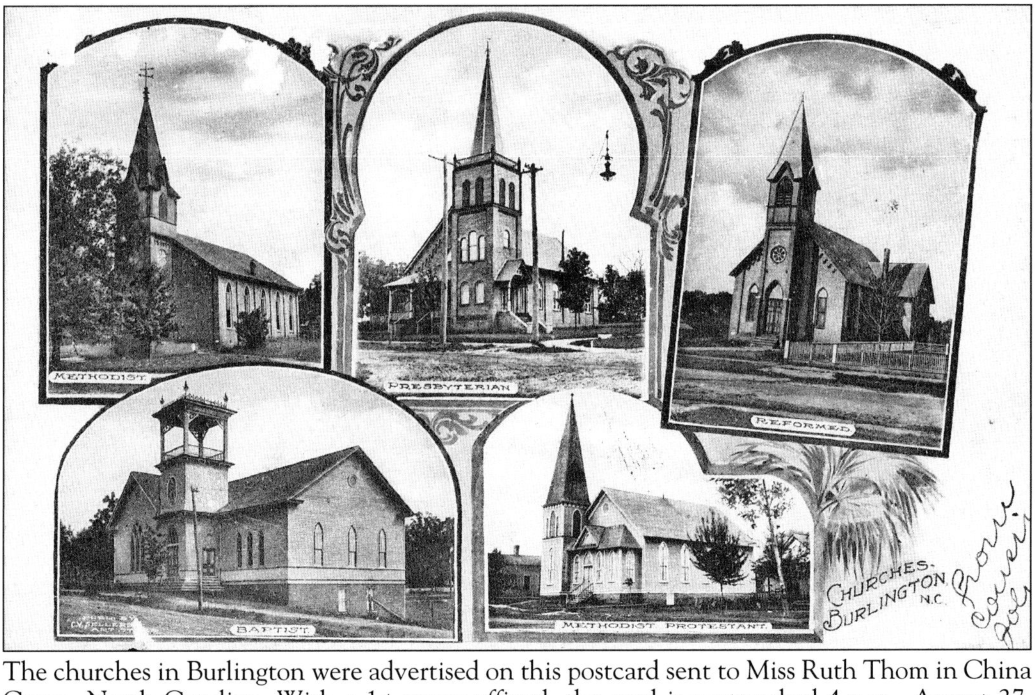

The churches in Burlington were advertised on this postcard sent to Miss Ruth Thom in China Grove, North Carolina. With a 1¢ stamp affixed, the card is postmarked 4 p.m., August 27, 1908. Before the completion of the above structures, the congregations of these denominations and more met in the Union Church Building in Company Shops. (See page 82.)

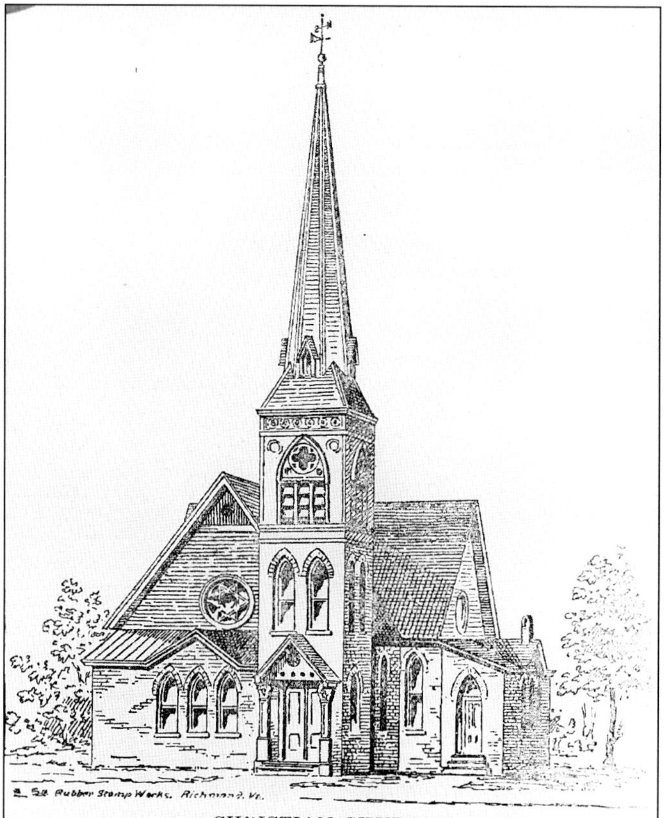

CHRISTIAN CHURCH.

This artist's rendering is of the first building for the Christian Church in Burlington. Completed in November 1893, at a cost of $3,935.10, it was located on the southeast corner of Davis and Church Streets. This original structure was replaced in March of 1920 by a newer building located on another corner of the same intersection.

This building served as Burlington's First Presbyterian Church from 1909 to 1953. It was a remodeled and enlarged version of the structure on the previous page, which had been built in 1891. The church stood at the corner of Front and Church Streets where the fire department headquarters is now located.

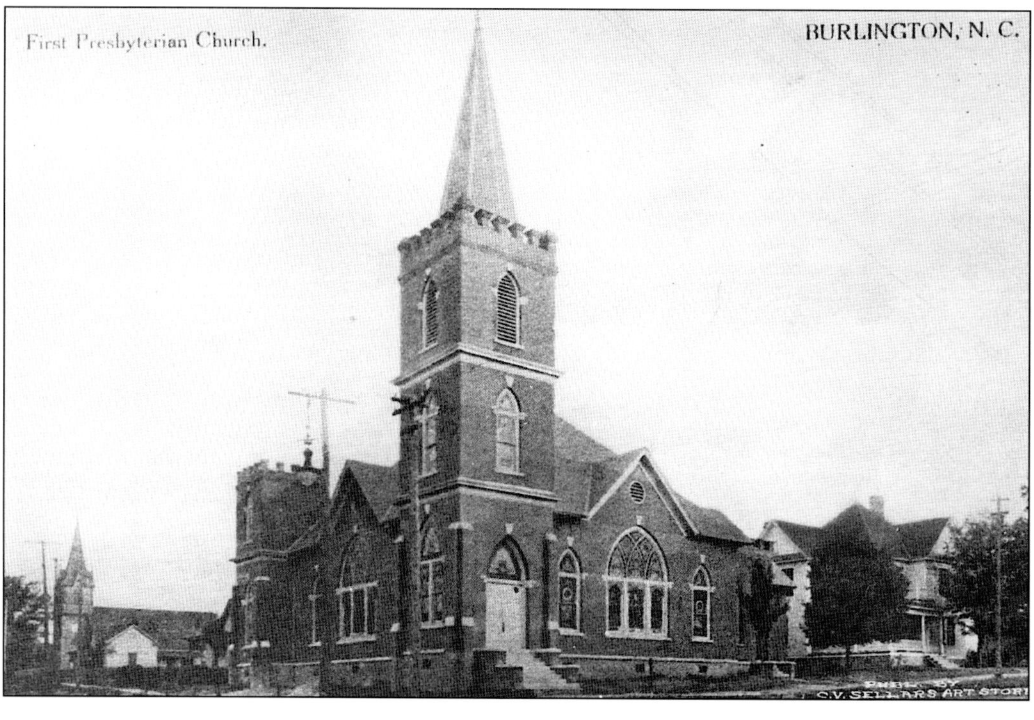

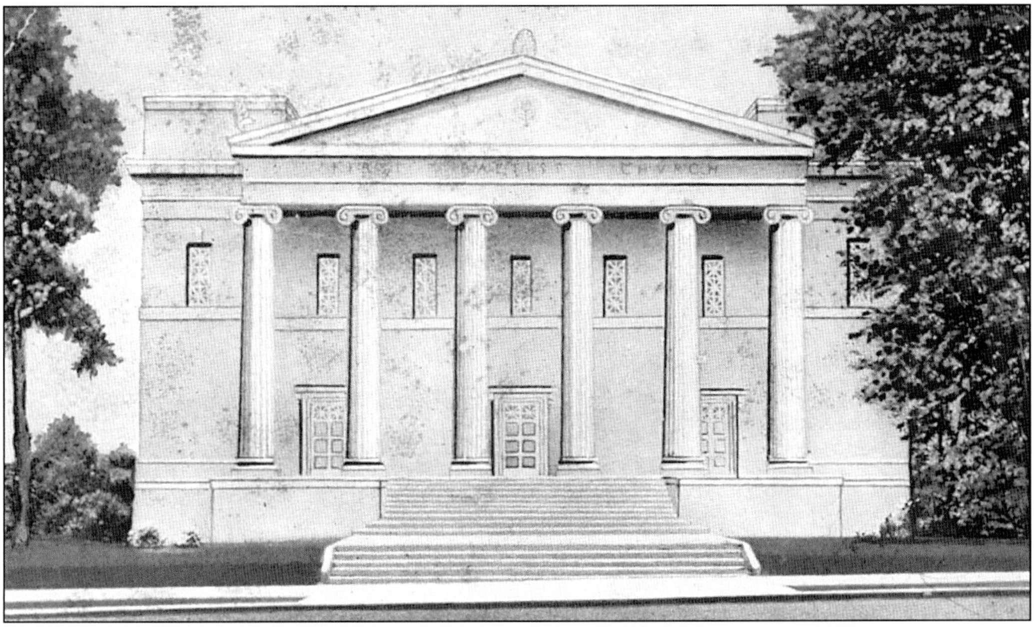

On this postcard is an artist's view of the First Baptist Church in Burlington. This location opened for services February 24, 1924, on Broad Street at the Davis Street intersection. Before that, a building across the street, pictured on page 95, had served the congregation since 1891.

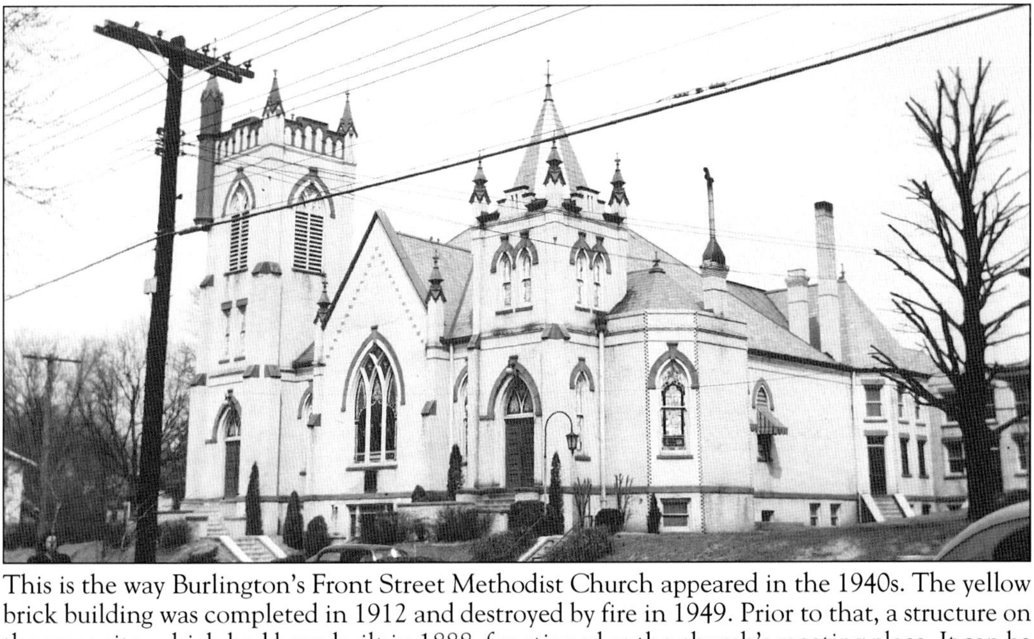

This is the way Burlington's Front Street Methodist Church appeared in the 1940s. The yellow brick building was completed in 1912 and destroyed by fire in 1949. Prior to that, a structure on the same site, which had been built in 1888, functioned as the church's meeting place. It can be seen in the postcard on page 95.

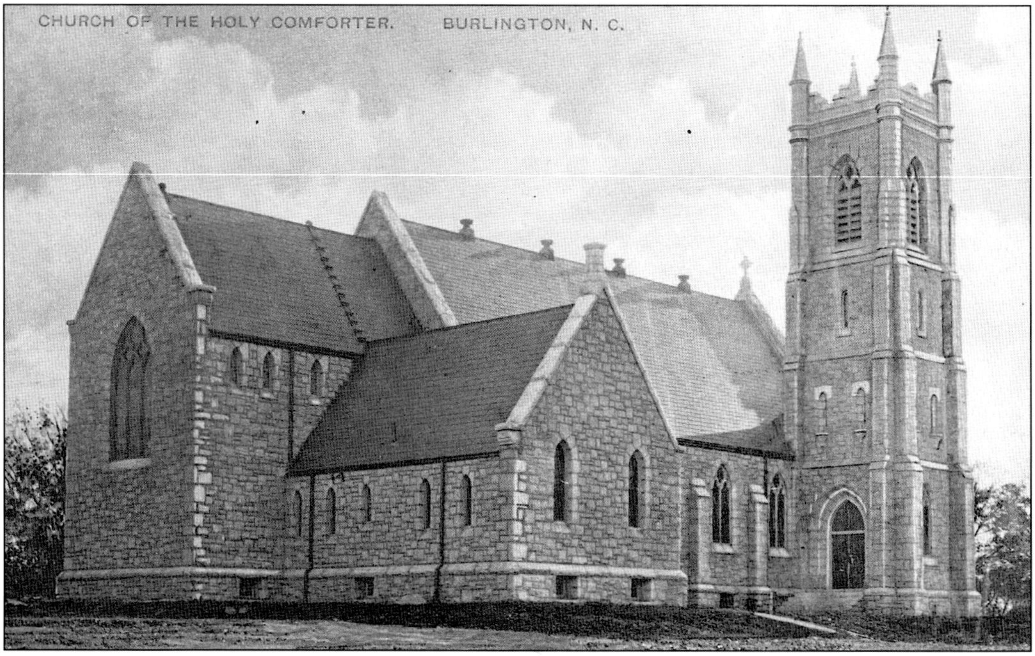

The Episcopalians built the Church of the Holy Comforter on Davis Street in Burlington. This postcard image offers a good representation of the beautiful building designed by architect Hobart Upjohn. (Courtesy Alamance County Historical Museum, Inc.)

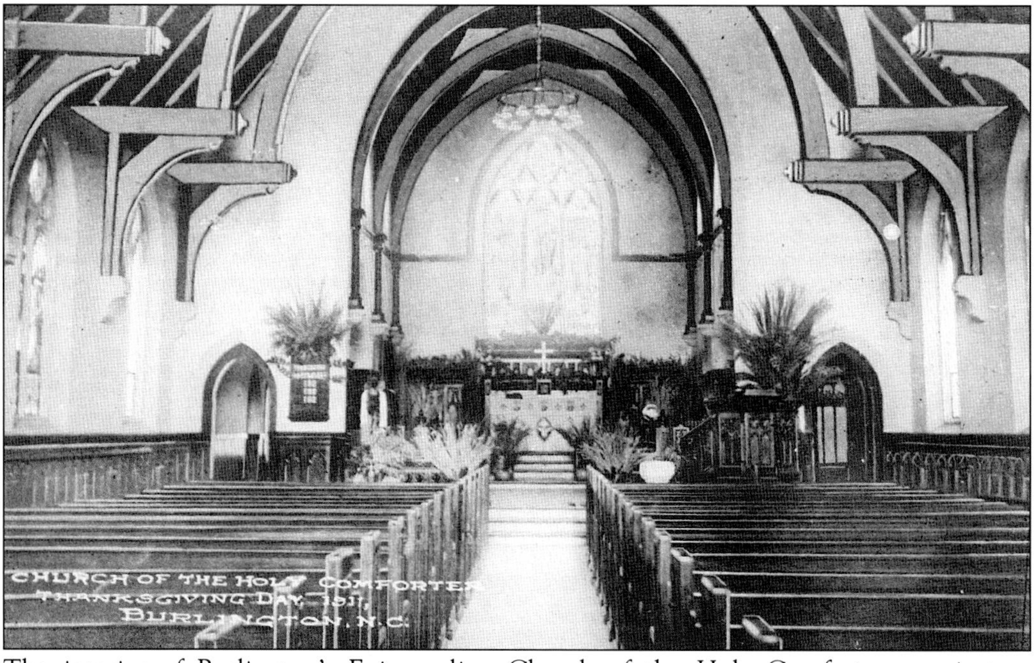

The interior of Burlington's Episcopalian Church of the Holy Comforter was just as interestingly designed as the exterior. This postcard view captured the sanctuary on Thanksgiving Day in 1911, soon after the new building opened. (Courtesy Alamance County Historical Museum, Inc.)

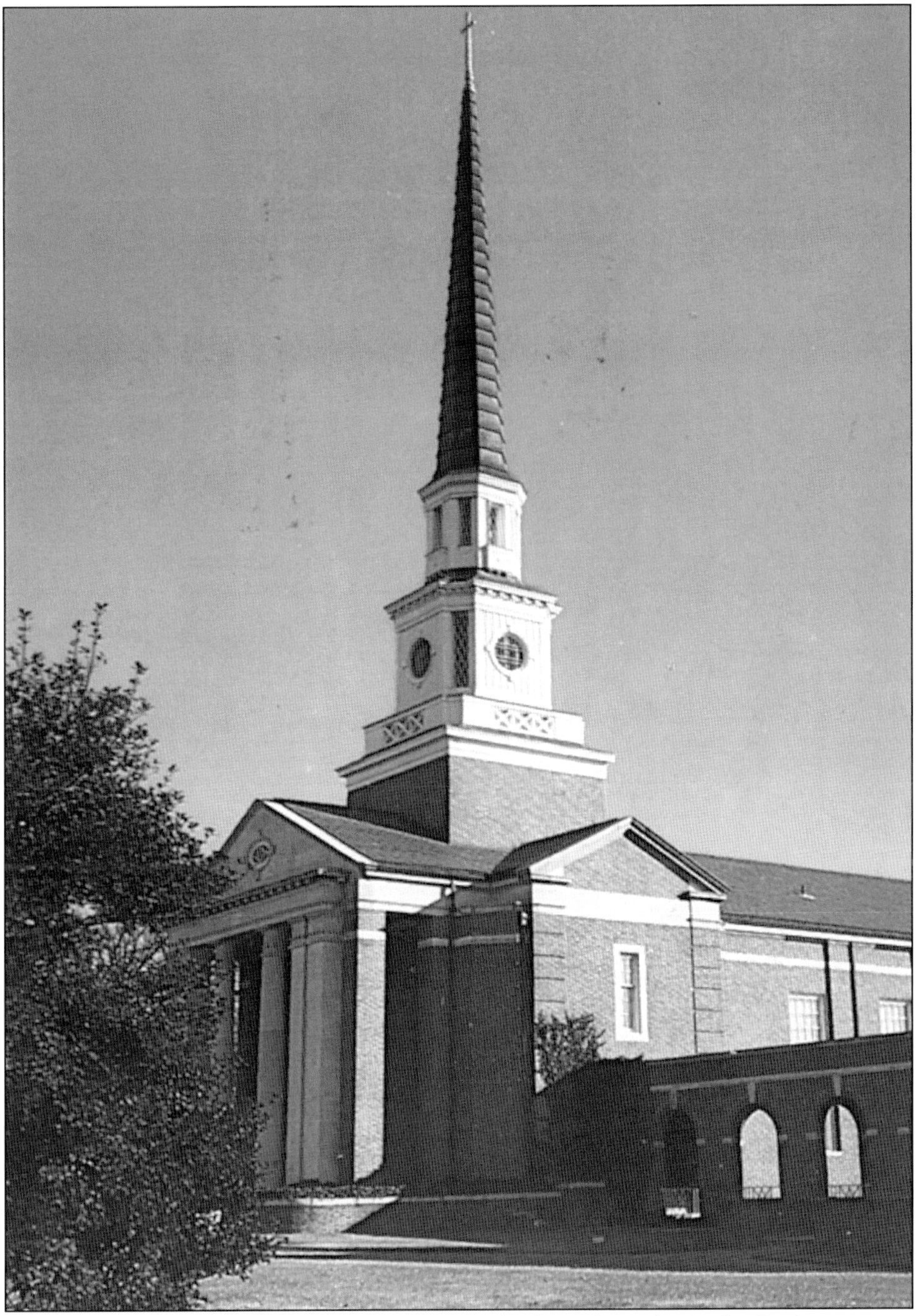

One company held a photography session that took place throughout the Burlington area on February 22, 1960. This resulted in a large quantity of photographs to be used for postcards. This picture of the First Presbyterian Church was among the images created that day. The building at 508 West Davis Street was completed in May 1953, at a cost of approximately three quarters of a million dollars. Many Alamance County natives remember receiving their kindergarten education at such area churches before the public school system began providing that service. (Courtesy Alamance County Historical Museum, Inc.)

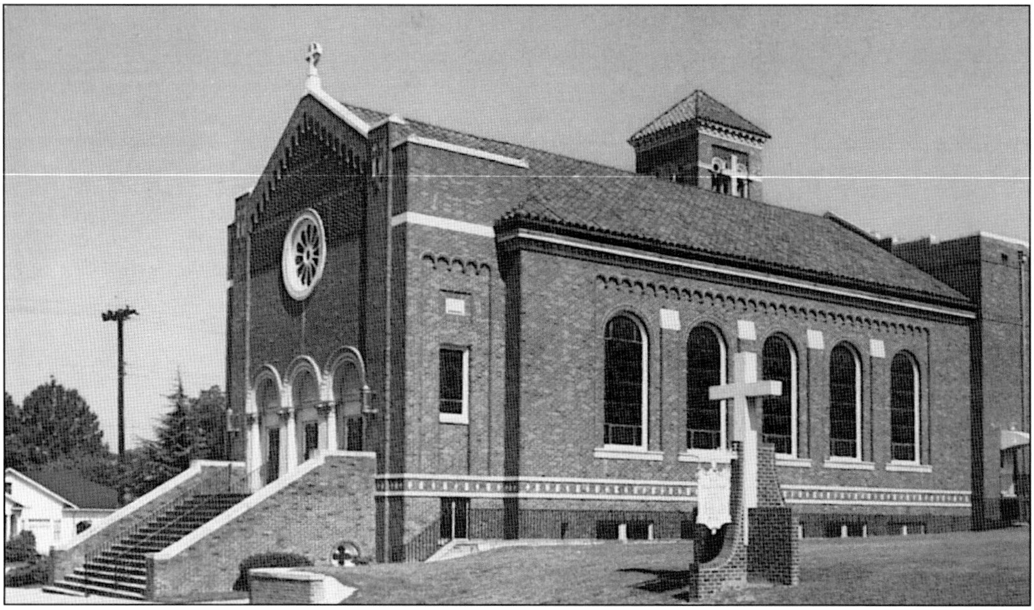

This postcard view of the First Reformed United Church of Christ in Burlington was made on February 22, 1960. The building was dedicated on October 12, 1941, as the First Evangelical and Reformed Church at 513 West Front Street. It replaced an older structure that opened on January 6, 1901 (pictured on page 95). (Courtesy Alamance County Historical Museum, Inc.)

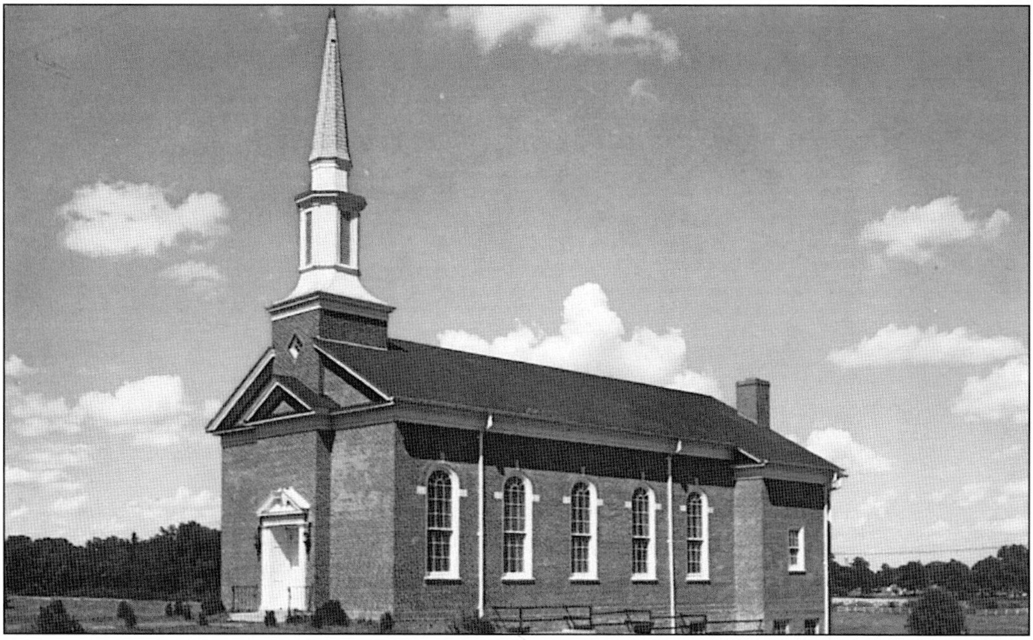

This is yet another postcard image snapped on February 22, 1960. Shown is Holt Memorial Chapel of the Congregational Christian Home for Children at Elon College. (Courtesy Alamance County Historical Museum, Inc.)

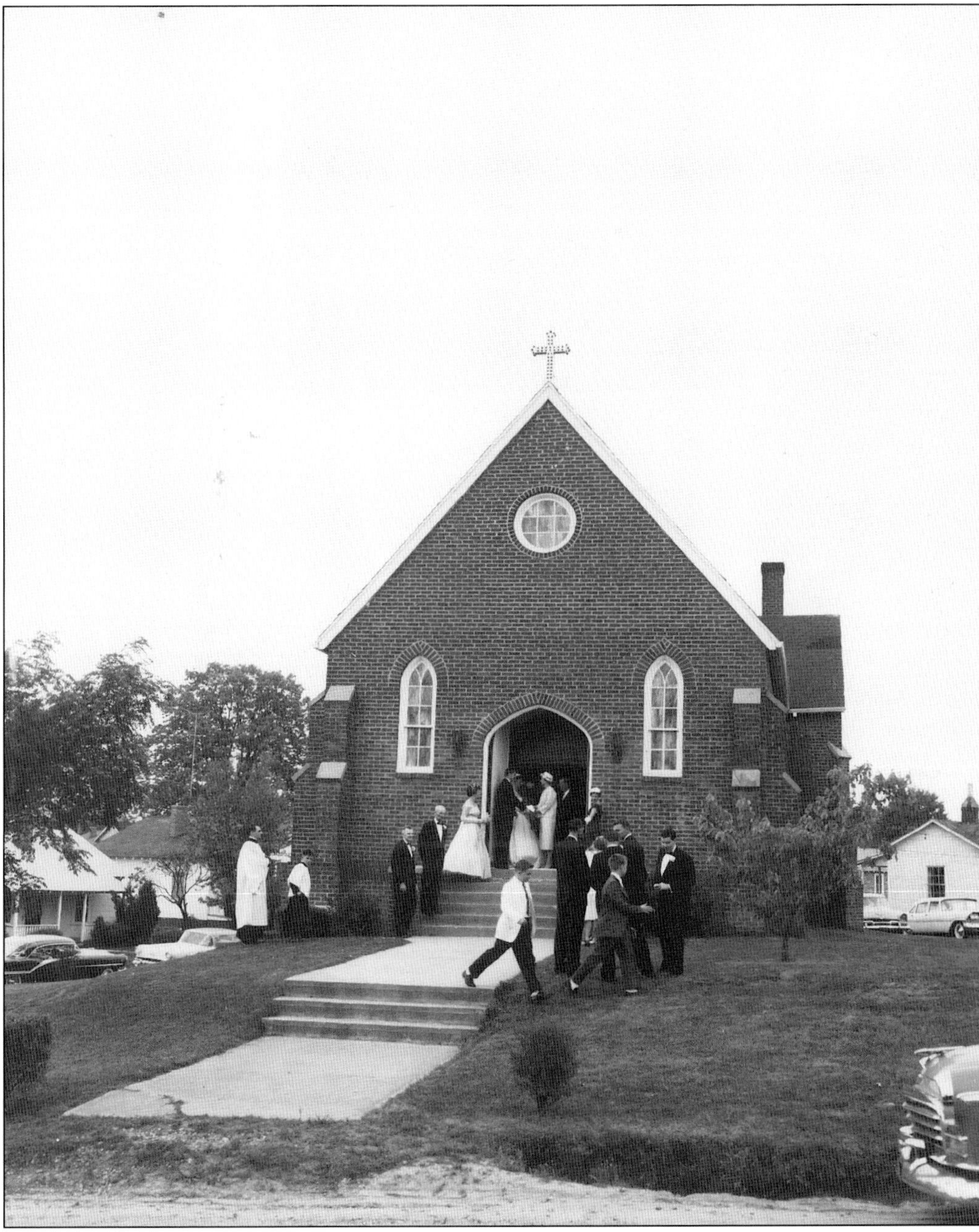

A wedding took place at Calvary Chapel Episcopal Church on April 30, 1960. Calvary Chapel, a mission of the Episcopal Church, was located on the corner of Piedmont Way and Oklahoma Avenue. The small congregation disbanded several years later and its members moved to the Episcopal Church of the Holy Comforter in Burlington and St. Andrews Episcopal Church in Haw River. The structure now houses a Baptist church.

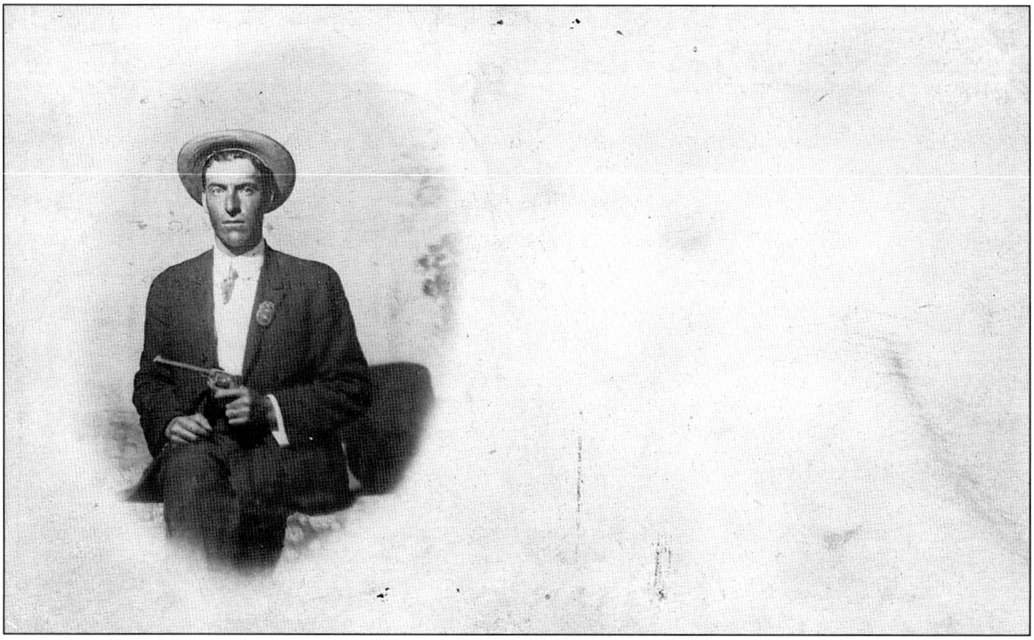

This postcard portrait showcases Crawford "Croff" Ray, who served as deputy sheriff of Alamance County and constable of Haw River. The card was postmarked April 1907, and mailed to Miss Hattie Ray in Hillsboro, North Carolina. (Courtesy Haw River Historical Association Museum.)

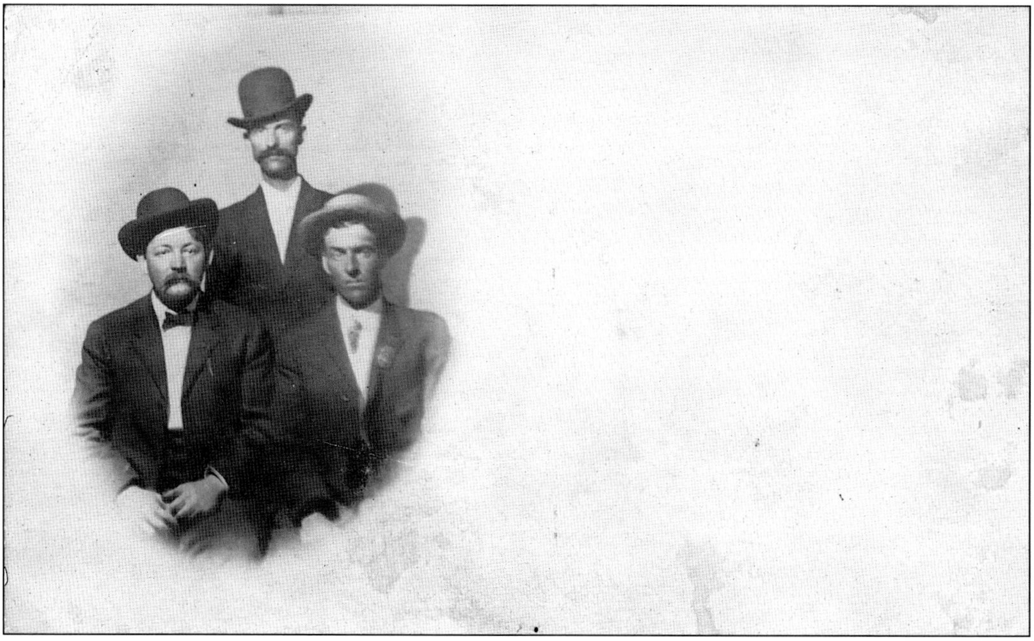

Joining Deputy Sheriff Ray in this postcard are A.L. Thompson and Ellias Williams, *c.* 1907. (Courtesy Haw River Historical Association Museum.)

Nine

A Sampling of People

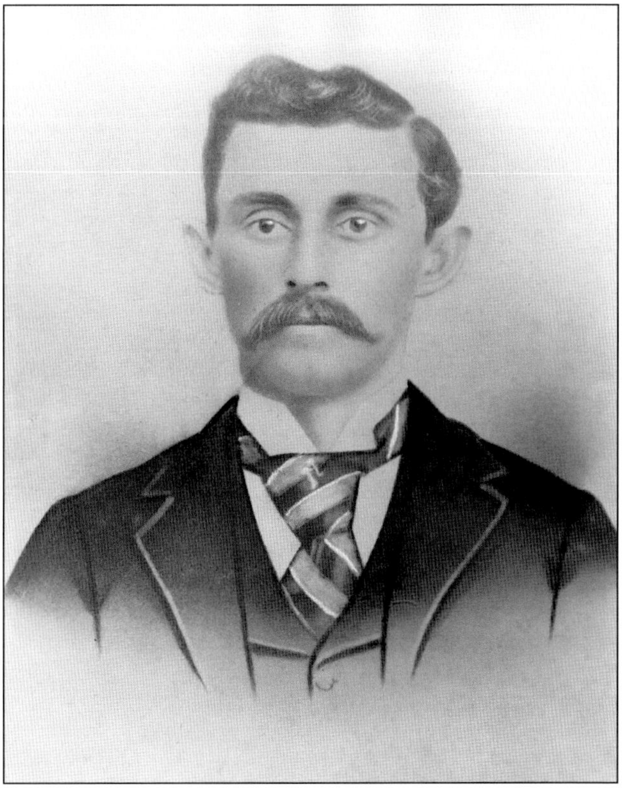

An image of cartographer W.L. Spoon was preserved in this flattering portrait. In 1893 Spoon did a great service to area citizens by undertaking and completing the task of making a detailed map of Alamance County using his professional skills. (Courtesy Alamance County Historical Museum, Inc.)

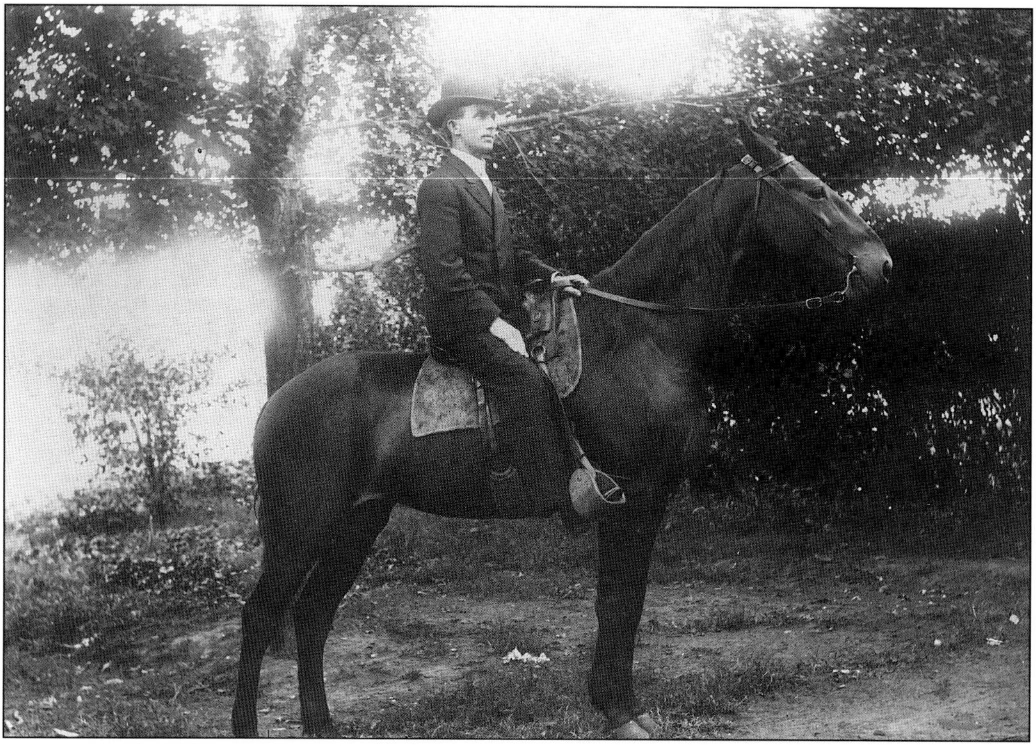

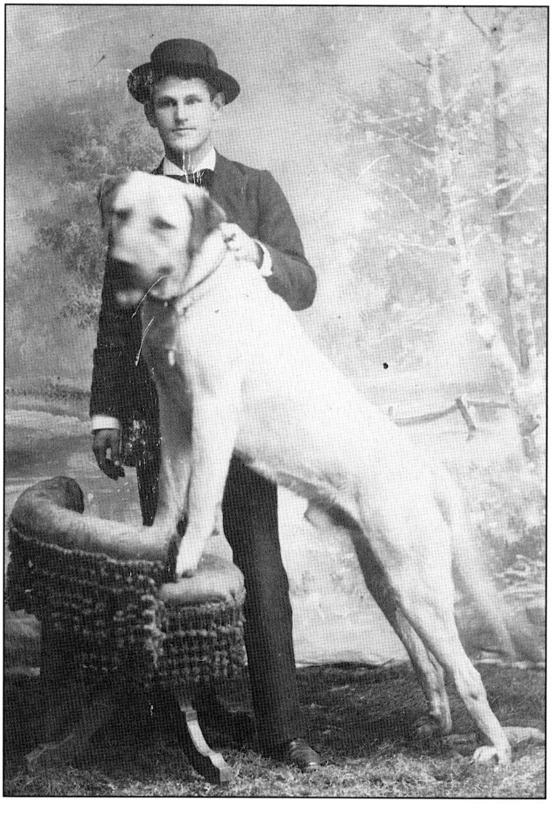

In the early 1900s, Dr. Samuel Dace McPherson practiced general medicine in Haw River. This view of him astride his horse was a common sight. In 1910 Doctor McPherson left Haw River and later opened McPherson Hospital in Durham. (Courtesy Haw River Historical Association Museum.)

This grandson of cotton mill pioneer Edwin Michael Holt indulges himself with a portrait of pet and master. (Courtesy Austin Holt McCormick.)

Lynn Banks Holt (1842–1920), son of Edwin Michael Holt, ran the Alamance Mill with his brother after their father retired in 1866. L. Banks moved to Graham in 1886 and built a mansion on his 500-acre plantation. (Courtesy Austin Holt McCormick.)

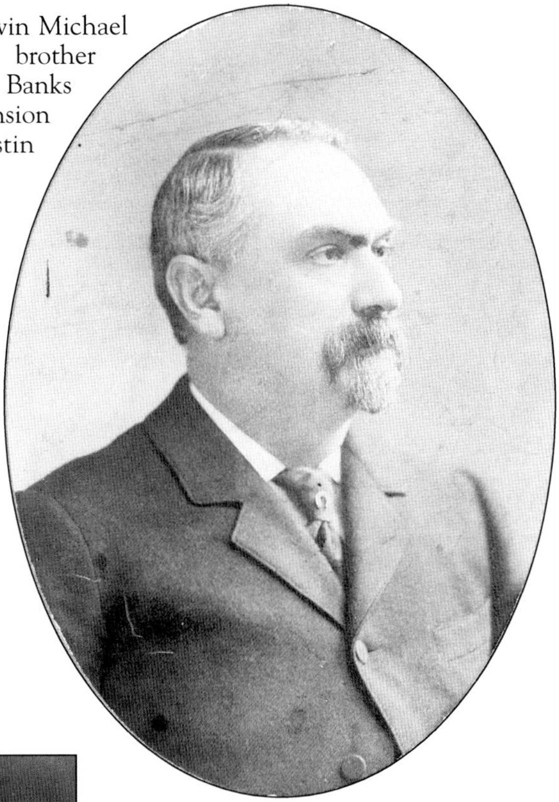

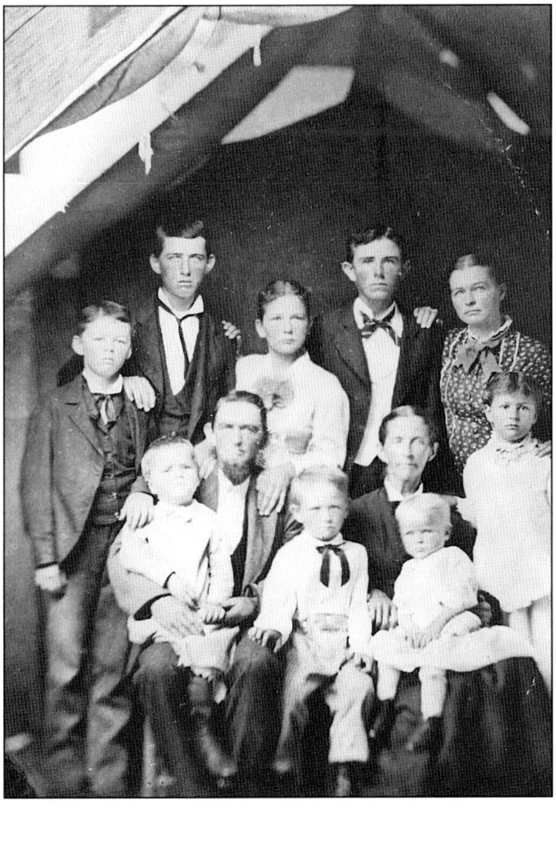

This tin-type photograph shows Colonel Jeremiah Holt (1795–1877); his wife Sarah Foust (1801–1875); and their nine children, *c.* 1840. (Courtesy Austin Holt McCormick.)

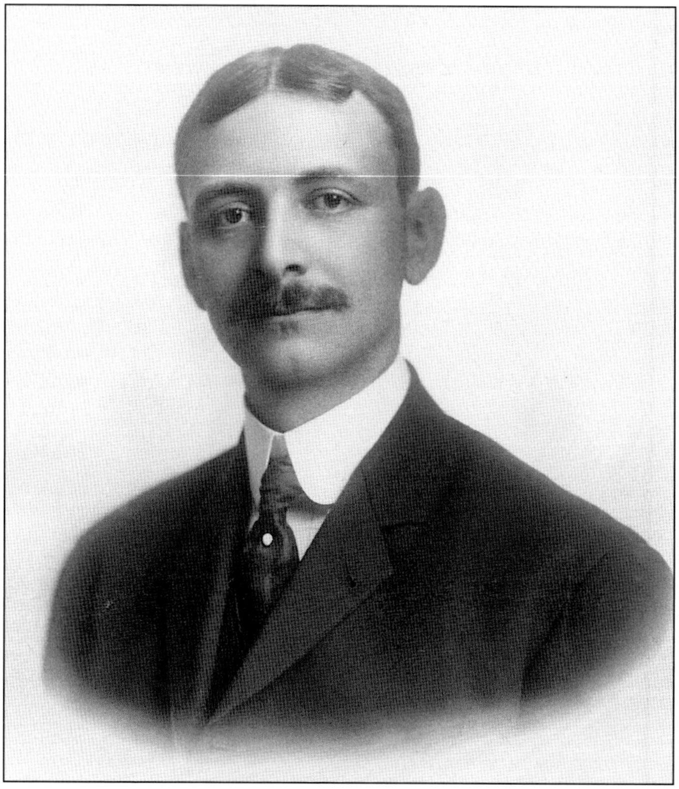

This photographic portrait is of Alamance County citizen Erwin Allen Holt. He provided most of the information for Julian Hughes's 1965 book *Development of the Textile Industry in Alamance County*. (Courtesy Alamance County Historical Museum, Inc.)

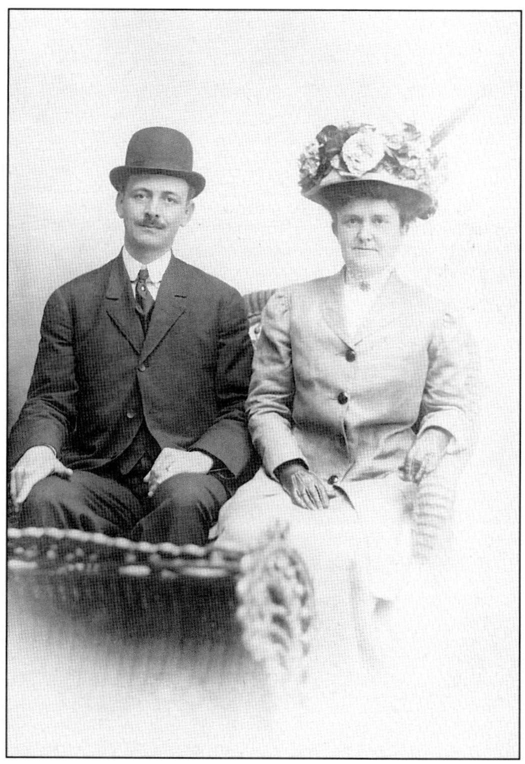

Erwin Allen Holt married Mary Warren Davis. Later, they posed for this postcard image. (Courtesy Alamance County Historical Museum, Inc.)

Erwin Allen Holt (standing) managed to get his picture taken with baseball legend Connie Mack. Not surprisingly, Holt had the photograph made into a postcard. (Courtesy Alamance County Historical Museum, Inc.)

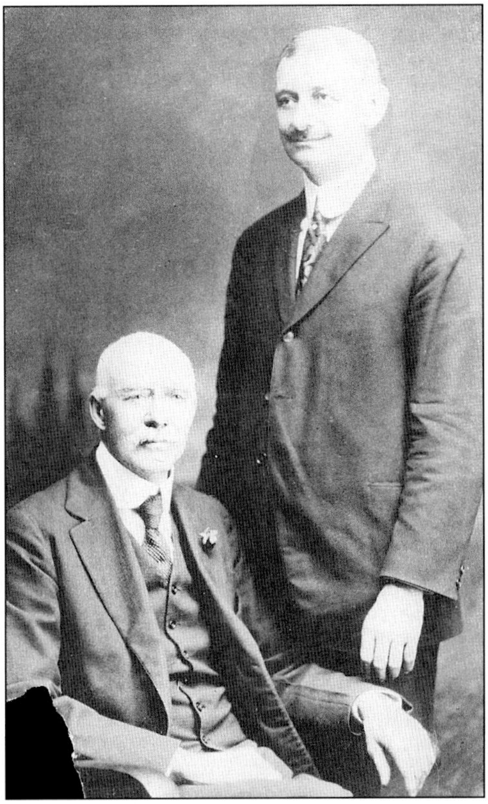

After working for a while as a conductor for a railroad, Robert Edward Lee Holt Sr. returned to his native Burlington and ran a hardware and construction company. He shared this picture with his wife, Hattie, and eight of their 13 children, c. 1918. (Courtesy Austin Holt McCormick.)

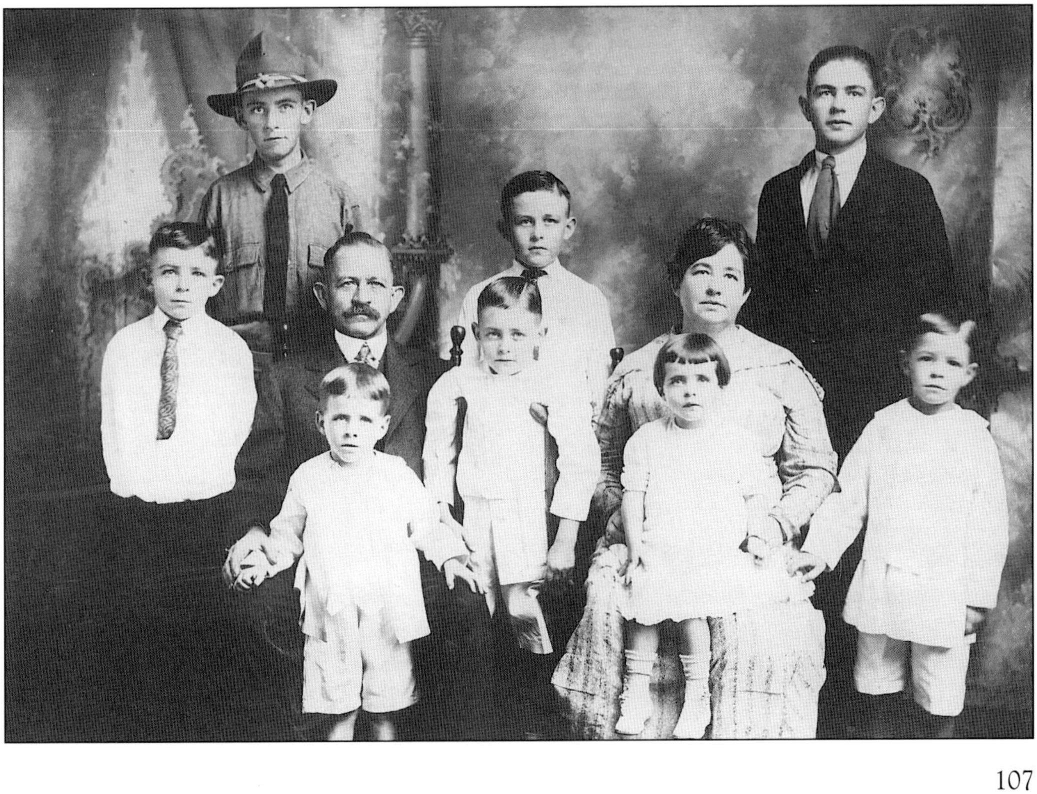

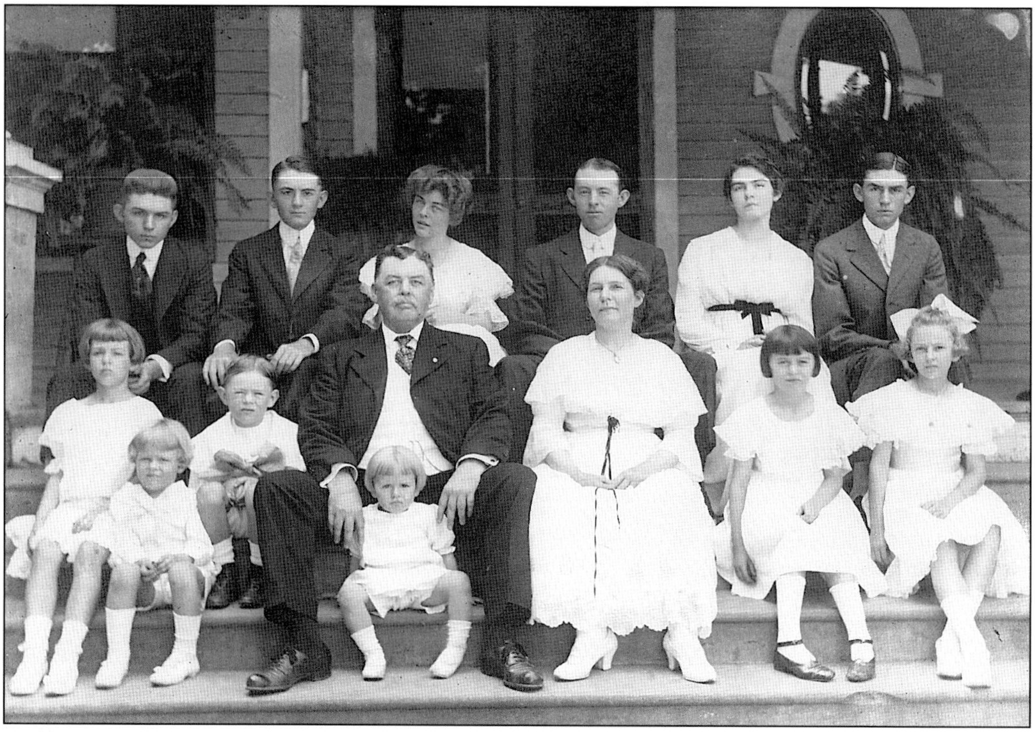

William Kirkpatrick Holt was in the hardware business and married Maude G. May in 1890. Here they show off 12 of their 14 children. (Courtesy Austin Holt McCormick.)

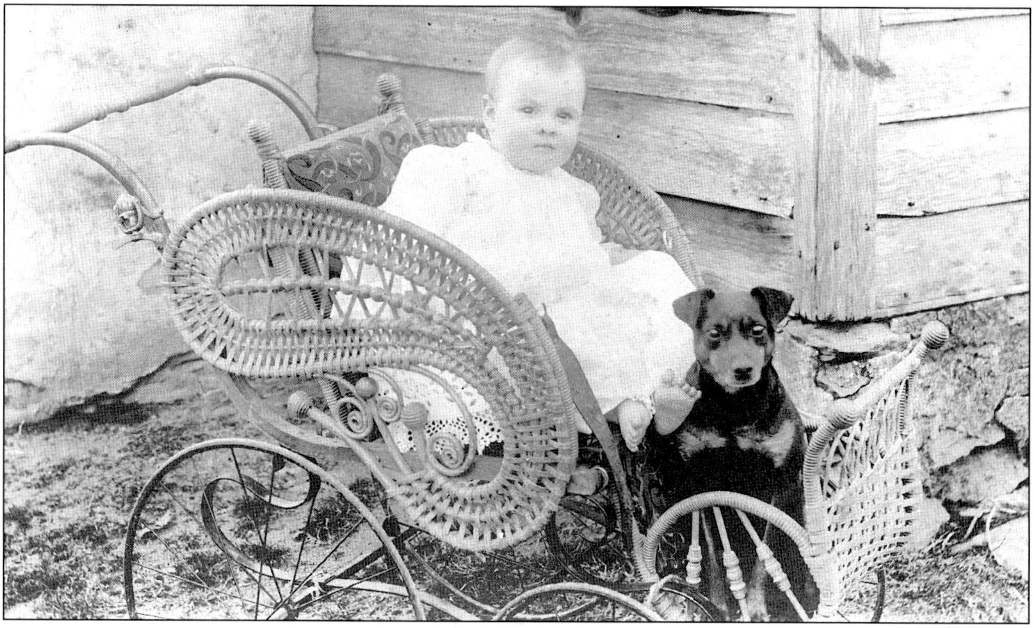

Ten-and-one-half-month-old Frances Estelle Hurdle rode with her pet dog in an ornately designed baby carriage. (Courtesy Alamance County Historical Museum, Inc.)

William Winslow Lasley, with his brother, had established a mercantile business in Burlington by May 1882. Lasley was one of the original 1889 trustees of that same city's First Presbyterian Church. He also served for a number of years as president of the First National Bank of Burlington. The house that Lasley built in 1890 still stands at 415 West Davis Street.

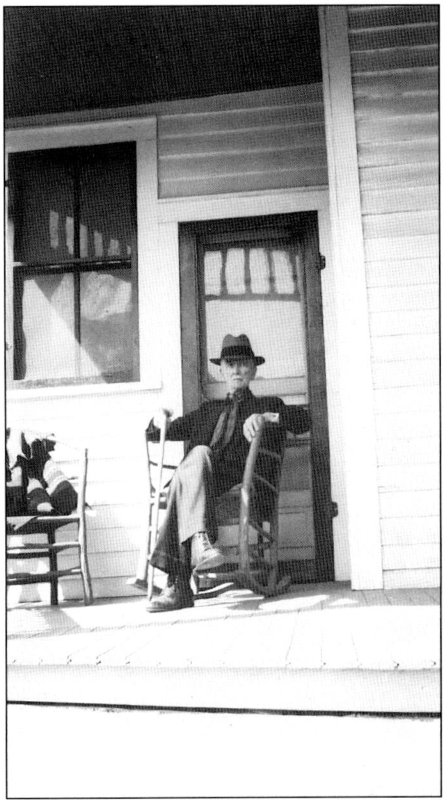

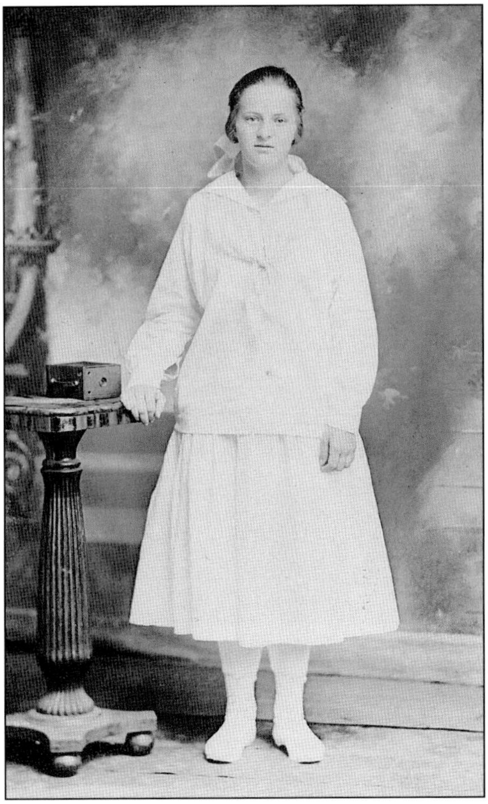

This postcard from Haw River pictures Miss Thelma Cates, noted schoolteacher for more than 40 years. There is a memorial to her at the Haw River Civic Center. (Courtesy Haw River Historical Association Museum, Inc.)

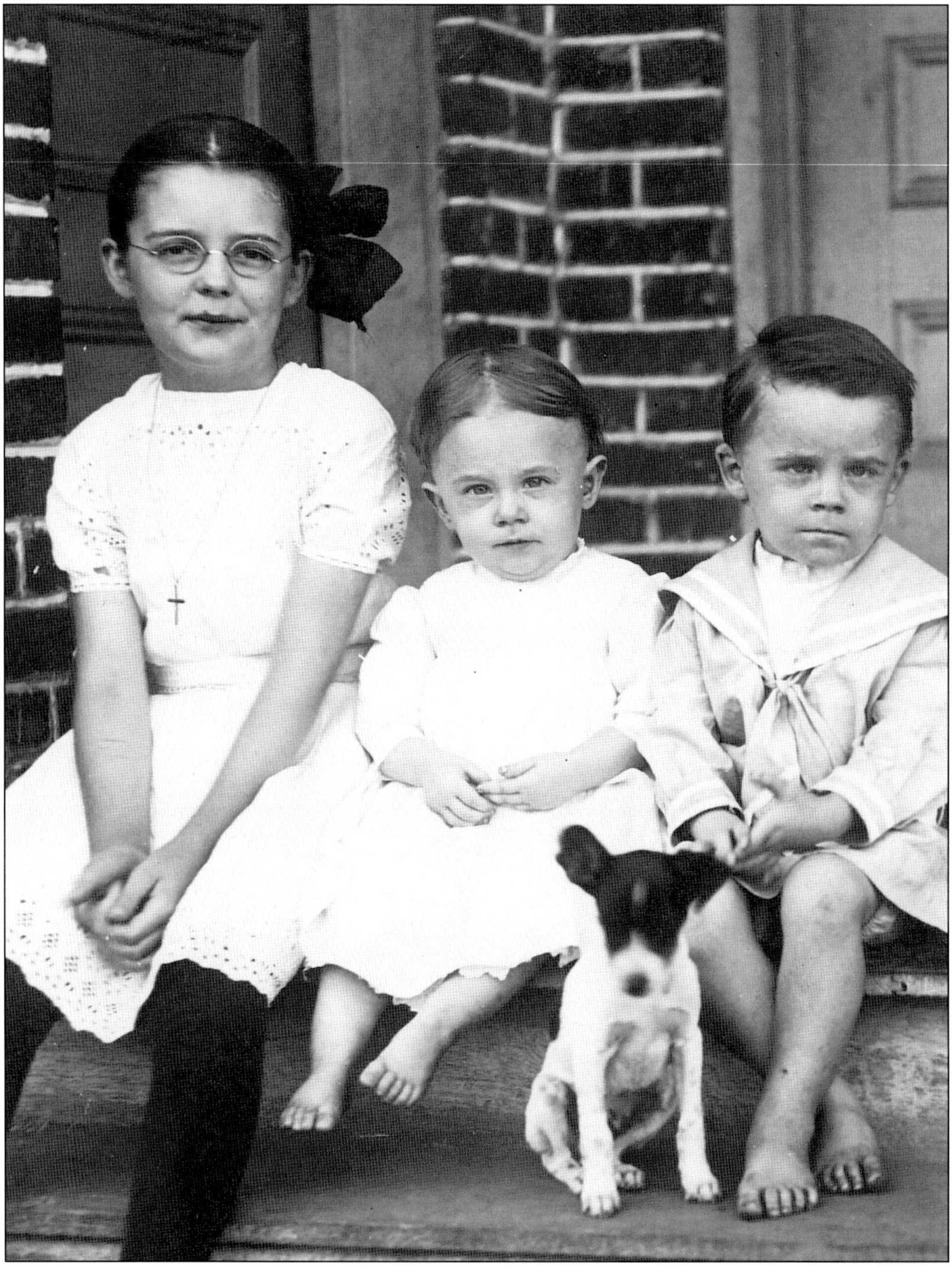

In the Haw River of 1910, Ella, Ethel, and Harry Childrey sit on the front porch with their best friend. (Courtesy Haw River Historical Museum.)

Once upon a time, while at home in Haw River, Miss Daisy Blackmon became a postcard image. (Courtesy Haw River Historical Association Museum.)

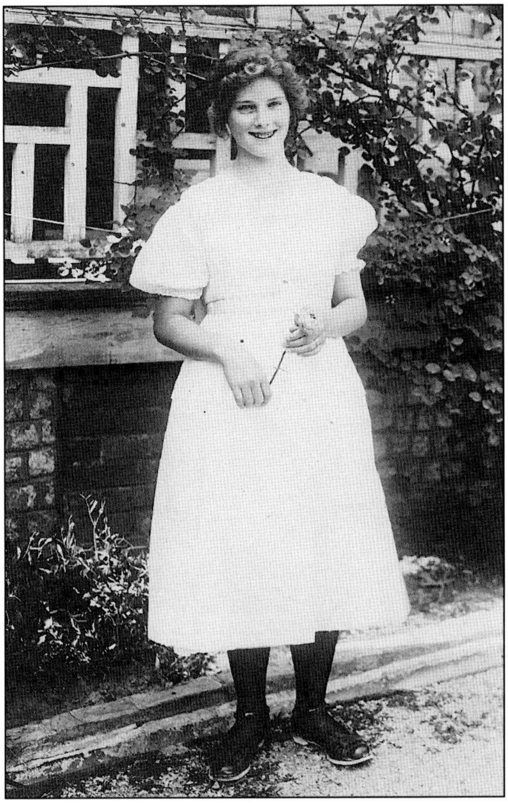

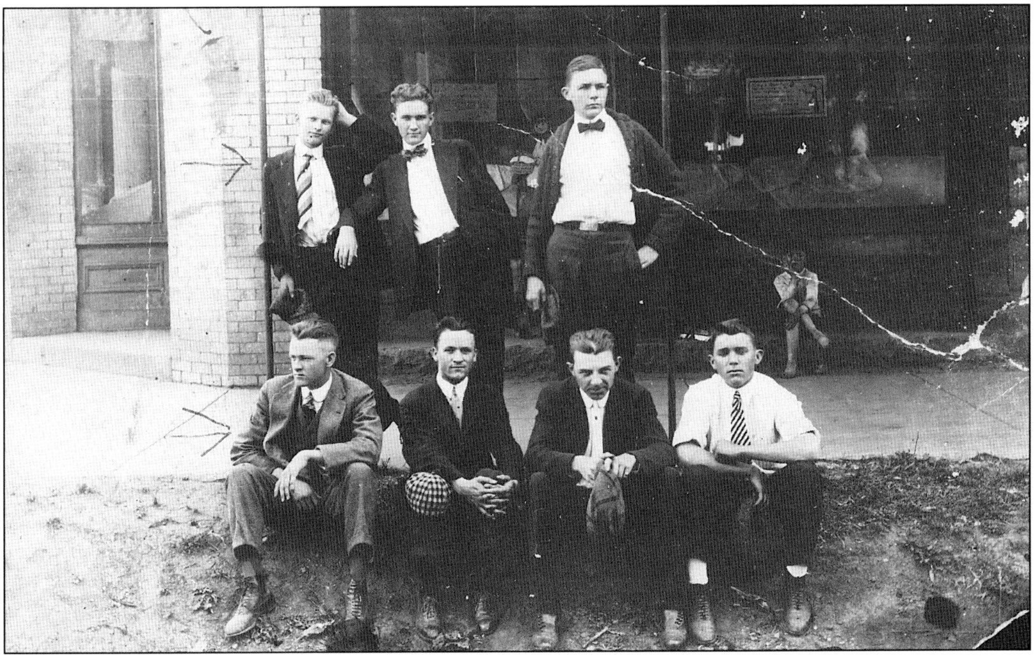

In the 1920s, some friends joined Jim and Haywood Simpson on a corner at Elon College. (Courtesy Haw River Historical Association Museum.)

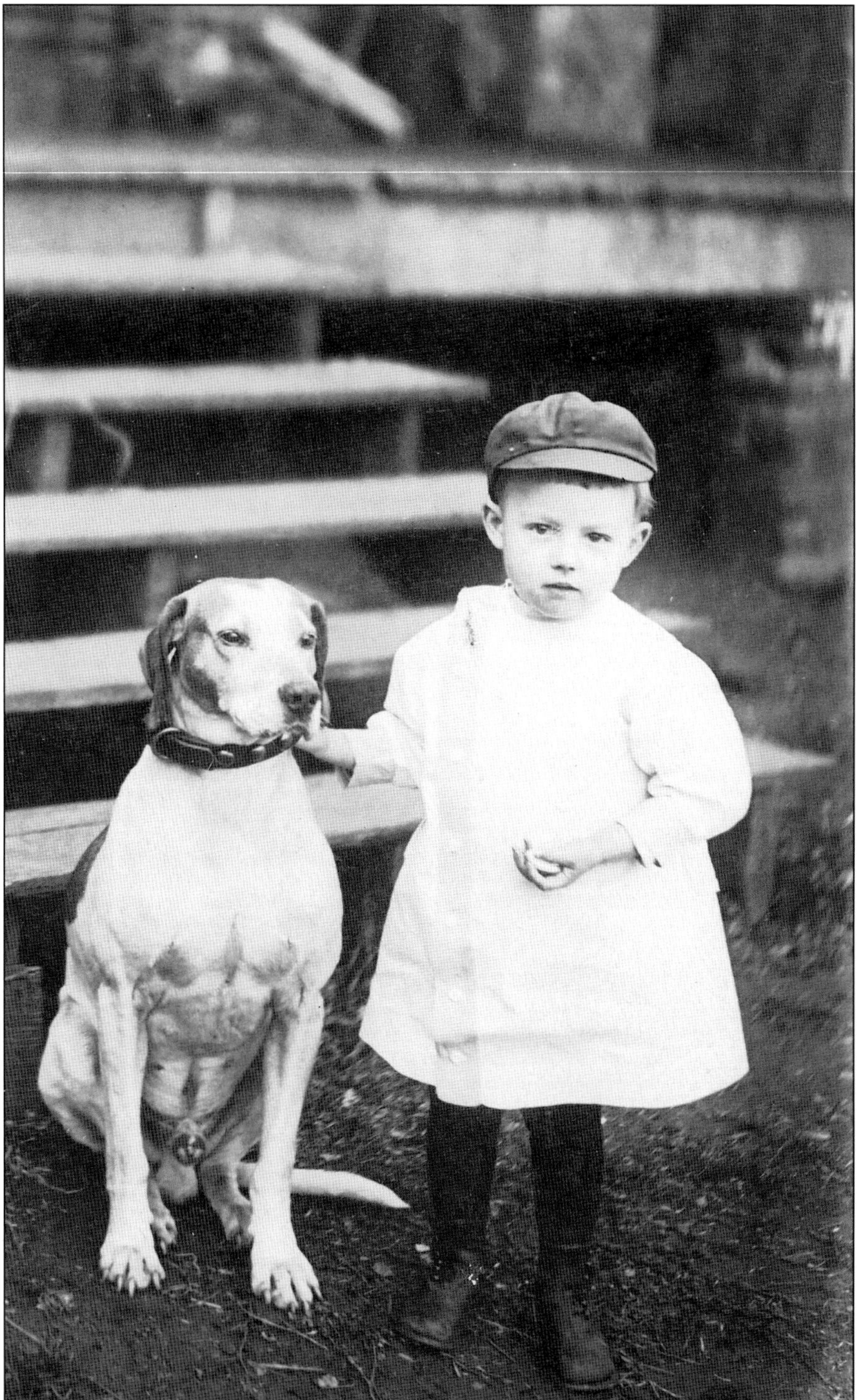

Jerry Bullard and Spot helped to create a great-looking Haw River postcard. They posed before some front porch steps at Brick Row beside Trollinger Cemetery. (Courtesy Haw River Historical Association Museum.)

Ten

LIVING IN ALAMANCE COUNTY

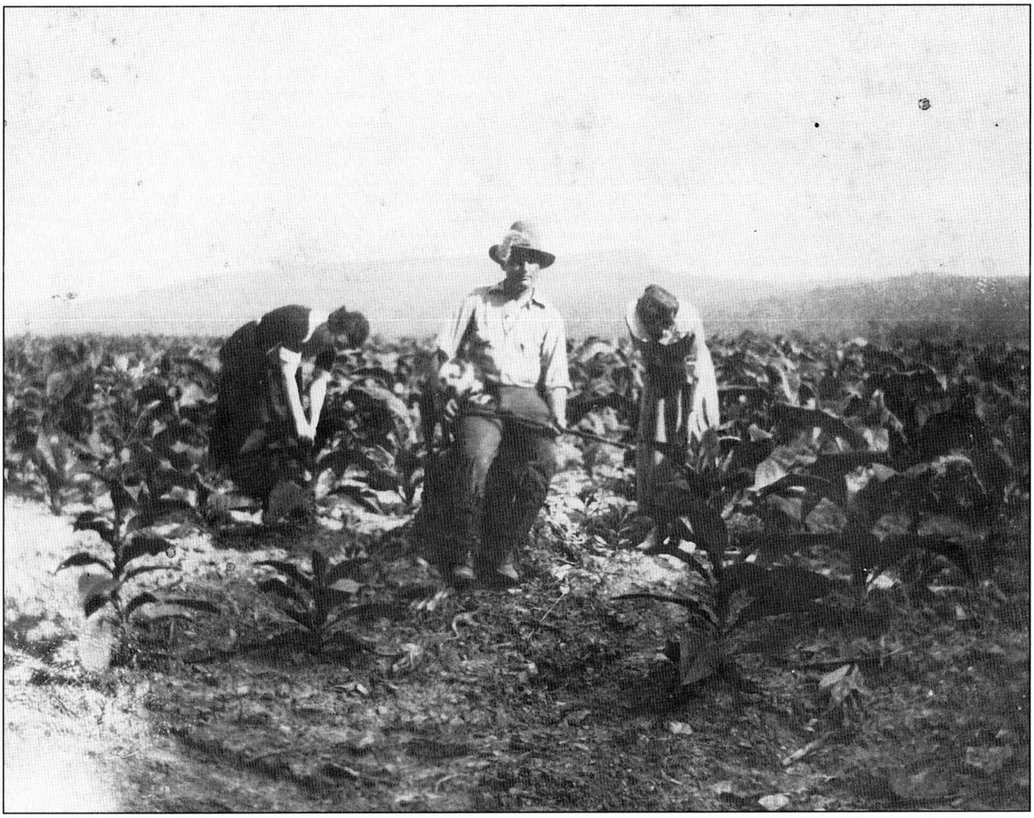

In the middle of the twentieth century, there were more than 2,700 farms in Alamance County averaging 80 acres in size. The principal crops raised included tobacco, corn, and hay. Above we see Ada Brooks, Max Leiberman, and Nell Brooks picking tobacco near Haw River in the 1920s. (Courtesy Haw River Historical Association Museum.)

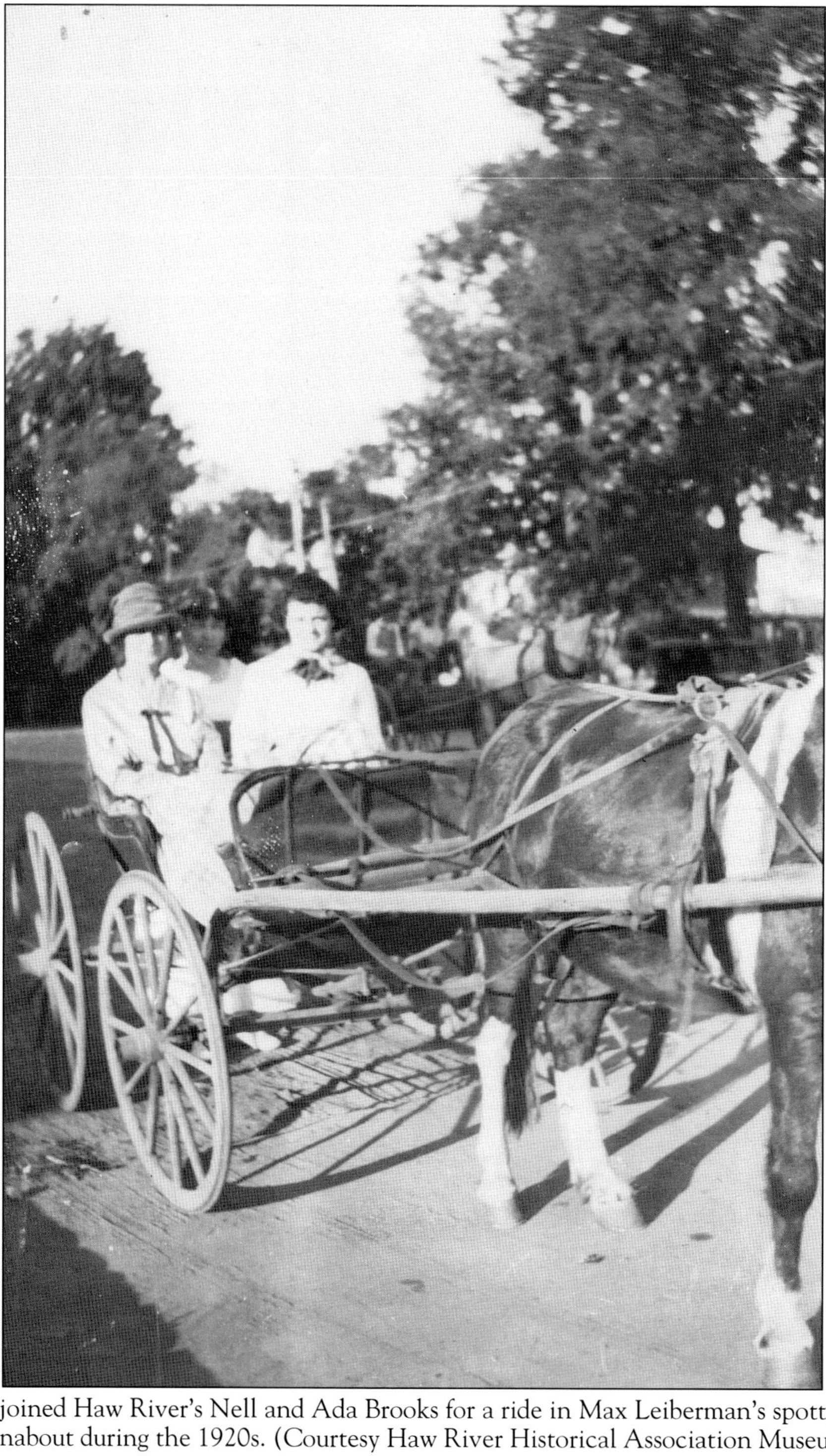

A friend joined Haw River's Nell and Ada Brooks for a ride in Max Leiberman's spotted pony-driven runabout during the 1920s. (Courtesy Haw River Historical Association Museum.)

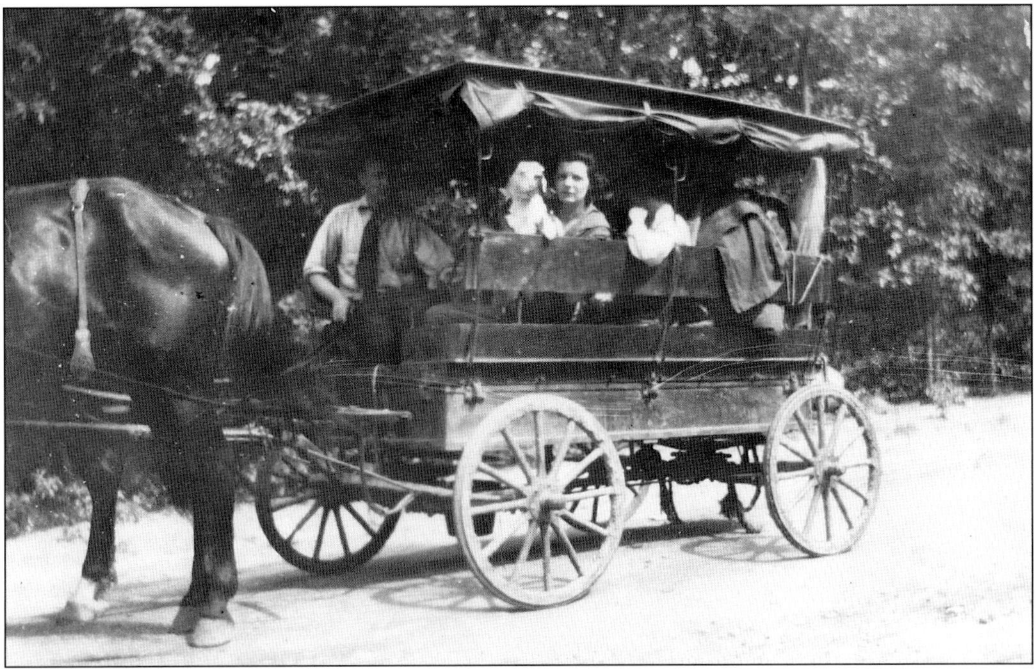

Max Leiberman gave his friend from Boston, Massachusetts, a tour of Haw River. (Courtesy Haw River Historical Association Museum.)

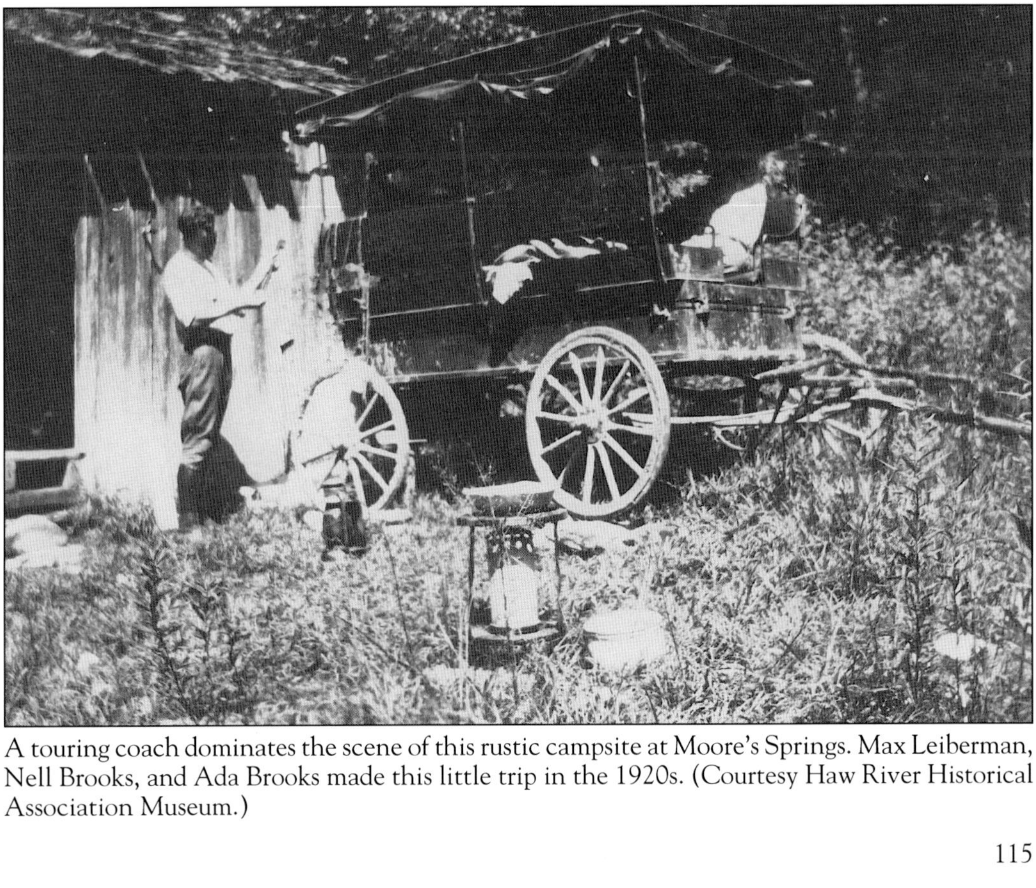

A touring coach dominates the scene of this rustic campsite at Moore's Springs. Max Leiberman, Nell Brooks, and Ada Brooks made this little trip in the 1920s. (Courtesy Haw River Historical Association Museum.)

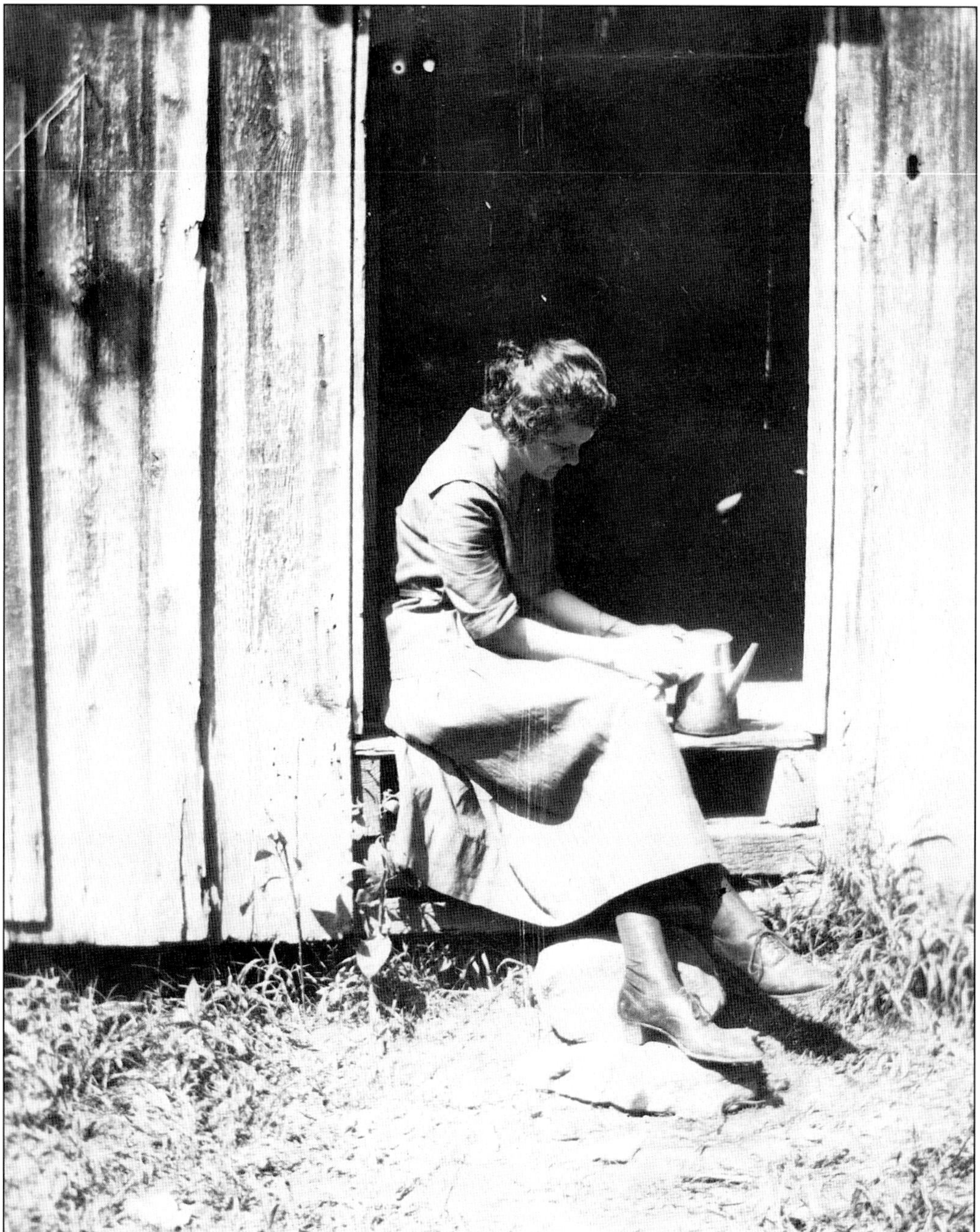

This photograph was taken on a camping trip that Nell Brooks took to Moore's Springs in the 1920s. With coffee pot in hand, she sits in the doorway of a cabin at the campsite. Nell later married fellow Haw River native Jim Simpson. Born in 1897, she is still, as of this writing, able to reminisce about the earlier times in her life. (Courtesy Haw River Historical Association Museum.)

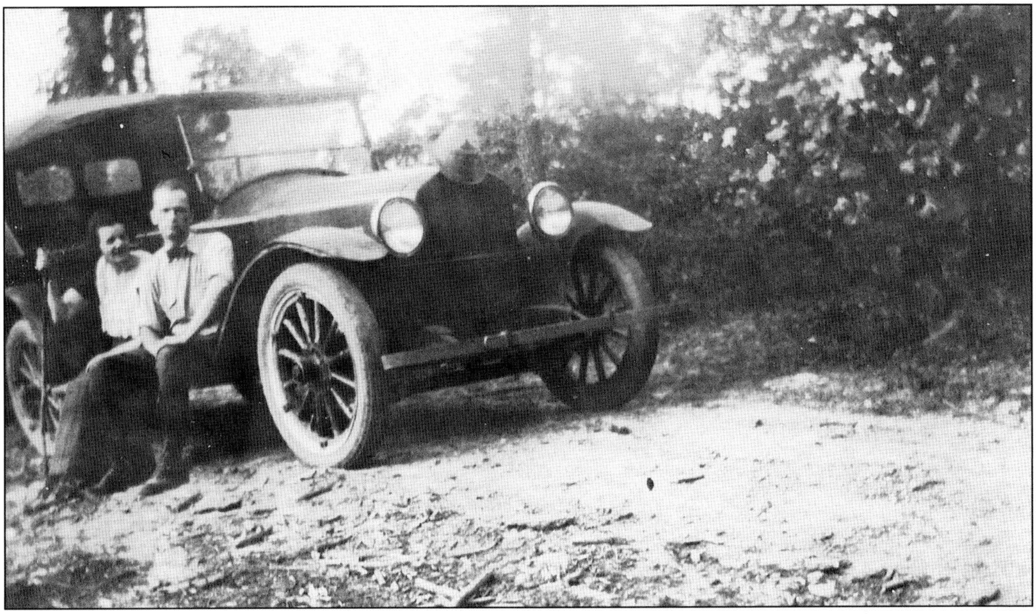

Jim and Nell Brooks Simpson relax on the running board of his Studebaker in the 1930s. Studebakers first came to Alamance County in the form of wagons, c. 1870. (Courtesy Haw River Historical Association Museum.)

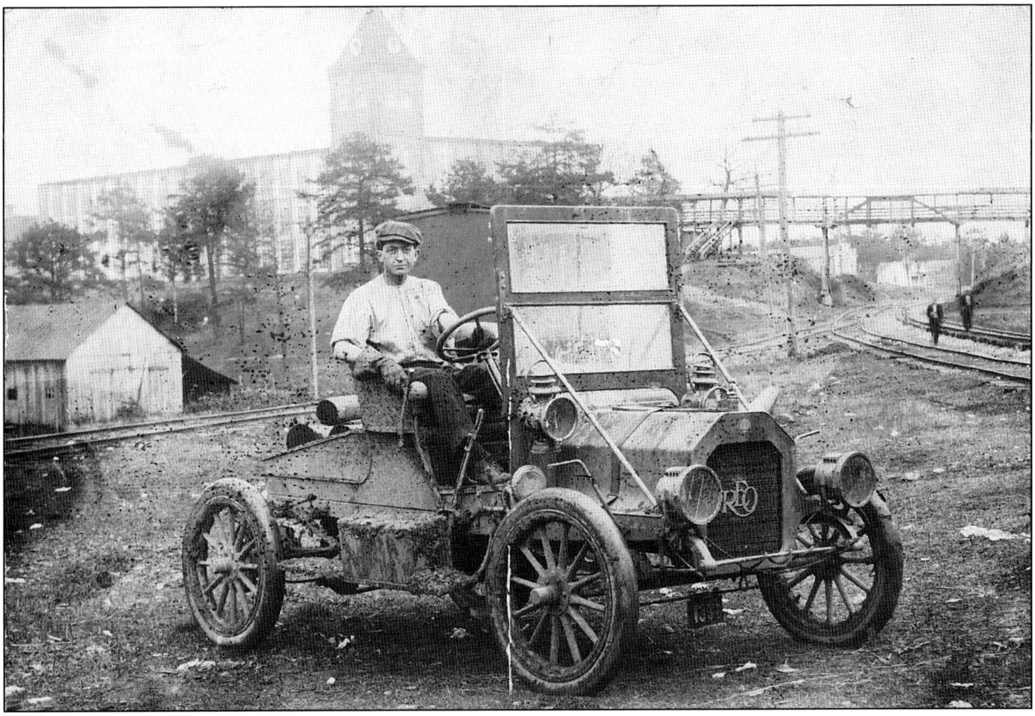

Haw River's Julius Thomson shows off his new REO with a background view of the Thomas Holt Mill. The elevated walkway on the right led to the Cora Mill. (Courtesy Haw River Historical Association Museum.)

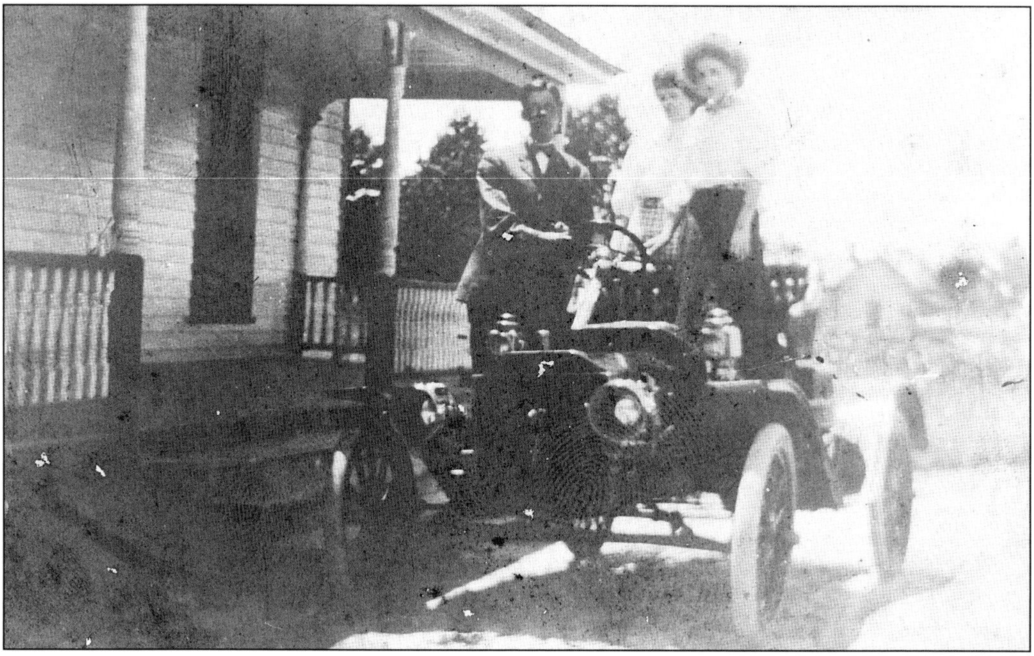

W.S. Fix, Mrs. Pauline Thom Lasley (1881–1971), and Miss Lola Jeanette Lasley (1888–1963) prepare for an automobile ride around Burlington in 1906 or 1907. Pauline was the wife of William Blair Lasley and became the mother of William Thom and John Kerr Lasley. Lola later married Edgar Samuel Williamson Dameron, a Burlington lawyer. (Courtesy Nell Holt Lasley.)

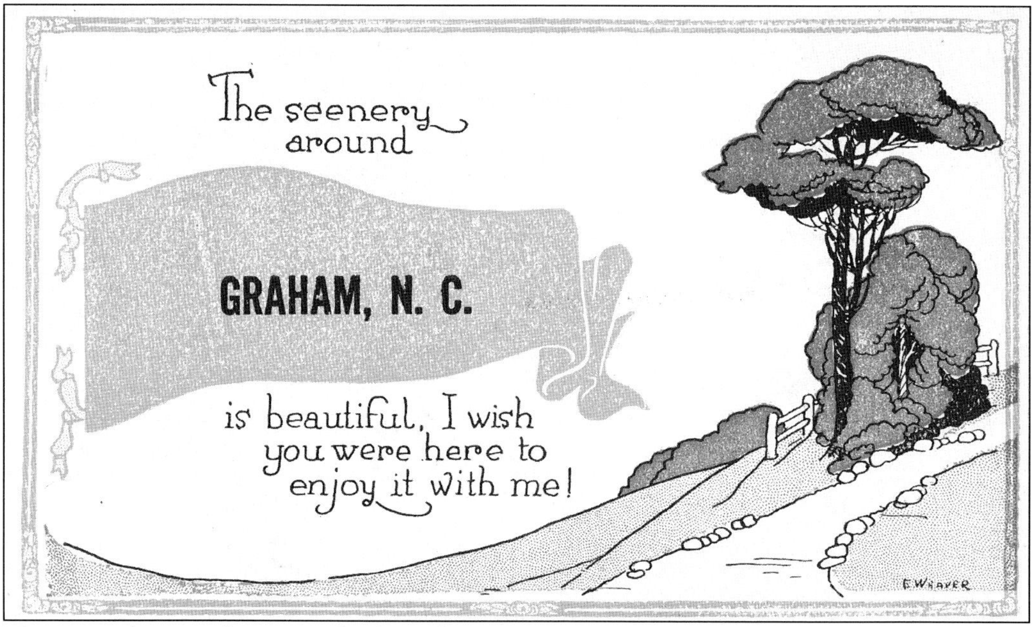

This type of postcard was popular from the turn of the century through the teens. The generic format allowed the postcard distributor to add the appropriate place-name to the banner. The town of Graham, named for North Carolina governor William A. Graham, is the county seat and was incorporated in January of 1851. (Courtesy Alamance County Historical Museum, Inc.)

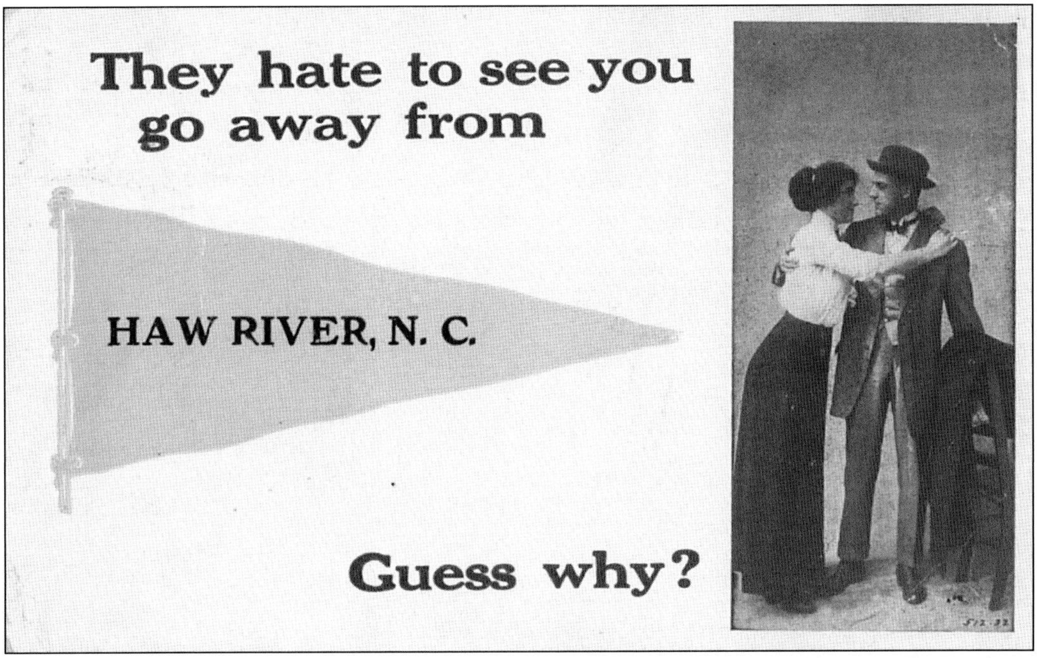

Postmarked July 20, 1913, this card was sent to Mr. Ollie Boggs in Venable , North Carolina. (Courtesy Haw River Historical Association Museum.)

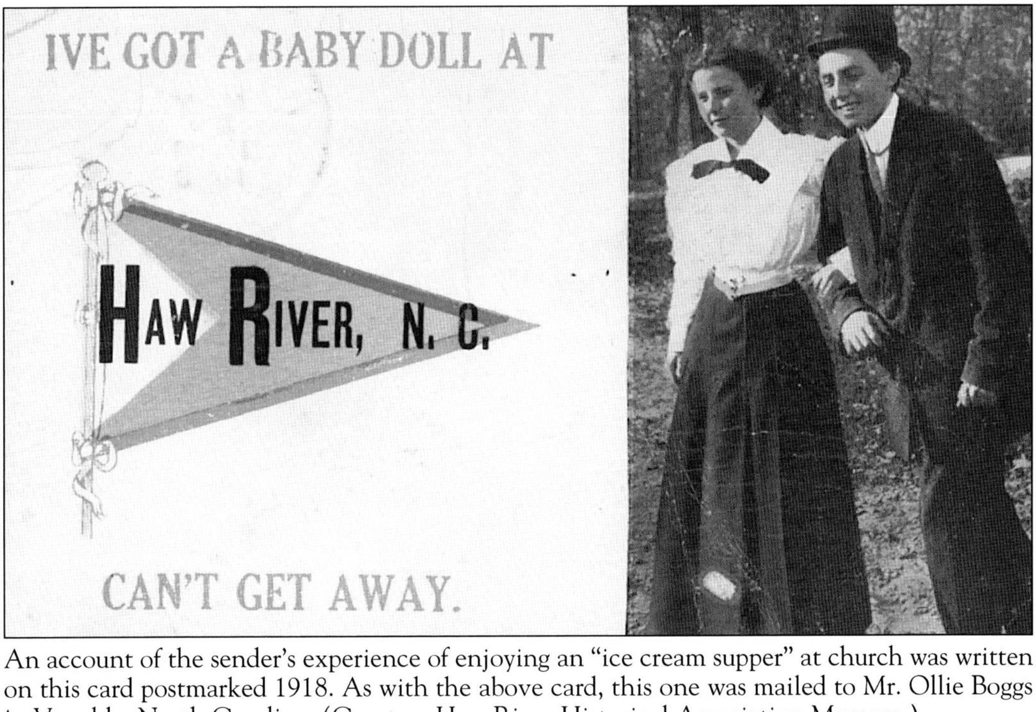

An account of the sender's experience of enjoying an "ice cream supper" at church was written on this card postmarked 1918. As with the above card, this one was mailed to Mr. Ollie Boggs in Venable, North Carolina. (Courtesy Haw River Historical Association Museum.)

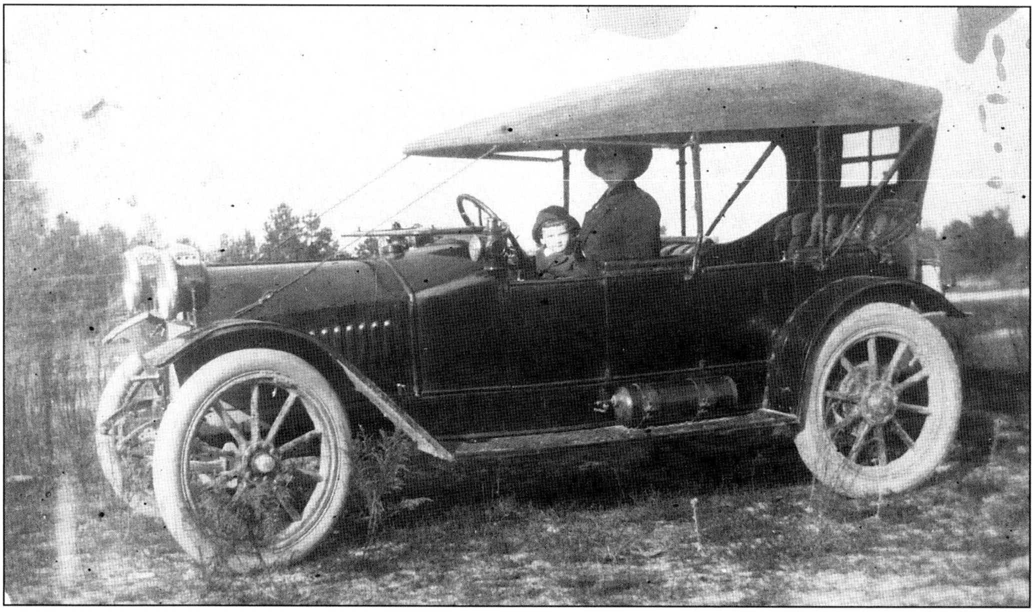

Little W.T. Lasley and his mother, Pauline, sit in a Hupmobile touring car, c. 1914. W.T. would later serve as Burlington's assistant postmaster for 12 years, retiring in 1972. Hupmobiles were made from 1908 to 1940. In the teens and '20s, they were popular among Alamance County residents as ideal family cars. (Courtesy Nell Holt Lasley.)

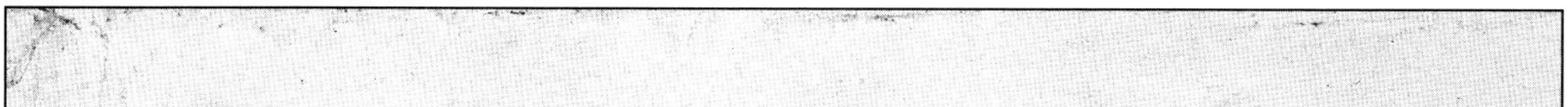

In the early 1890s, brothers Burton and Will H. May bought a controlling interest in the failing Daisey Hosiery Mill. By the late 1920s, May Hosiery Mills, Inc. was a well-established thriving business. Employees received Christmas bonuses in envelopes such as the one above. The business later became part of the May-McEwen-Kaiser Corporation, a division of Burlington Mills.

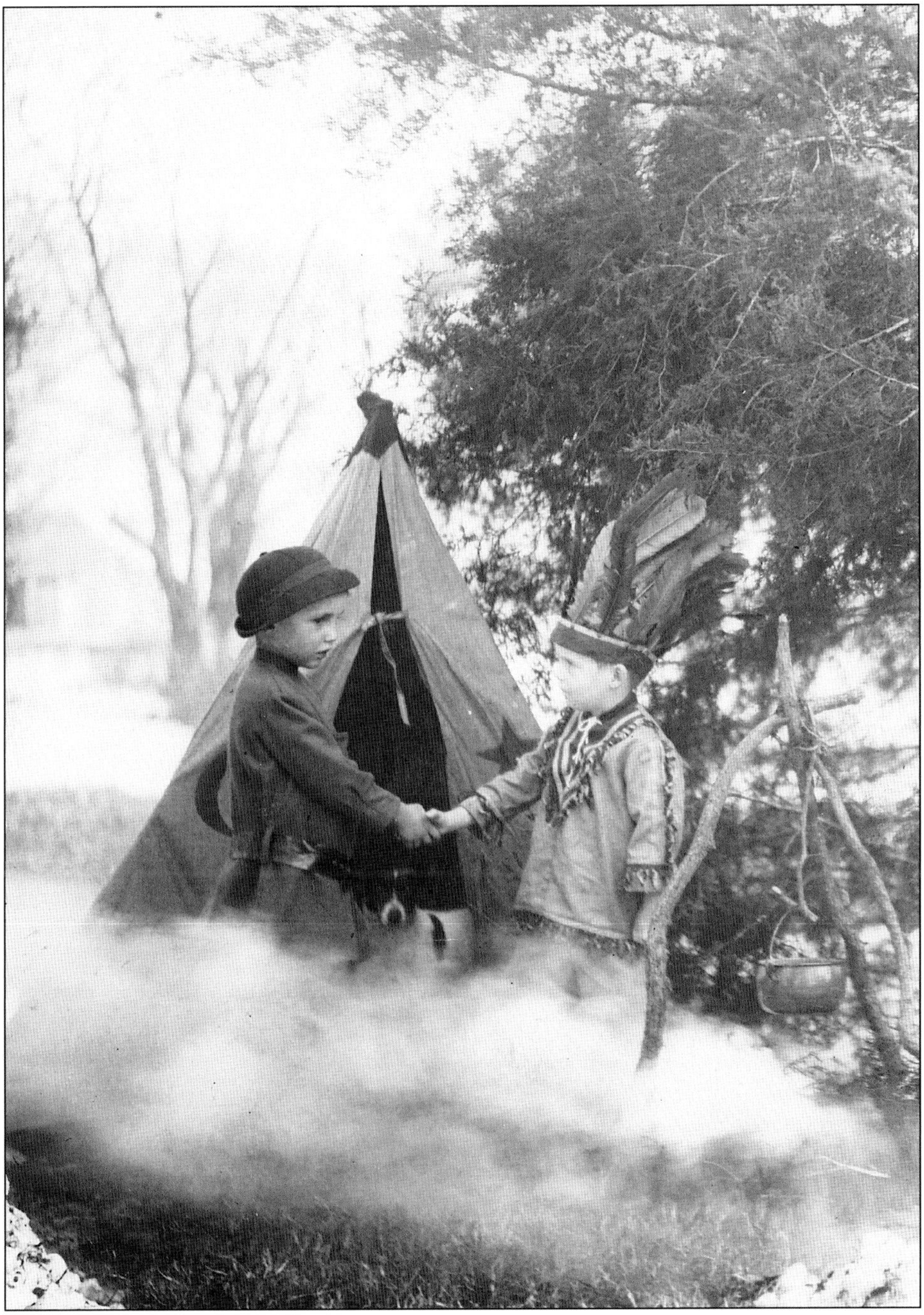

Standing between a smoking campfire and a tepee, Harry Childrey greets Bill Aldridge in Haw River. Perhaps the boys were imagining a possible encounter that occurred while German explorer Doctor John Lederer was on an expedition through Haw's Old Fields in 1670. Or maybe the playmates were re-enacting a meeting between John Lawson and an Occaneechi villager. Lawson, surveyor general for His Majesty's Province of North Carolina, set out on an expedition in 1700 and passed through what is now Alamance County. (Courtesy Haw River Historical Association Museum.)

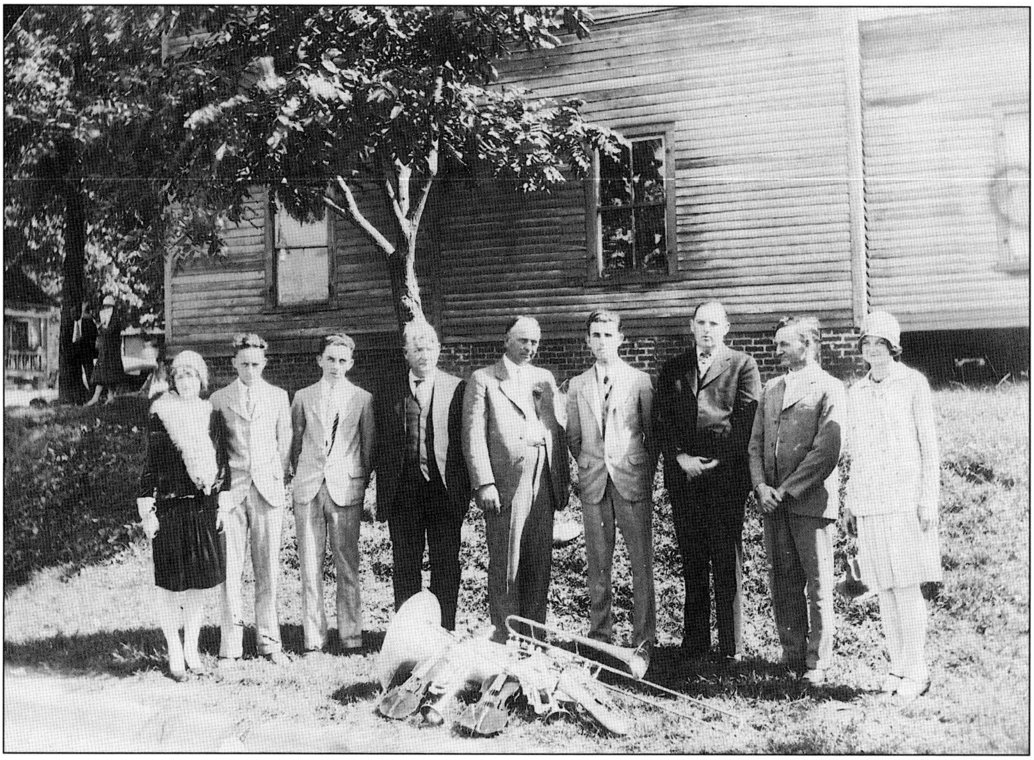

After inexplicably shedding their instruments, A.L. "Allie" Thompson (fourth from the left) and his fellow band members from Haw River pose for a group shot in the 1920s. (Courtesy Haw River Historical Association Museum.)

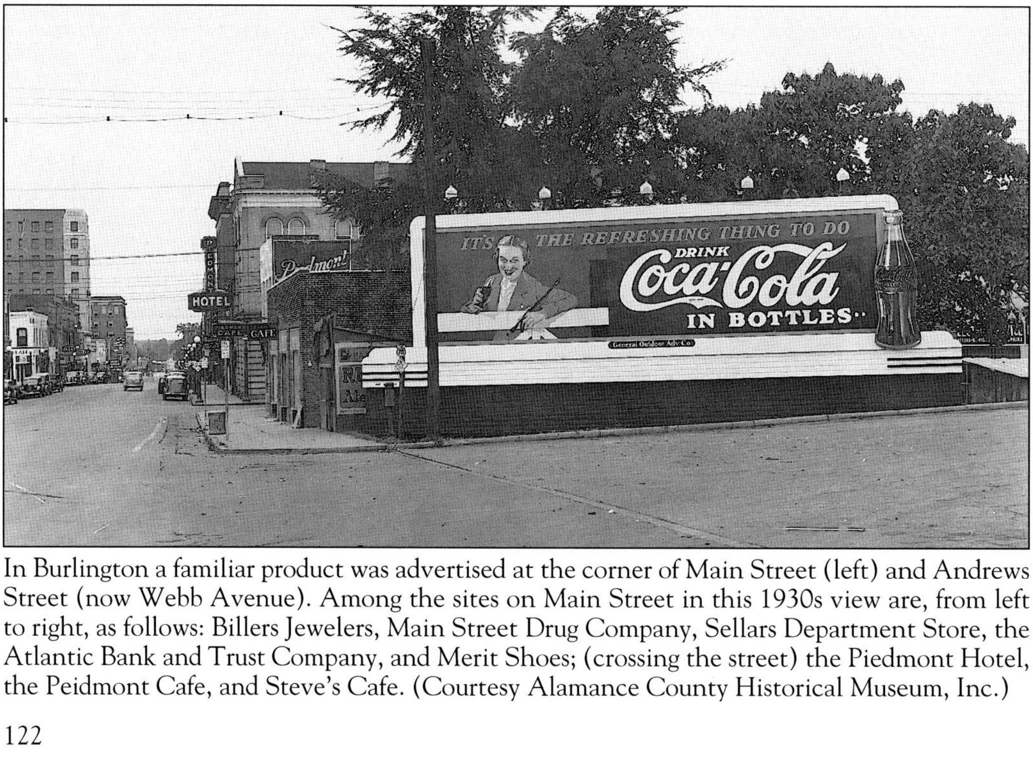

In Burlington a familiar product was advertised at the corner of Main Street (left) and Andrews Street (now Webb Avenue). Among the sites on Main Street in this 1930s view are, from left to right, as follows: Billers Jewelers, Main Street Drug Company, Sellars Department Store, the Atlantic Bank and Trust Company, and Merit Shoes; (crossing the street) the Piedmont Hotel, the Peidmont Cafe, and Steve's Cafe. (Courtesy Alamance County Historical Museum, Inc.)

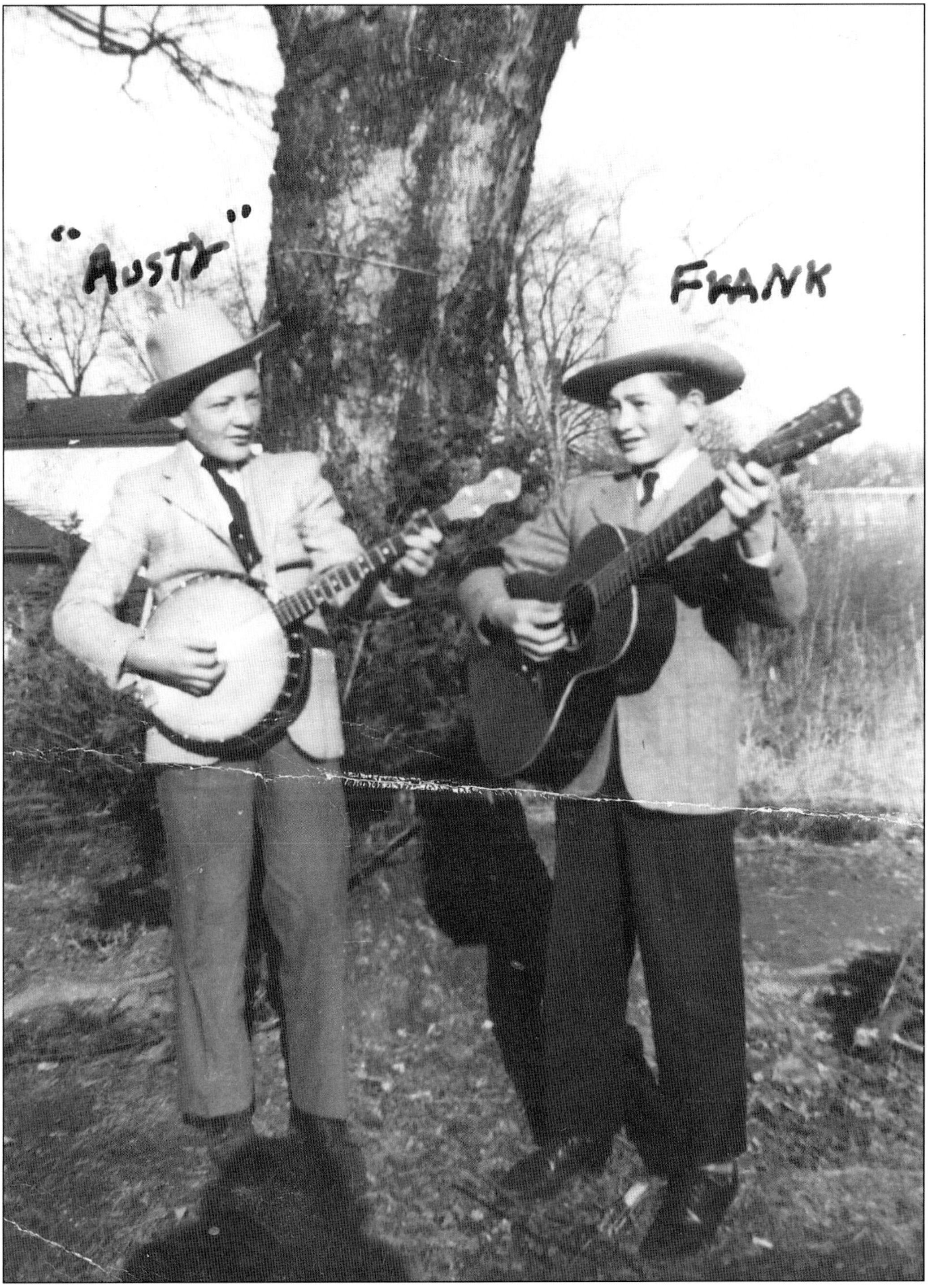

Banjo player Rusty and guitarist Frank livened up Haw River as "The Thompsons," *c.* the late 1940s. The term "country music" was not in widespread use at that time, and the label "country and western" was an even later creation. The pieces that these boys performed were then popularly known as folk songs. (Courtesy Haw River Historical Association Museum.)

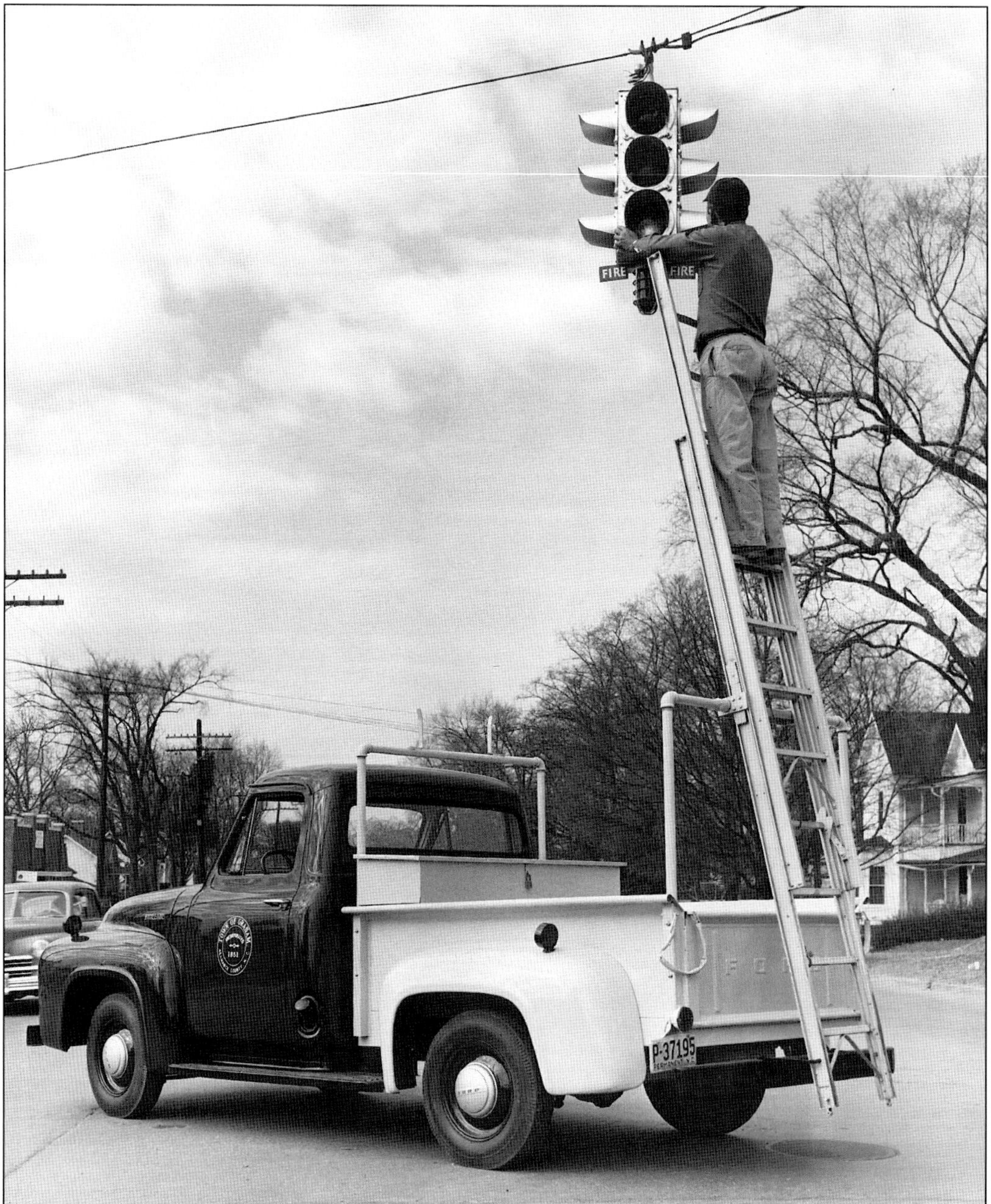

In the 1950s, a Graham maintenance man works on a traffic light. The beacon on the underside of the light flashed whenever a fire alarm was raised. As indicated on the door of the truck, Graham was still officially a town and not yet a city in the 1950s. (Courtesy City of Graham.)

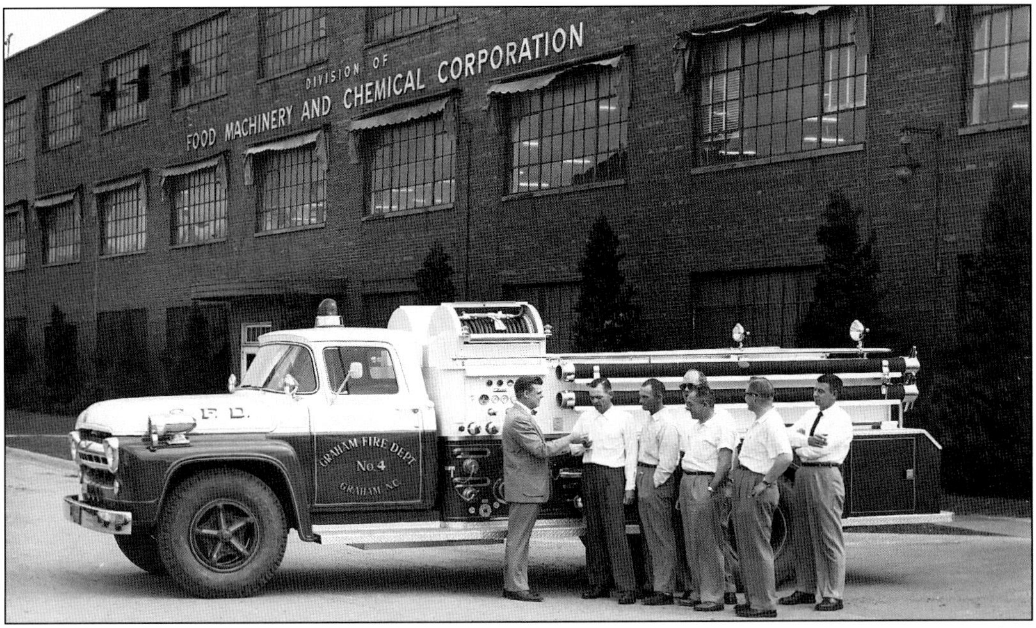

The Graham Hose Company, the town's first volunteer fire-fighting group, was organized in 1904. Above, members of the Graham Fire Department pick up a new truck in Ohio, *c.* 1956. Meeting with the salesman are as follows: (on the left) E.M. Todd, Kenneth Evans Jr., Foster Hughs (in sunglasses), Charlie Ivey, Marion Simmons, and Russell Thompson. (Courtesy John Andrews and Chief Kenneth Evans of the Graham Fire Department.)

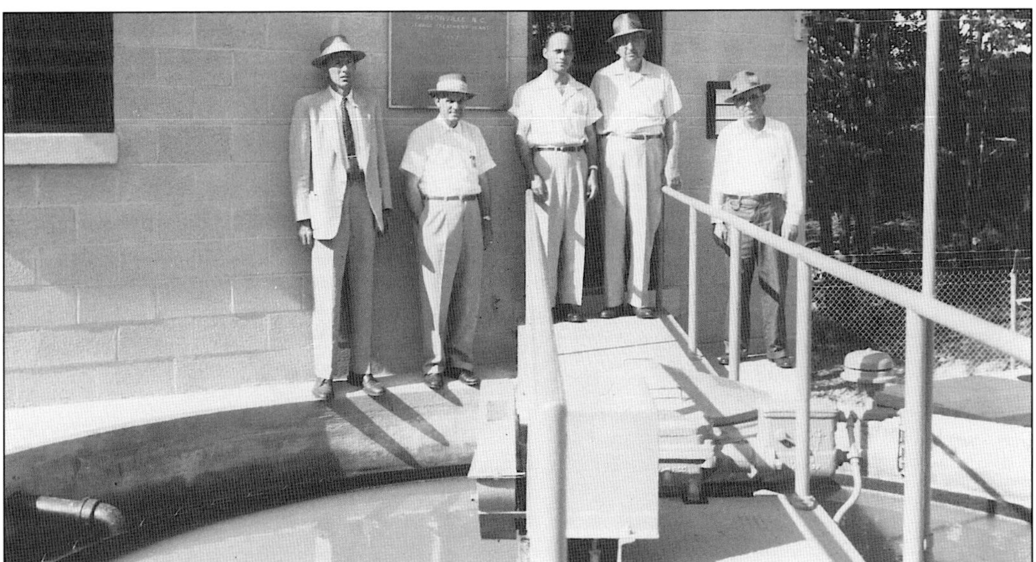

This photograph was taken at Gibsonville's Northside Sewage Plant, *c.* 1957. The facility closed in 1978 after Burlington began handling the sewage. From left to right are as follows: Alderman Melvin Randolph (town clerk), Melvin Wyrick (manager), J.O. Harper (alderman), G.B. May (fire chief and water superintendent), and Charlie Whitsell (public works department). (Courtesy Town of Gibsonville.)

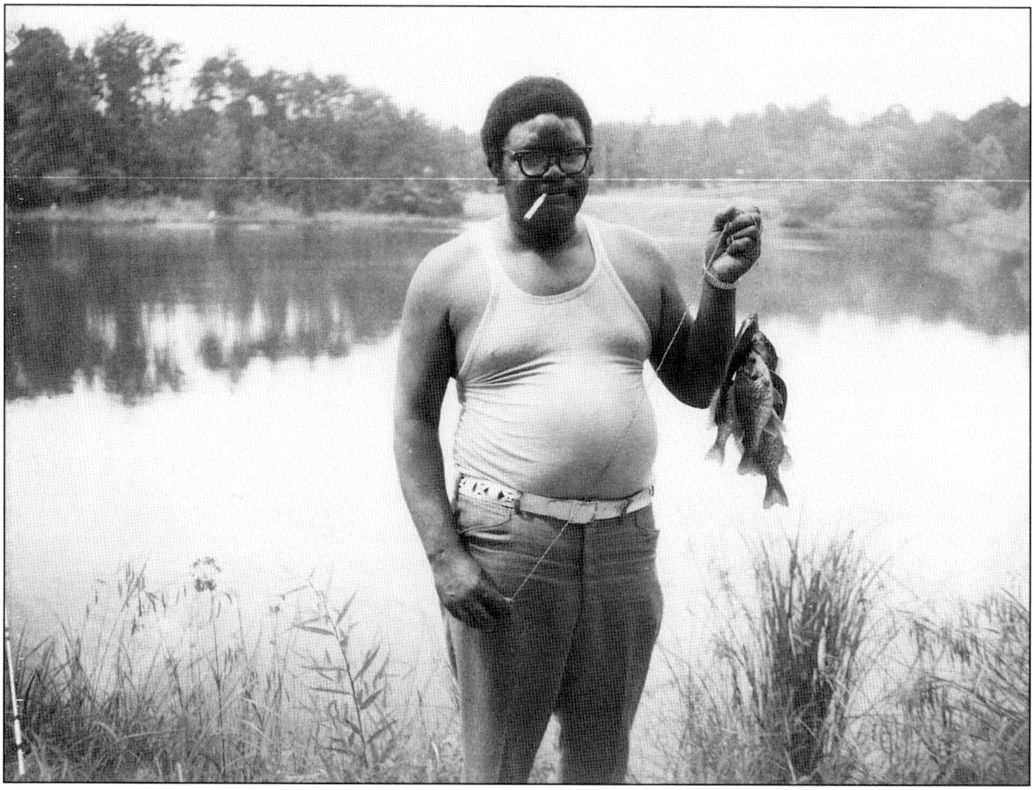

Junious Rogers worked in the prep-department at Cone Mills in Haw River. In the 1960s, he displayed this string of bream that he caught on a company outing. (Courtesy Haw River Historical Association Museum.)

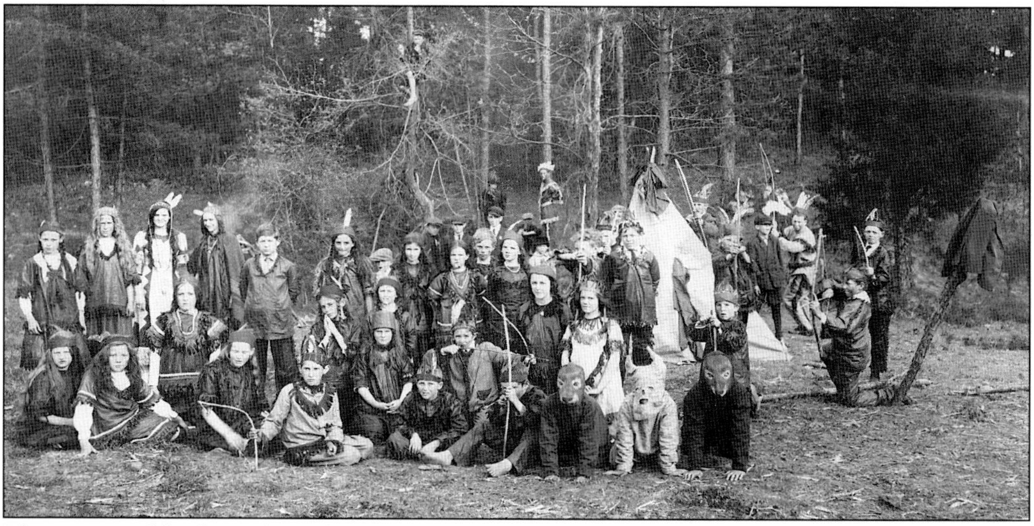

This vision of feather-adorned young people comes from some time during the first half of the twentieth century in Haw River. One may assume that a fun and interesting time was had by all who participated in this outdoor event. Perhaps the idea was to acquaint themselves with how the Sissipahaw natives lived on the very same land not long before. (Courtesy Haw River Historical Association Museum.)

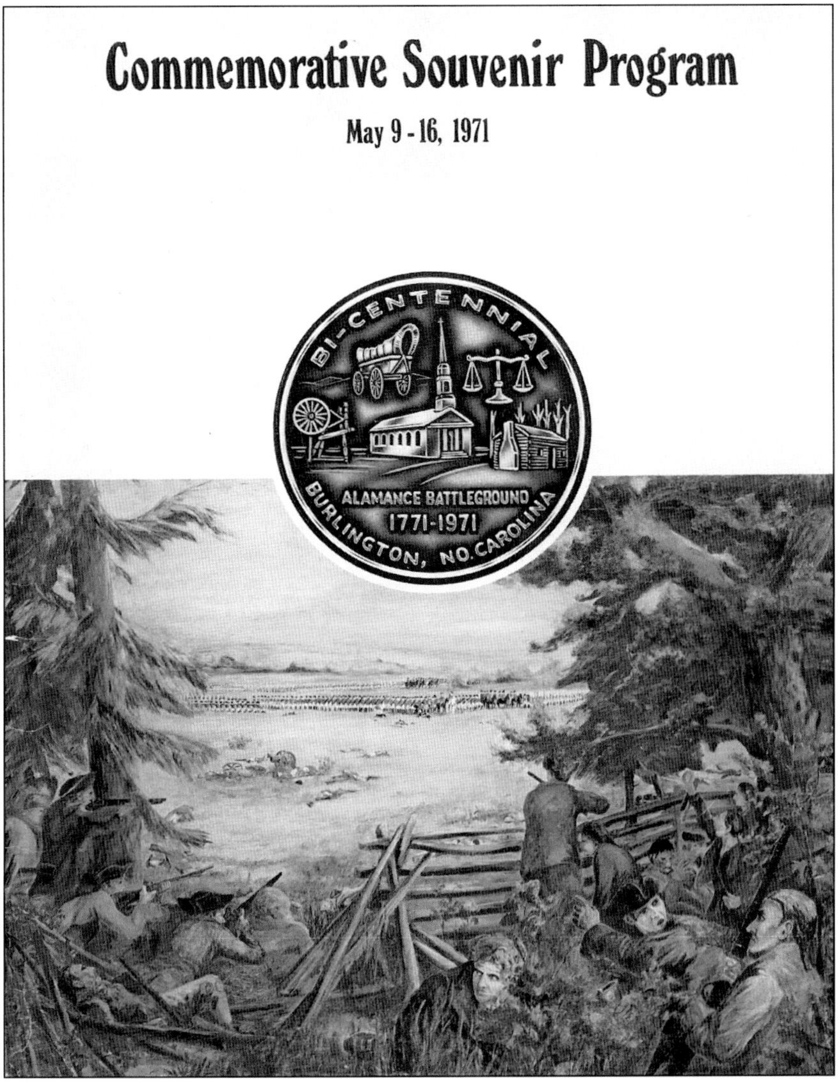

The story of Alamance County came full circle in 1971 as citizens commemorated the legendary event that would forever bring pride to those who live there. The Battle of Alamance Bicentennial Celebration included a fashion show, band performances, historical dramas, a parade, an auto show, sales at area businesses, gospel singing, entertainment by various choirs and choruses, and many other events. It was all about remembering what happened on May 16, 1771 (see page nine). On that day, the settlers at Alamance were the first to stand against oppression from the royal government. Years before the American Revolution officially began, colonists from this area gave their lives to begin a war for independence. Two centuries later, county residents remembered that early sacrifice, which was the first spark of the epic struggle for freedom. The artwork used on the above program cover is a painting by Margaret Thompson. It adequately depicts the fear and determination of those brave men who deemed themselves "Regulators." One survivor named James Pugh was among those later hanged for their part in the uprising. At his execution, he had this to say about the action that had enshrined Alamance County as the place where an important line had been drawn: "The blood that we have shed will be as good seed sown in good ground, which soon will reap a hundred fold."

Bibliography

Alamance County Bicentennial Commission. *Historic Sites of Alamance County*. P.N. Thompson Printing, 1976.

Euliss, Elinor Samous. *Alamance County: The Legacy of Its People and Places*. Greensboro: Legacy Publications, Inc., 1984.

Hughes, Julian. *Development of the Textile Industry in Alamance County*. Burlington: Burlington Letter Shop, 1965.

Stockard, Sallie Walker. *The History of Alamance*. Raleigh: Capitol Printing Company, 1900.

Stokes, Durward T. *Company Shops: The Town Built by a Railroad.* Winston Salem: John F. Blair, 1981.

Trelease, Allen W. *The North Carolina Railroad, 1849–1871, and the Modernization of North Carolina*. Chapel Hill: The University of North Carolina Press, 1991.

Whitaker, Walter E. *Centennial History of Alamance County: 1849–1949*. Burlington: Burlington Chamber of Commerce, 1949.

White, Robert D. and Frances W. *Centennial History of First Presbyterian Church, Burlington, North Carolina: 1879–1979*. Burlington: First Presbyterian Church, 1979.

Newspapers

Burlington Daily Times-News, 1951–1993. Burlington.

City-County Newspaper, 1977–1983. Burlington.